THE SPY WORE SILK

THE SPY WORE SILK

Aline, Countess of Romanones

G. P. PUTNAM'S SONS
New York

G. P. Putnam's Sons
Publishers Since 1838
200 Madison Avenue
New York, NY 10016

Library of Congress Cataloging-in-Publication Data

Aline, Countess of Romanones, date.
The spy wore silk / Aline, Countess of Romanones.
p. cm.
ISBN 0-399-13613-4
1. Aline, Countess of Romanones, date.   2.Spies—United
States—Biography.   3. Spies—Morocco—Biography.
4. Hassan II, King of Morocco, 1929-
—Assassination attempt, 1971.   5. Morocco—Politics and
government.   I. Title
E839.8.A68   1991   90-22098 CIP
940.54′86′73092—dc20

Designed by Rhea Braunstein

Printed in the United States of America
1   2   3   4   5   6   7   8   9   10

This book is printed on acid-free paper.
∞

For Miguel

For Miguel, my son
For Miguel, my grandson

"Though those that are betrayed
Do feel the treason sharply, yet the traitor
Stands in worse case of woe."

—WILLIAM SHAKESPEARE

Author's Note

In my books I recount what I believe to be the most dramatic intelligence operations with which I have been connected. In this one, as in others, I have been obliged to protect the identities of people who for a wide variety of reasons do not care to be or should not be recognizable. In some cases dates have been changed; in others, where a name change did not sufficiently conceal a character's identity, a composite character has been created. The woman Fatima has been disguised, as has, I trust, the woman called Salima. Nevertheless, the story is true, and the people are real.

In order to make the book move smoothly, a few dramatic moments have been left out, as well as some insignificant events. What I have attempted is to inform and to entertain while giving my reader the clearest possible picture of this intelligence operation. I have studied archives, old letters, newspapers, and magazines of that period, and spoken to people who were close to the coup or were present during the attacks. Conversations have been re-created, of course, but always with an effort to reflect as exactly as possible the personality of each character and event. My intention throughout has been to capture the essence and flavor of the places, events, and conversations that actually took place.

Those of us who work in intelligence do not always learn the answers to all the questions, as is shown in this story. Also, many brave people of our intelligence services, whose names I am unable to mention, contribute to collecting information, similar to that in this story, and in doing so help maintain the security of our great country, and it is to them I dedicate this book.

Prologue

Saturday, July 10, 1971

The air that July night in Washington, D.C., was as humid and heavy as the Malaga bullring in August. My plane from Madrid to New York had arrived late and I'd missed the connection to our capital. It was, therefore, just about midnight when I entered the hotel. Although I was elated to be again in my country of birth, I was exhausted from the long trip. The man at the reception desk apologized for the porter being occupied and, handing me a key, said that my luggage would be delivered as soon as he returned. In Madrid it was six hours later and the time change was now adding to my fatigue as I slowly made my way down the long hallway, looking for the room. Maybe that added to my being woefully unprepared for the shock when I swung the door open and stepped inside. A huge television set somehow had been left on, and there, in the darkness on the screen, a familiar man faced me. I'd met him only three months before. It was the face of King Hassan of Morocco.

I rushed to turn up the sound and stood in front of the screen. It was a news bulletin about Morocco. King Hassan's photograph was replaced on the screen by the serious face of the anchorman, who was speaking forcefully and quickly. What he said seemed impossible, and for several moments I listened without comprehending. Then the terrible reality of what had happened struck me and I sank to the carpet, my heart racing. The coup we had decided was no longer a threat, at least for the time being, had taken place!

The commentator was saying that it was not known whether the King was alive. Many had died. Flashing in rapid succession on the screen were views of the gardens of the Moroccan Royal Summer Palace with armed troops firing automatic weapons, exotic tents being ripped apart, bits of decorations flying through the air. The facts marched inexorably one by one before me, hard and undeniable, soldiers in combat gear, inert bodies lying on the bloody ground. This was not a bad dream, although much of what I saw was strikingly similar to the nightmare I'd had in the recent past.

The next morning at six I called down to the desk for the newspapers. The first edition of the *New York Times* arrived with the story of the coup on the front page: SOLDIERS ATTACK MOROC-CAN SUMMER PALACE, the headlines began. 10 OFFICERS LED 3-HOUR RAID BY 1,400 MEN. MONARCH SAYS 3 GENERALS WERE KILLED—HE ACCUSES LIBYA OF INCITING UPRISING. Impatiently, I scanned the article, skipping whole paragraphs in my haste to get the story.

Moroccan Army troops attacked the Summer Palace of King Hassan II outside Rabat yesterday . . . The Libyan radio previously announced that Libyan troops were ready to help the Moroccans in the event of foreign interference.

Palace sources reported that the Belgian Ambassador, Marcel Duprat, had also been killed. Among those reported to have been wounded was the King's brother, Prince Moulay Abdullah.

It was reported that when the shooting first broke out, some of the King's guests thought the shooting was from fireworks.

Then, according to witnesses, they began to fall, struck by machine-gun bullets.

There was a photograph of handsome General Oufkir in a battle helmet. The caption read, "Gen. Mohammed Oufkir, Interior Chief, assumed civil and military powers." The story around it told me the details:

Palace sources said that King Hassan has authorized the Interior Minister, Gen. Mo-hammed Oufkir, to take over all civil and military power to regain control of the situation.

The names I was reading, those of the living and the dead, I knew well. They were people who had been my companions a short time before, when we had shared many wonderful experiences together. The awareness that if I had done my job properly, this catastrophe would never have occurred left me weak. I put one hand on the table and leaned on it, drinking in the bitterness of failure. The room seemed airless and suffocating, pressing on me with the weight of the dead bodies. I could almost feel the air pulsing with their ghosts, or was it just the pounding of my heart?

THE SPY
WORE SILK

Chapter 1

I'd become involved in the Morocco case about three months before, almost by accident. My husband, Luis, was going to Rabat for the yearly General Board meeting of Riff Mines, the iron ore company his grandfather had founded sixty years before. Luis and I had made so many trips to Morocco that this time I was thinking of not going, when I received a call from Fatima Aziz, an old friend of mine. She was having an exhibit of her custom-designed jewels in Casablanca at the same time as Luis's meeting and wanted me to come to the opening; and after that we would stay on at her house a few days so we could go to a . . . something . . . her sister was giving in Rabat. "You'll enjoy it," she said. The bad telephone connection made it hard to hear.

"Enjoy what, Fatima?"

"The party—a lovely party."

"Oh, no. Thanks. I won't be able to go to a party. This time I'm not accompanying Luis. He only intends to stay two days, and I have things I must do here."

"Oh, please change your mind," she had responded. "It's important." Her voice became persuasive. "I need you, Aline. Something's come up that . . . I think you could help me with."

I couldn't refuse. Fatima had been my friend since the day many years ago we happened to meet while picking up our children at Rosales, our boys' school in Madrid. Our five-year-olds had been in the middle of a group of little boys who were wrestling. Fatima and I had bumped into each other, trying to extricate our children from the squirming mass. Although I didn't know it at the time, she was the wife of a Moroccan diplomat who had recently been assigned to Madrid. In a torrent of Arabic, she had scolded her child and pointed with obvious exasperation at his jacket, which was torn and buttonless.

I had laughed. "Isn't it incredible how little boys love to fight? Mine come home almost every day with the buttons ripped off their jackets."

She had looked at me. I'd been struck by this unusually beautiful woman, but more than anything by the black, almond-shaped eyes—more striking, perhaps, because of the thick arched eyebrows. She was tall and slim, with long legs and broad shoulders; her lips were full and her perfect teeth gleamed startlingly white, in contrast to her olive skin. Later I learned that, ten years before, when she'd been living in the United States with her father, who was then the Moroccan Ambassador to Washington, a totally infatuated American had committed suicide because she had refused to marry him. Evidently her admirers had been many and quite unusual in their reactions to her beauty. Another, a wealthy Argentine, had stopped traffic in Washington, D.C., when, from a helicopter hovering over the Moroccan Embassy, he had dropped two hundred envelopes, each enclosing a simple *billet doux*—"Mario loves Fatima."

Fatima and I had soon become friends. I met her husband and was surprised to see that the man she had selected to marry was neither attractive nor charismatic. Squat, bald Raoul Aziz was at least twenty years older, but very wealthy, influential, an important figure in Moroccan politics, and was rumored to be in line for a cabinet post. I had no doubts that Fatima's beauty and intelligence, as well as her own powerful family, had contributed to her husband's successful career.

As we flew to Rabat, my thoughts dwelled upon Fatima's impressive background, which Raoul Aziz had proudly related to me one evening. Realizing the importance of a modern education, her father had sent Fatima, then a young girl, to the École Briamont in Lausanne, Switzerland, and then to an exclusive girls' school in America. She had subsequently graduated Phi

Beta Kappa from the University of California. Despite all that, however, Fatima had remained amazingly Moroccan, wearing traditional garb in her home and placing family and national customs above personal whims.

The Iberia flight from Madrid was not long, only an hour and fifteen minutes. Luis went across the aisle to talk to another board member, and Alberto Lorca, the Spanish choreographer, who was on his way to Morocco for the opening of the Spanish Ballet, moved into the empty seat next to me. Our in-flight luncheon was served just after he sat down. "This is delicious," I commented, as I tasted the shrimp in a pink sauce. "It reminds me of the first time that I saw you," he said. "It was in a restaurant, must have been well over twenty years ago. It was shortly after you arrived in Spain, so that must have been—what? About 1944?" He looked at me with a smile. "I can even remember what you wore. You were the first American girl I'd ever seen. I was bewitched. We all stared at you."

I laughed. Spaniards were like that—always generous with their exaggerated compliments. "Well," I said, "I was about the only American girl in Spain then, and that must have been what made you notice me. My clothes were different from the Spanish girls', my hairdo . . . it took me a while to get used to it all."

His words reminded me of those early years in Spain, after I had completed three months in the United States' first foreign espionage school. In those days I had been awestruck by the beauty and the old-world lure of Madrid. I had also been worried that I might botch my operation and be sent back to Washington, D.C. I couldn't tell Alberto that when he had seen me, though only twenty years old, I was already a spy. That mission hadn't been easy. Hitler had been constantly trying to pressure General Franco to join the Axis so that German troops could march through Spain and attack the Allies in northern Africa. There had been over six hundred Gestapo undercover agents working in Spain in this endeavor. As it was, Franco's neutrality had not only helped the Allies liberate France and England, but had also helped save North Africa.

Back in those days I never suspected that I would marry a wonderful Spaniard, a man who happened to be a grandee of Spain, or that I would spend the rest of my life in that country.

No one ever knows, I reflected, what adventures lie ahead. As it ensued, I was about to embark upon another.

Soon we were circling the sparkling blue waters of Casablanca's bay; several transatlantic liners were in dock, and a number of merchant ships as well. Zigzagging across the water were hundreds of little white sailboats. It was about three-thirty when we stepped off the plane. Men in long gray-and-white-striped djellabas and cotton turbans milled around the small terminal, and ankle-length, black-robed women with large black eyes stared at us over thick veils. Voices were soft; there were no crowds, nothing reminiscent of the boisterous racket in other international Western terminals. Already, I was light-years away from Europe.

Fatima, elegant as always, was waiting, and after a warm welcome, escorted us through customs. Soon we were in a black Mercedes on our way to her house high on a hill overlooking the city. As I looked out the window at the lovely old city, I remembered that as far back as the tenth century, Morocco had possessed a highly developed culture with universities that had attracted scholars from all over the Islamic world; many important buildings and homes had also had refinements that included running water at a time when Europeans were still living in primitive conditions.

The flat roofs and round domes of Fatima's house loomed ahead. Its austere high white walls had no windows, but I knew that inside, it was cozy and beautiful, with many rooms opening onto decorative patios and lush gardens. Arabic homes were like that, isolated from the outside world. As we entered, I was once again captivated by the exquisite Oriental atmosphere and the beautiful architecture. Servants in white turbans and floor-length djellabas took our luggage and padded silently away through spacious salons with ornately colored tiled walls and high ceilings carved in colorful, intricate designs. Our hostess led us across a marble patio into an arched room, where we sat on an upholstered red banquette in front of a low round table resplendent with shiny Oriental teapots, silver trays, and pyramids of cakes and almond cookies. The scent of incense was in the air, and the surroundings were silent except for the sound of birds and a splashing fountain.

Fatima was preoccupied. I could tell by the way she poured the mint tea that she was hardly interested in what Luis was telling her about our trip. Although I was aware from our telephone conversation that she was upset, her attitude still surprised me. Usually, my women friends were charmed by my attractive husband. He was handsome, witty, fluent in many languages, and an expert in everything from golf to games of chance. Luis was the product of an era and a family that bred men to be kind, polite, and courteous at all times. Although he did not go to the office at regular hours, he efficiently ran his ranches and family companies. He was also a brave man. When he'd been sixteen years old, the bitter Civil War had broken out in Spain, and Luis had left his home, lied about his age, and enlisted. A year later he had been badly wounded and left for dead on a battlefield. Only the good fortune of being recognized by a family friend had saved his life.

Fatima kept glancing at me, indicating that she wanted to talk to me alone. However, we didn't get a chance that night, and it was not until the next morning, after Luis had left for his board meeting in Rabat, that I began to have an inkling of what was on her mind.

Fatima came to my room, where I was basking in the sun on the small terrace overlooking her exotic garden. Her almond-shaped eyes were blacker than ever, and her sultry voice was soft and low.

"It's about my sister, Salima. She's become such a problem." Fatima played nervously with the fringe on the ancient fabric of the upholstery, and sighed. "I'm sorry you've never met Salima. She's been studying and working in New York for the past six years. Much too long. And now she's depressed because she is obliged to live here. I'm hoping you can help me, Aline."

I sat up and nodded. "I'll be glad to do what I can, but tell me more."

"She hadn't intended to come back at all, but our father put a stop to that idea. You know he can be very forceful." She smiled at me, and the crinkling around her eyes made them curve in a way that reminded me of the story about the man who had committed suicide.

"What was Salima doing in New York?"

"She was working in advertising and public relations, and had formed her own company with some American friends. You see, just as I did, Salima went to school in Europe and then the United States. I too found it difficult to come back home after so much freedom and independence, but Salima was tormented by the prospect. So she simply stayed in New York. First it was one excuse, then another, always some project she had to complete. For a while she got away with it. She's always been my father's pet. Finally he had enough and asked me to go to New York and find out what she was doing. That was a little over a year ago. I discovered that she was determined to stay there, and when I came back to Morocco, I was obliged to tell my father that she had no intention of returning. I hated to do it, but you know how powerfully Moroccan fathers control their families. I don't think Salima's quite forgiven me."

"How sad for her," I said. "After building a career for herself, to have to give it up."

"It's more serious than that." Fatima looked uncomfortable. "When I went to New York to see Salima, I also discovered that she had married an American, a frightful man called Alexander Coburn, without my father's permission, another reason she did not want to come home. In this country and in this family, marrying someone of a different religion is simply not acceptable. According to our laws, since he was not Mohammedan, the marriage was invalid. She'd only been married a couple of months when I arrived in New York, but of course I had to tell my father that, too." Fatima's sigh was almost a moan. "It was awful. Two days later my father flew to New York and took her bodily from the apartment and brought her to Casablanca. And, as if that was not enough, about two months after she arrived here, we learned that she was pregnant." Fatima was silent for a moment. "We had to hide her until she gave birth."

"But didn't her American husband complain?"

"He tried to, but my father paid him handsomely not to contact Salima. He also had him investigated so that he could never come back, asking for more money. Papa does things thoroughly. It turns out that a few years ago the man was arrested for pushing drugs, though never convicted, and his own father kicked him out of the house. And as if that were not enough, after they had been married only a few weeks, this terrible man started to go out with other women and left Salima alone. One afternoon she returned to her apartment to find that another woman had been in her room, in her bed. He never bothered to try to hide the telltale signs, and when she complained, at first he just smiled. But one day, Salima told me, he lunged at her and slapped her across the face so hard she fell to the floor. That was shortly before my father went to New York to bring her back to Morocco. But despite such an impossible situation, Salima wanted to stay in New York; she really seemed to be in love with this awful man."

Fatima walked over to the small table and poured herself a pink liquid from the line of multicolored crystal vases containing fruit juices. "My sister's looks are sensational, especially here in Morocco, because she has light hair and white skin, a terrific figure, and enormous pale blue eyes—very much like my father's grandmother, who was Swedish, I am told. Ever since she was a little girl, she's created a sensation, playing the role of the beautiful, lovable child to get whatever she wanted. When denied, she could cry on cue, looking at the offending person with huge, wide blue eyes, tears rolling down her pink cheeks. She manipulated everyone outrageously, especially my strong, strict father." Here, Fatima paused to shake her head. "Nobody could deny Salima anything. She was consistently being dismissed from one school after another; she became the darling of the paparazzi, always giving them a beguiling or provocative picture. Right before her move to New York, she went too far at Cannes, posing on the beach in the briefest of bikinis, the top dangling over one arm. My father summoned her home, lost his temper, something I'd almost never seen him do before, shouting that her outrageous conduct had brought a strong rebuke from the King. I thought he was going to strike her. But Salima fell to her knees, crawled to Papa, wrapped her arms in supplication around his legs, lifted those tear-filled, beautiful blue eyes, and begged his forgiveness. He raised her to her feet and embraced her. I was astonished to see my strong, powerful father talking to Salima as if she were still four years old. When her crying subsided, Salima stepped back and ceremoniously bowed to Papa. He smiled and completely forgave her. As she left the room, she winked at me." Fatima's sigh was loud and long. "I love her—she's my sister—but what a difficult girl!

"There were no more incidents after that. Salima returned to New York City, where she had been studying, and became a different woman, working hard in the company she had formed, handling movie openings, introductions of new products, new restaurants, social balls, charities. Then she fell in love, and you know the rest, Aline. When she left New York with Papa, she did not yet know she was pregnant. Then Papa decided to find Salima a proper Moroccan husband and oblige her to marry and take her place in Moroccan society. At first Salima was shattered. I could hardly believe it, but she was really in love with that terrible man. By now I think she's getting over him, but what a blow to her self-respect! At least, in some ways the shock has improved my very spoiled sister. She seems to have learned that her beauty is not going to protect her from disaster, and that my father is not going to give in to her anymore."

"What happened to the child?" I asked.

"It died during childbirth. That was over six months ago. Salima's never been quite the same. She really wanted that baby. What a difficult situation! You know our strict Moroccan customs. How could my father explain that Salima had given birth to an illegitimate child without ruining her chances for a proper Sunni marriage? And what would we have done with that baby if it had lived? Salima could never have recognized it as her own. Just lately, my father brought her back to Casablanca to live at home. No one knows anything about all this. Salima spent the months of pregnancy in the house of an 'aunt' in Ceuta and gave birth there."

Fatima shook her head. "Salima's always been a rebel and independent. My father allowed her to stay on in New York too long."

Now Fatima was on the verge of tears. Something else was bothering her that she was not telling me. The words came tumbling out, like an old-fashioned gramophone at the wrong speed.

"Ever since Salima returned to Morocco, she's been terribly depressed. She hardly eats. She's lost the will to do anything.

Now she'll hardly even talk to me, at least not frankly. I understand that. She sees me as a traitor. All her sorrow and bitterness are directed against me. And when we do talk, there is such hate in her eyes!"

Fatima's shoulders sagged and the tears in the beautiful eyes swelled. I was extremely uncomfortable. As much as I cared for this family, I did not want to become involved in a private emotional affair. My reaction was to remain silent. And, in a way, I sympathized with Salima. I couldn't see how a girl accustomed to American ways could return to ancient Moroccan customs.

A few years back I had learned just how different those customs could be. One evening, when I had been visiting Fatima and we were dining at her parents' home, we women were seated on poufs, big pillows, around a low circular table in a corner of the large rectangular room. Fatima's mother faced us on the banquette which bordered the room. In an opposite corner, their father had dined alone. It was not customary, they told me, for the man of the family to eat with the women.

Fatima wiped her tears and started to speak again. "What's really bothering me is that Salima's capable of doing something that could devastate my father. She might run away—or even marry another foreigner—anything to show her independence. Our family's good name could be destroyed—our reputation for reliability, our loyalty to our religion, to our customs. My husband's career could be affected. Even our relationship with the King is at stake." Her black eyebrows arched. "You know our traditions, Aline. They're centuries old and no deviation is permitted. That's why I need your help. She's always admired you. You're American. I think you can make an impression on her. You might give her some ideas about a job, or, if worse comes to worst, suggest she go to Madrid and help find something for her to do there. After all, Spain is more old-fashioned than America and there are usually appropriate young Moroccan men working there who could entertain her. Perhaps she might fall in love with a suitable one. Knowing that you would be looking out for her would be such a help. Please don't think I'm being selfish, Aline. We want Salima to be happy—and I more than anyone—but we fear she might destroy her own chances for happiness." She looked at me pleadingly. "If she likes you, you can help enormously. I want her to understand that life doesn't have to be black-and-white, that this isn't a question of Morocco or America. It's a matter of reconciling one's education and goals with one's culture. She must realize she cannot just turn her back on the world she came from."

Fatima stood up. I sensed the conversation about Salima had concluded. Despite my qualms I decided I had to do something. Maybe with time Fatima would accept the fact that Salima's education abroad would make it improbable that she could ever again adapt to a conventional Moroccan family life. The way things were, I doubted that Salima had much chance for happiness. Perhaps when I talked to her some solution would occur to me.

Before I could do so, however, I was faced by another, much greater problem.

Chapter 2

That night Luis returned so late from the board meeting in Rabat that we barely had time to dress for the dinner we were going to with Fatima and her husband. He came into the room from the bathroom, drying his head with a towel and saying something about his old friend Abdul Nabil, but I couldn't hear him clearly. Little did I know that what he was telling me would change my life significantly for the next few months and beyond.

"I can't hear you," I said impatiently while struggling with the zipper on my dress and knowing that everyone was already waiting for us in the garden.

"Abdul told me," he repeated, as he put down the towel and grabbed his shirt. "He's very worried, but more than that, he's frightened."

I listened with only half an ear. "What's it about?" I asked, beginning on my chignon, with one eye on the clock.

Luis was now knotting his tie. He paused with hands in mid-air, addressing my reflection in the mirror in front of him. His next words gave me a shock. "Aline, he thinks there's a plot to assassinate King Hassan."

My earlier impatience about being late was replaced by a new one: to hear everything—quickly. A hundred questions popped into my mind, but I could see that Luis had more to say, in his own calm way, so I controlled myself and waited.

"And," he went on, giving his tie a final tug, "Abdul wants me to ask you to secure the American Ambassador's help."

"Luis," I said vehemently, "I don't even know the Ambassador. How could I speak to him about such a thing?"

"According to Abdul, the Americans are the ones who should investigate this rumor. He dares not. He fears the ringleader of the scheme could be an associate, so he's understandably afraid to mention his suspicions to anyone he knows. He also believes Libya is involved in this thing, and maybe the Soviets as well."

"But why doesn't Abdul speak to the Ambassador himself?"

"He says that if he went into the American Embassy, those plotting the coup would find out. There's always some local employee who informs about these things. He probably would be murdered—simple as that."

"But how would I get the American Ambassador interested in a local matter that may only be the product of Abdul's imagination? He's always been a bit exaggerated. You know that."

Luis nodded. "You're right. But he's provided me with evidence. I wouldn't suggest your speaking to the Americans without it. He showed me a report a relative sent him from Libya. I told him you would need a copy of the papers he showed me to get the Ambassador's collaboration."

"Well, did he give you a copy?" I paced restlessly. Luis always took so long to tell a story. Although I realized that his habit of weighing words was preferable to leaping recklessly into statements, as I often did, tonight his slowness made me impatient.

Finally satisfied with the knot of his red-and-navy-striped tie, Luis turned to me. "Of course. I wouldn't have mentioned this otherwise." He took his jacket off the clotheshorse, removed a speck from the lapel, and put it on. "As you know, Abdul works for the Moroccan government in the department of foreign relations. Evidently this relative of his works in the Libyan foreign office, and gave him copies of two reports received by a Libyan far-left radical group from an unidentified senior Moroccan official. Both refer to a conspiracy inside the Moroccan government to remove the King." Luis walked to the desk and lifted the top of his leather briefcase. From a zippered section inside, he removed some papers, which he handed to me.

The two photocopied sheets were in Arabic. I turned them over, hoping to find a translation on the back.

"Abdul says those reports come from a Moroccan who signs the code name of *El Hadj*. He claims that they not only serve as proof of a *coup d'état*, but they also refer to the collaboration of top Moroccan officials, although naturally they are referred to by code names only. I can't verify that, but I'm sure the Ambassador has reliable translators who can. One thing I'm certain of is that Abdul is an honest man and he's incapable of lying about something so important." Luis took the photocopies from my hands. "Until you see the Ambassador, they are safer in my briefcase. In my opinion these papers provide more than sufficient reason for you to bring the matter to his attention."

"I suppose so, but still this sounds far-fetched, don't you think?"

"Not if what Abdul says those papers state is true." Luis closed his briefcase and locked it with a small key. "Think of what a coup would mean, Aline. Morocco is one of America's greatest allies in Africa. A successful coup would deprive the United States of potential bases, perhaps change the entire political climate of northern Africa. And we're just a few miles across the water—think what a leftist nation in Morocco could mean for the potential political health of Spain. Not to mention"—he made a wry face—"the potential health of our mining interests here."

Something struck me. "I don't understand why Abdul just doesn't tell the King. He's close enough to him, isn't he?"

Luis looked at me and shook his head. "He did tell the King— and the King didn't take him seriously! He just told him to stop worrying so much. He was confident none of his close associates would ever plot against him. As for the reports, Abdul said the King had met his Libyan relative once, years before, and never liked the man, and when Hassan doesn't like someone . . . well, nothing that person does is right. So that's why Abdul decided to come to us."

While I finished my hair, Luis continued to ruminate. "I've the feeling Abdul knows much more than he's telling me. Of course, I understand that the situation is delicate, and that it might not be prudent for him to tell me more than is absolutely necessary. But while Abdul was talking to me, I could see how worried he was. I feel sorry for him. . . ." Luis shook his head. "Abdul tried hard to convince me that the Americans could investigate this better than the Moroccans anyway. He says the CIA operates several espionage networks inside his country—I suppose you'd know more about that than I would. And he insisted that after the King's reaction he dared not take this plot to their own secret service. Abdul feels that with the Americans working on it, there would be no danger of the guilty knowing he was trying to uncover those involved, and he would be safe. By the way, Abdul also asked for anonymity. So don't mention his name to the Ambassador unless absolutely necessary. He was adamant about that."

"Do you realize, Luis," I said teasingly, "this is the first time you've ever actually encouraged me to get involved in something to do with intelligence work. Usually it makes you furious."

His reaction was fast. "Bringing the matter to the attention of the Ambassador is very different from your accepting a mission which could put your life in danger, as you've done before," he said. "I don't mind that my life is jeopardized, but I do mind when espionage endangers our three children. On some of those cases you've become involved with, anyone who wanted to blackmail you could have kidnapped them." He threw his hands in the air, then moved his head in a familiar gesture that I knew indicated he was getting impatient. "But anyway, this is different. I'm not asking you to do anything dangerous, just show these papers to your Ambassador here, then let him take it from there. No more than that. In and out. And if you have any more doubts about Abdul, I'll tell you what: he'll be at the dinner tomorrow. Talk to him then and see for yourself."

I decided to accept Luis's advice, and put off calling the Ambassador until I had talked to Abdul myself.

In the meantime Luis and I drove to Rabat the next afternoon to attend Fatima's exhibit. During the forty-five-minute drive, I told Luis the story Fatima had told me about her sister. The narrow two-lane highway skirted the coastline, and I turned to gaze out at the sun-bathed, glistening sea.

"The girl sounds wild to me," commented Luis. "She'll create some new difficulty, wait and see. If she made such a mistake with that American, she'll probably pick a scoundrel next time, too."

As we entered the city, we passed the Royal Palace, where the King's black guard stood at attention with their spectacular red-and-white uniforms—red jacket and exotic white bloomers, and white turban circled with a red ribbon. We continued along the Rue Mohammed V to the Palace Hotel, where Fatima's exhibition was being held. The hotel was modern and in the heart of the ancient metropolis—the streets were filled with men and women in traditional ankle-length djellabas, many with capuchas; sometimes the capucha hung down the back and, instead of being used to cover the head, held packages. There were wagons and donkey carts transporting everything from ancient water jugs to modern electric appliances. It was not yet dark when we arrived, and the sky loomed above like a patch of torn gray silk, through which the faded remnants of a sunset were dimly visible. Whole parts of the city were lost in shadow, while others appeared to be on fire in the blaze of the last rays of the sun.

The exhibit was crowded, and although I knew the growing reputation of Fatima's designs, I was still surprised to see so many people. I was wearing a tiger-shaped pin Fatima had made for me years ago, which I particularly cherished for reasons she never could have guessed. Of course she didn't know, nor did most others, that Tiger was my code name for undercover work.

As Luis and I milled in the crowd, greeting old friends and gazing into the glass cases where the jewelry was displayed, I kept an eye out for Salima. I hoped I would recognize her from the family pictures Fatima had shown me, and when my eyes found a tall, slim girl who was easily the best-looking woman in the room, I had no doubt it was she. She was standing alone, gazing at a pair of glistening gold earrings in the shape of half-moons, from which dangled three tiny rubies on gold chains. I was immediately struck by her grace and a certain magical quality in her face. Her skin was the flawless, creamy white of seashells, her eyes were enormous and pale blue, like her father's. The neck was unusually long, her thick hair was golden blonde and hung loose down her back; she was tall and very slim, and had an openness and an innocence of expression that was appealing, but perhaps it was the pale eyes more than anything else that gave her that special quality. I felt immediately drawn to her. All the Karam girls were famous for their looks, but now I understood why Salima, the youngest, was reputed to be the most beautiful. She was different, not only from them, but from any girl I'd ever seen.

When I introduced myself, she greeted me warmly. "Aline, I feel as if I knew you already, I've heard so much about you," she said, in a musical voice that reminded me of Ava Gardner's. "When I was vacationing in Spain two years ago, I tried to contact you, but you were out of the country. In fact, I almost went back again last year. I had some problems." Her smile disappeared. "And at first my father thought of sending me there. But he changed his mind."

"I admire your father, Salima, but I'm sorry he didn't send you to Spain. If you want to come again, I'll always be delighted to have you stay with me. Fatima tells me you're quite a businesswoman. If you don't find interesting work here in Morocco, perhaps you might in Spain."

She smiled again. "Thank you. It would be wonderful if that were possible." Her tone had become less formal, and I felt we were closer than we had been a few minutes before. Salima turned to the vitrine. "These earrings are my favorites," she said, looking back inside the case at the half-moon gold pendants. I looked, too, and found them exquisite—delicate and decorative at the same time. "Your sister is extremely talented," I said.

"I know," she replied. "And she's lucky to have an interest she can pursue in Morocco. My specialty is not in much demand here."

I feigned ignorance about her situation, and Salima repeated what Fatima had already told me about her job in New York. "Sometimes I don't know how I'll survive if I'm forced to stay here," she said.

"But this country is beautiful."

"That's easy for you to say, because you're not Moroccan. There's no way you can understand the pressures on a Moroccan woman. The lack of freedom, the idea that women are supposed to cater to men's wishes and sublimate their own personalities. In New York I was so happy! I loved my life and my work, and the people, and the hours, too." She sighed. "I could breathe there. Here, I'm suffocating with tradition and expectations."

I nodded sympathetically. Pretending I knew nothing about the husband or the child, I said, "I understand. How well I remember trying to adapt when I was first married in Spain. Staying in bed until eleven, lunching at three and dining at ten-thirty, and not working at anything. Yet, when I began to get used to the night hours, which meant rarely going to bed before two A.M., I soon took up their morning hours as well. And do you know, Salima, today I live like any other Spanish woman, and I find it quite normal."

She shook her head impatiently. "Yes, but to be in New York! To know I can do whatever I please that evening, that week, my whole life . . . to me, that's exciting and mysterious. The freedom to try to become successful on one's own merits."

At that moment Luis and several friends joined us and I introduced Salima. Courteously, she shook hands, but directed her attention to Luis, who seemed to lift her spirits remarkably. A short time later she turned and drifted away. Luis's eyes followed her until she had crossed the room and disappeared.

"Now I understand why that girl gets into trouble," Luis commented. "She's more than just *guapa*. She has an interesting quality, an intensity which contradicts the innocence in her manner."

"She's also unhappy," I added. "Or at least she was until she met you, darling. You have a way of cheering women up." I took his arm and as we strolled through the room, admiring the exhibit, I wondered how I might help Salima. Now that I'd met her, I understood Fatima's concern, but as I watched her, I could not reconcile this sweet girl with the wild rebel Fatima had described. Fatima's designs were magnificent, but the real star of the show was Salima, who attracted admiring glances as she walked around the room, wearing her sister's jewels, speaking enthusiastically with possible buyers. She seemed to be doing everything possible to help, without a trace of the bitter hostility Fatima had referred to. It occurred to me that perhaps Fatima had misunderstood Salima's animosity.

By the time we left to rush to our hotel to change, it was almost dark. The sky was a dim molten red—the reflection of the feverish lights of the city. And against this dramatic backdrop, we passed the ancient palace where we would be dining later on. I looked at it in wonder. The stuccoed walls as white as eggshells were washed with a faint, reflected red sheen, and the three huge domes loomed like luminous moons in the sky. The aged palace was wrapped in an atmosphere of drama and adventure.

At nine o'clock the arched entrance of the old Moroccan home glowed with the light of oil lanterns, their orange flames shooting meters high into the air, making shadowy designs dance over the whitewashed walls. Two maids in long white djellabas and white head scarfs knotted at the nape of the neck stood at the door, welcoming the arriving guests with dates and camel's milk. One girl dipped a glistening silver ladle into a bowl of creamy milk and filled a small crystal glass, which she handed to me. This custom, I had heard, was a throwback to the times when Moroccans were nomadic, and dates and camel's milk were the most precious nourishment. Men in elegant ankle-length white djellabas and women in glittery silk brocades of lavish colors gave the grand entrance salon an air of Lawrence of Arabia. I wished I were wearing one of the beautiful kaftans instead of my evening gown, which until then I had thought exquisite.

The dining room was all red—tapestries, carpets, the velvet banquettes bordering the walls, even the painted designs in the thirty-foot-high carved ceiling, and in each corner was a low round table with centers of red roses entwined with bougainvillea. I found my place card and sat down on the floor, and, imitating my neighbor, took the velvet pillows scattered nearby and placed a triangular one under my arm, a long thick roll at my side, and a large round cushion for my back.

The man seated on one side had been introduced to me by

Fatima at the exhibit. His name was Michel de Bonville, and I remembered him because of his good looks. Although not very tall, he had a self-assurance that made him immediately comfortable to converse with. In no time he informed me that he was the French representative for a company involved in manufacturing men's and women's leather goods, and that he had been recently transferred to Rabat to oversee a factory, and to improve sales in Morocco. "And how do you intend to do that?" I asked, with Salima in mind.

Though he was sophisticated and well-mannered, I was surprised to note that my question seemed to catch him unprepared. "I'm not completely sure," he admitted falteringly. "I only arrived a few weeks ago, and I'm still trying to analyze the problem and become familiar with the factory. As I spend more time here, I hope I'll have a better idea."

"Don't you think this might be done by improving your public relations program? Perhaps your company is not spending enough on advertising."

His face brightened. I noticed that the large wide-set eyes were an indeterminable shade of grayish brown. His light brown hair, thick and bushy, sprouted from his head like an overgrown crew-cut. He was wiry but strong-looking and, I suspected, a good athlete. "As a matter of fact, I've been thinking about that," he said. "I suspect my company would be willing to explore that possibility—but where would I find someone experienced in advertising and promotion here?"

Oh, no, I thought, this was just too easy. Not wanting to press too hard yet, I murmured something noncommittal and let the topic drop—but I resolved to introduce him to Salima later in the evening.

Meanwhile I had become conscious of another man opposite me, whose staring was making me uncomfortable. Eventually we began to speak across the low table, and in no time discovered we both had a special interest in horses. By the time the sixth course appeared, a huge silver tray with steaming couscous, the good-looking foreigner—it was obvious he wasn't Moroccan—had managed to change places with Michel de Bonville and had invited me to accompany him to the races the following Sunday. I told him regretfully that we were leaving

Sunday morning and couldn't go, and at that moment, Fatima approached and overheard our conversation. She pulled up a few pillows and sat down next to me. As soon as the man's attention was elsewhere, she confided, "It's a good thing you didn't say yes. That fellow you've just been talking to is from the Soviet Embassy. His name is Serge Lebedev. I don't think Luis would have wanted to accept that invitation, not the way he feels about Communists."

I was surprised to learn he was Russian. I had thought he was French, since that was the language he spoke and his accent sounded like that of the Parisians I knew. Suddenly the possibility of seeing him again became more attractive; fraternizing with the enemy had always appealed to me, perhaps because I usually learned something new about their tactics and mentality. But I knew Fatima was right. There'd been Soviet Communists in Madrid during the three years of the bitter Spanish Civil War, which had seen nineteen of Luis's family killed. Although Luis spoke little about that war, I knew he had not forgotten the tragedies. Most Spaniards had not. Over one million out of a total population of twenty-seven million had died.

Before everybody moved from the tables, Fatima told me more about the blond Russian. "He's been here for over five years, and until lately he's always remained distant. Ambassadors come and go, and yet he stays on. It's strange, but I suppose his remaining here is due to his late wife, who, it is said, refused to return to Moscow. The new French Ambassador, who had known them before, told me the most heartrending story about Serge, and ever since I've tried to be kind to him. You've never heard anything worse. Serge and his wife had two children—a boy and a girl. The boy committed suicide when he was fifteen by shooting himself with his father's revolver. And then the daughter, who was seventeen, threw herself in front of a speeding truck five months after her brother died. Two suicides! And their only children! The French Ambassador said the children were emotionally unbalanced. The wife had spent a great deal of time in a psychiatric hospital in Moscow, so undoubtedly the children inherited their tragic weakness from their mother. But she was beautiful. When I first met her at a dinner in the French Embassy, I didn't know about this tragedy. She was perfectly normal as far as I could see. Anyhow, when she became ill about three years ago—she died only last year—no one knew him well enough to be able to offer much sympathy. Serge was inconsolable for the longest time, and he's only lately started going out."

At that moment Abdul finally made his way to me, and despite Fatima's fascinating story, I was obliged to turn my attention to him. I'd always been very fond of Abdul—he and his wife had visited us often during the summers in Marbella. Thanks to their help we'd been able to fill our house there with Moroccan antiques. Soon, mint tea and coffee were served and people began to mill about. Abdul indicated that he wanted to talk to me, and took my arm, directing me toward the patio. He said nothing of consequence until we neared the fountain, where the jets of splashing water blurred our voices.

"Did Luis give you my message?" he began.

I nodded.

"There's no way I can stress the importance of avoiding this catastrophe," he said as we circled the splashing water. "Not only for my country but for America as well. The person I suspect to be masterminding the plan is here tonight, but I dare not mention his name—I may be wrong. But if I'm right, it's someone close to the King, and to me as well. For that reason I cannot tell anyone about this." He glanced nervously at two men coming in our direction, one in a Moroccan uniform and the other in a red fez and a long white djellaba. Abdul lowered his voice still more. "However, of one thing I am certain. Libya is behind this plot. You are aware, I'm sure, that the Libyan government supports leftist causes and is sympathetic to Communist doctrine—it's natural they would support any movement to annihilate our King. This thing would be a disaster—for us, for you, for everybody. Please say you'll help."

I had already decided it could do no harm, and I nodded. A wash of relief spread across his features, and then, with the robed figures now quite near, Abdul hurriedly changed the subject.

On our way back to the house I had an opportunity to introduce Michel de Bonville to Salima. As soon as Michel had said hello and shaken Salima's hand, her face lit up. "You're French," she said.

"I moved here recently," he replied. "I'm from Paris."

"I love Paris—almost as much as New York, which is my favorite city in the world," she said. "I came to love Paris when I went to school there. Apart from the beauty of the city, it is a wonderful place for a woman to work. I miss that kind of challenge."

"I confess I feel the same," he admitted. "Working in Paris gives one so many opportunities. The competition is stimulating—the people from all over—not to forget the glamour."

I saw that they had hit it off well enough, and chose that moment to mention Michel's job.

"You know, Salima has been working in advertising and public relations in New York," I said. "She's experienced and has a university degree in advertising—and she's very clever."

"Really!" he said. "Do you have a job at the moment?"

"No, that's not easy in Morocco. That's why I would like so much to be living in New York or Paris. I'm not sure how long I'll be obliged to stay here." She scanned the room, probably conscious that dissenting family members might overhear.

"Salima is Fatima's sister, by the way," I said, hoping Michel might realize how helpful her important family might be to his business.

"It happens that we may be hiring someone to handle our Moroccan public relations and advertising," he said to Salima with an amused glance at me. "If you're interested I'd be happy to speak with you, say, tomorrow? In my office?"

Salima took his card, barely able to conceal her pleasure. Michel soon moved on to talk with other people, and I was glad I had seized the opportunity to put them together.

"Oh, Aline," she cried. "If he gives me the job I don't know what I'll do to repay you. This is the first time I've felt any hope for so long!"

Chapter 3

When I called the American Embassy the next day, I was informed that the Ambassador was out of town, but his secretary arranged a meeting for me with his deputy, who received me that same afternoon. We spoke in the attaché's office, and I told him about my past services for the CIA and OSS, and also that Jupiter had been my spymaster since the beginning. Then I informed him of the reason for my visit and showed him the photocopies of the secret communiqués. He insisted on knowing the name of the person who had provided the reports, and with regrets I complied. As soon as he heard Abdul's name, and without even requesting a translation of the reports I had shown him, he became very concerned and suggested I speak to someone in their CIA office.

"Our Chief of Station is out of town, but his assistant would be the person to assess this information." He picked up the telephone and dialed a number, and I heard him request someone to see me immediately.

A few minutes later I was ushered into the airy office of Henry R. Rice, a bespectacled, curly-haired young man of about thirty. It didn't take long before I realized that he was a pompous novice in the business of espionage, and much impressed with himself. This was obviously his first post overseas, and he wanted to make it known that he ruled the roost—alone.

I explained my past espionage services while he sat impatiently in his swivel chair, swinging from one side to the other.

Perhaps his nervous motion and disrespectful attitude led me to transmit Abdul's worries without sufficiently defining its enormous importance.

Rice started by telling me that my news was difficult to believe, since they had capable agents throughout the country and would have known about such a plot if one existed. When I suggested he contact Jupiter about the matter and get his opinion, he became frankly offensive. "Old-timers like that fellow you call Jupiter don't impress me. In my opinion they should all be retired—obligatorily." He smirked. "And you'll have to forgive me if I tell you that in my opinion you're all behind the times. We run things differently now. Operational Approval is required before recruiting an agent. The first thing that should be done with this fellow, in order to know whether he's reliable, would be to have him fill out a PRQ."

I looked at him in amazement, tempted to laugh at the self-importance with which he spoke. But trying to control myself, I asked, "What in the world is a PRQ?"

"Personal Record Questionnaire," he answered pompously. "All modern intelligence agencies use this type of form. We need detailed information about our future controlled-agents for our files back in Langley. Can't take a chance on people whose background and political history is not available to be checked."

I shook my head in disbelief. "I never said this friend was going to become an agent. He'd certainly refuse. He's an important government official and a friend of the King. He would never work for a foreign government. And as for the PRQ, whatever it stands for I know nothing about it, nor do I intend to find out. I've been working at this business since our country first had a foreign intelligence service, and my superior never requested anything like that. I wouldn't think of complying if he did. The people who provide my information are all persons I trust personally, and information is often wheedled from them without their being aware. I couldn't think of compromising them. No. No," I said. "I see we don't understand each other at all."

"Well." Henry Rice shrugged his shoulders and raised his eyes to the ceiling and then, in a conciliatory tone, said, "I'll send a note to headquarters. That's our custom when anyone comes in with a request, but I doubt you'll hear from us."

I grabbed the documents which were lying on the desk, picked up my handbag, and stuffed them inside to indicate that our meeting was over. I got to my feet, struggling to keep my tone matter-of-fact. Repeating my request about the cable to Washington, I told him the Company would know where to find Jupiter. Henry Rice stood up, again saying something about sending a note on to headquarters, but I was so furious I could barely hear him, and anyhow I doubted he would send the kind of cable that would bring any reaction from Langley. As I walked out the door I vented my indignation, telling the egotistical young amateur that there were many agents he called old-timers who knew more about foreign operations than he, who had no experience out in the field.

I swept through his outer office, determined never to return and never to have anything to do with this office again. If the style of my exit attracted attention, so what? I was never going back. I sailed through the corridor, almost tripping over a cleaning woman who was on her hands and knees washing the red tile floor. Only when I saw the Moroccan receptionist staring at me did I slow down and try to regain my composure.

As soon as Luis saw me, a few hours later when we were boarding the plane on our way back to Madrid, he asked about my conversation with the Ambassador. We were surrounded by friends, so I had to wait until we were airborne to tell him what a failure the visit had been and how rudely the young CIA official had behaved. Luis turned to me. "May that be a lesson to you, and to me. I never should have told you about Abdul's worries." He took a cigarette and tapped it on the silver case. "The last thing I want is for you to get involved again with your old colleagues. No. I was wrong in telling you about Abdul's request: I intended your efforts to be limited to speaking to the Ambassador—no more."

Gazing out the window, I could not help but think about our old friend Abdul. I remembered his children and our three boys playing together in the swimming pool in Marbella. Now he had asked for my help—but there was nothing I could do.

* * *

It was some three weeks later that I received the call from Jerry Haversmith, the local Chief of Station in Madrid, asking if he could come to my house. The matter was urgent.

Jerry was a stocky fellow who looked more like a prizefighter than an espionage agent, yet he could speak six languages fluently and imitate any accent. Although his nose was red and bulbous and his skin showed signs of acute acne, for me his charm had always overcome his appearance. We'd made a point of becoming friends ever since he and his family had arrived in Madrid; Luis and Jerry even played golf together, so it was quite normal for Jerry to drop by now and then without arousing suspicion.

That day when I came downstairs to meet him, he was standing in the library, apparently absorbed in studying a document we had recently received from the Spanish Ministry of Justice. He was a history buff, and especially interested in Luis's famous ancestors. "This is really fascinating," he said, fingering a framed genealogical chart. "You never told me Luis was descended from Christopher Columbus. It says here that at the end of the eighteenth century, Luis's great-great-grandfather was Columbus's direct heir and that he had one son and one daughter."

"And that the daughter was Luis's great-grandmother," I said. "These things impress me, too, but not Luis. Columbus's main heir carries the title of Admiral of the High Seas and the amusing title of Duke of See Water, which in Spanish is Duke of Veragua, bestowed by Isabel the Catholic in 1492. That, of course, always went to the male heir, but Luis's great-grandmother inherited the archives and papers. She also inherited our ranch in southwestern Spain where you've visited."

Jerry nodded. "I didn't know I'd been in a property belonging to Christopher Columbus."

"Let's say to his descendants. That ranch has been in Luis's family since 1231, way before Columbus discovered America. The funny thing is, the archives show the family was not especially impressed with him when he married into it."

We walked into the next room and sat on a sofa where I could keep an eye on the garden, where my son and a friend were kicking a soccer ball. It was a lovely afternoon, and long shadows from the fading sun zigzagged over the yellow-and-blue d'Aubusson carpet. The setting was ideal for secrets.

Jerry reached into his pocket and brought out a piece of yellow paper. "I was told to show you this."

He said nothing more while I concentrated on the typewritten sheet. It turned out to be a transcript of the cable from Henry Rice in Rabat. As I read through it, my emotions went from astonishment to despair and fury. For a few moments I could say nothing, weak from the news he had brought me—Abdul Nabil had been murdered. The message provided no further explanation other than the last two sentences: "This leads us to believe that Tiger's information may have a serious basis after all. Would greatly appreciate her assistance."

At that moment the butler came in with the tea. We said nothing until he had left the room. Jerry waited for me to pour him a cup of tea and then looked at me.

"What do you say, Aline? Are you willing to go down there? To help us? This could mean a major crisis in northern Africa."

I shook my head vigorously. "Not a chance." I kept moving my head from side to side. Maybe it was the shock of my friend's death, but it was also the worry that I had been responsible. I had mentioned Abdul's name in the Embassy that day. Had it been leaked? Who knew what passed for cocktail-hour chatter among the local diplomats, or what uncalled-for inquiries about Abdul that fool Rice may have made without stopping to think about the danger the man was in? It took a few minutes for me to tell Jerry that I did not intend to work with the Rabat CIA man, who I now believed could have saved a good man's life if he had paid heed to my warning. Stumbling and stuttering with emotion, I told Jerry how Rice had behaved with me in his office a few weeks before.

"Now that the damage is done—my friend dead—I don't think there's any way I could help. Let that ridiculous inexperienced Henry Rice try to figure out the problem."

For another twenty minutes Jerry tried to convince me to help. "Just one short trip to Morocco to visit your friend Fatima. It's so little to ask. You could talk to Nabil's widow while you're there. Find out something," he pleaded.

But the memory of Rice was still too fresh in my mind, and

I suspected that Nabil's wife would not be able to help me, since Abdul most certainly had not told her anything—in order to protect her if nothing else. I continued to refuse. Then I went on to explain just how difficult espionage always made my life. I told him that Luis opposed these missions and that, if my cover were blown, my in-laws and my friends would be scandalized to learn that for years I had been working as a secret agent. I tried to convince him that the strain of leading a double life was disruptive to my marriage and my peace of mind. "I always want to collaborate, but I owe it to my husband to keep my promise not to get involved in espionage anymore. It's just not fair to him," I explained. When Jerry left I was still insisting that I did not see how I could be of any assistance.

The next day, when I returned from riding at the Club del Campo, my maid Maria Luisa told me Señor Derby had telephoned twice, from someplace called Boca Raton. "A silly name," she said. "Imagine calling a town 'rat's mouth.'" He would call back. However, it was midnight, which in Florida was only six in the afternoon, before Señor John Derby, alias Jupiter, reached me.

"I'm taking tomorrow's plane to Madrid," he said. "I hope you'll be there. I must talk to you urgently."

Jupiter had been my "spymaster," as I jokingly called him, since 1943, when he had recruited and indoctrinated me in espionage at the spy school referred to as The Farm, outside Washington, D.C. After a mission in Spain which had nearly cost me my life, Jupiter had sent me on assignment to France and Switzerland, until, returning to Spain, I had married in 1947. But soon Jupiter was after me again to take part in other missions, such as the one a few years before in Paris, when I had recruited the Duchess of Windsor. She had worked with me on an espionage mission for four months; it had been a great success and together we had uncovered a spy in NATO.

I always knew when Jupiter said he wanted to see me urgently, that his request was related to undercover work, despite the fact that he had other reasons to come to Madrid as well. Several years before, he had built a beautiful home on the outskirts of the city, surrounded by twenty acres of gardens and woods. He had often asked my help in finding a servant or to help form a guest list for a party, but this time I knew his visit had nothing to do with household matters. I wondered if I would tell Jupiter that, that very day, Luis had received an invitation from King Hassan to go shooting in Morocco.

The invitation had been arranged by our good friends Carmen Villaverde and her husband, Cristobal. Carmen was General Franco's only child, and one of those rare persons of whom even her father's enemies could find no basis for criticism. She was intelligent, considerate, and generous, and Cristobal was one of Europe's leading heart surgeons. The shoot was being given for them as a way to promote Spanish-Moroccan relations. The invitation would give me an excuse not only to return to Morocco, but also to investigate the coup . . . but I was still determined not to get involved.

Since Abdul had held an important post in King Hassan's government, the news of his death appeared in the *ABC,* the Madrid daily paper, the following day, but there was no mention of how he had died. Luis and I telephoned his wife, Myriam, as soon as we saw the paper, but she added nothing further and it was uncomfortable to ask questions about the tragedy on the phone. I called Fatima. She carefully intimated that Abdul's death had been suspicious, but she did not want to elaborate. "Of course," she said, "Abdul was buried immediately." There would be no funeral ceremonies for him. According to their customs, the relatives buried the dead as soon as possible with little fanfare. Their religion taught that the dead person had passed to a better existence, so there was no need to make a fuss.

The next day Jupiter arrived at my house; we embraced warmly, since we had not seen each other for some time. He looked better than ever—Jupiter had always stayed fit. Maybe it was part of his training for any unforeseen encounter. In fact, I knew of two occasions where his physical condition had saved his life. I hadn't taken a brush-up course in weapons or self-defense for years, but I was certain Jupiter had. Today, as usual, his face had that shiny scrubbed appearance, and he looked impeccable in his Savile Row suit. Flying rarely seemed to give him jet lag or change his aspect in any way. I suspected he slept better on a plane than in his bed. "Hate those Florida vacations," he began. "After playing golf every morning for a week, tennis in the afternoon, and those parties at night, I can't wait to get back to my office."

I laughed, because as far as I'd noticed, John Derby's office was a plane. He had offices—in many different countries—but he was never in them: he was always on an airplane going someplace. For years now I had wondered how often he did jobs for the Company and whether his recent business interests in the Far East had been initiated precisely for that reason. He had a large network of import-export transactions worldwide, which, of course, was an ideal basis for global espionage. But despite our long working friendship, I'd never dared ask if the real purpose behind his business was collecting intelligence. In our work there existed certain unwritten laws. One never inquired—ever—about anything; even the weather could sometimes be a delicate topic. But I suspected that Jupiter, like myself, would never give up completely; he truly enjoyed tracking down enemies of his country. We had done it too long simply to retire. Espionage was our second nature.

"Well, you know what I'm here for," he chuckled as he took the seat I indicated on our yellow sofa.

"Yes, and don't think for a minute that I'm going to work with that fellow from the Agency in Rabat," I began. "You can't imagine how rude—"

Jupiter lifted his hand to silence me. "I'm here to apologize for him. Rice will soon be recalled to Langley. George Allerdice, one of our best young fellows, will replace him."

"You're also here to induce me to go to Morocco," I said.

He smiled. "Don't be hasty in your decisions. What would you say if I told you we were going to do this together?"

"I don't know. First tell me what you know about Abdul's murder," I said.

"Abdul was assassinated at close range as he climbed into his car. His chauffeur, who had opened the door, was also killed. No witnesses. There were powder marks on his face. He must have recognized his killer."

"His wife dared not give me any details about his death, nor my friend Fatima, either. Can you explain that?"

"Maybe an investigation is underway and they've been advised not to talk about it. I'm sorry that you lost such a good friend." John Derby shrugged. "That's all I know for the time being. He was very concerned about saving his King's life, and he probably knew much more than he told you, or they wouldn't have killed him. I think Abdul even knew who the leader was, even though he didn't tell you. He probably wanted more proof before voicing his suspicions." Jupiter began to detail the way in which he wanted me to help. When he left, I gave him the copies of the Arabic documents Abdul had entrusted to me, but I still had not agreed to anything.

I also had not told Jupiter about King Hassan's shooting invitation. The trip, which would last nearly two weeks, in April, would take us to areas we had never been before, each night to be spent in a different place. Invitations to royal shoots were highly prized. They were lavish and luxurious and the guest list was always filled with outstanding personalities. I had no intention of missing this one, and I did not want to spoil it by trying to pick up intelligence at the same time—especially since my small intervention had ended in Abdul's death, for which I continued to feel partly responsible. The fact that I might combine our trip with espionage would certainly make Luis protest, but at the same time, if Jupiter knew, he would be still more insistent in my taking on the job.

That night, however, when I told Luis about my visit with Jupiter, his reaction surprised me. "I've been thinking, Aline," he said. "I said before that I wanted you to have nothing to do with this, but I also realize how disastrous this coup would be for Spain if it were successful—only our enemies would benefit if anything happened to King Hassan." He kissed me. "You must do what you think is right. And besides, we'll be together for the whole time.

"What could possibly happen?"

Chapter 4

King Hassan's shoot was still about three weeks off, and Jupiter left for Rabat almost immediately to study the situation, promising to send me a message before Luis and I left or to see me in Rabat when I arrived. Despite his promises, I had no news from him for two weeks, but during that time I almost forgot about the problem in Morocco, because Spain's Chief of State, General Franco, became ill. He was nearing eighty and we worried about the future of our country should he die.

Franco had designated Prince Juan Carlos as his successor two years before, but would the transition after his death be peaceful? That was the thought that worried all us Spaniards.

Fortunately, the General recovered, and after a sigh of relief, we were all able to continue with our plans. Then Jupiter's man in Madrid called to inform us of something new: several left-wing press articles had appeared in Rabat and in Casablanca, referring to Luis as a capitalist exploiter whose mining interests for years had robbed Morocco of millions. The article also implied CIA manipulation. We were astounded.

Luis was especially furious since his family's mining corporation had a reputation for being one of the fairest foreign companies in Morocco. Then, after reading the clippings sent by Jupiter, Luis had an idea. "It all has to do with the coup. The person who concocted this stuff must have overheard Abdul confiding in me at the board meeting."

"How do you know?" I asked.

"Because," Luis went on, "some of the statistics he mentions in this article"—he waved one of the clippings—"were brought up only at that meeting. One of the government officials who was present at our luncheon that day must be involved with the traitors. Over fifty men were present, though," he said glumly, "so there's no way to guess who it is."

"At least it's something to go on, Luis," I said. "That journalist criticizes you, instead of me, as an American who could be connected with the CIA. What worries me is his mention of the CIA—maybe he attacks you as a way to get at me. If someone reported seeing me coming out of the CIA office in Rabat that day and the journalist learned of it, that could have been his reason for mentioning CIA interference."

"An Arab is less likely to think a woman could play a serious role in a major intrigue," said Luis.

"There are some special assets," I replied, "to being a woman doing espionage in an Arab country." We dropped the matter then; neither of us could fathom what the Communists' purpose had been.

The day before our departure I received another call from Jupiter in Rabat. He was always cautious, and we spoke in a manner no one could understand. Decoded, Jupiter said he was unable to come to Madrid before I left, and expected to see me at the party in Rabat the night of our arrival in Morocco. "Our COS in Madrid will call you shortly," his words gave me to understand. "Be sure you see him before coming here."

As soon as Jupiter had hung up, Jerry called, asking if he could stop by. He arrived about a half hour later and wasted no time. "We've got a break. Jupiter has intercepted a message that could be proof Libya is involved in this plot." He showed me the transcribed cable from Jupiter and pointed to the last two lines. "These are the exact words," he said as his finger moved along the typed letters. "They were in code, of course, and in Arabic. Our translator is first-rate, so we're sure it's right."

My eyes concentrated on the lines to which he pointed: *El Hadj and his cohorts will move on Mecca in ten days.* I looked up.

"'*El Hadj*' meaning their leader, and 'Mecca' being the King?" I asked.

Jerry nodded. "And it's all planned to take place in ten days' time."

"How did Jupiter intercept this message?"

Jerry smiled. "A piece of luck. We obtained the info straight from the KGB. They're so damned clever, these KGB guys. And do you know, that fellow Henry Rice was not all bad. You must have impressed him more than you thought. After you left, he had his surveillance teams working overtime, following every damn employee in the Soviet Embassy. And in only one week's time, his efforts paid off. One of his men, who was trailing an embassy chauffeur, saw that the man frequently took the same road going out of the city and always stopped at the same empty lot. Then he would get out of the car and wander around until he picked up a stone, turned it over in his hand, and put it back where it had been. It didn't take much to figure out that the guy was servicing a dead drop, so after the chauffeur left the lot one day, our guy took a look. The stone had been hollowed out, and threads drilled into it so it could be screwed back together; the job was so well done that the crack was almost invisible, and our man spent hours picking up stones and turning them over before he located the proper stone with the message concealed inside. The first message stated, in plain French, 'Where's the money?' He put the message back and replaced the stone exactly as he'd found it. From then on we have had access to one of their dead drops. And that's where we got this message."

"Then we know that the Soviets are aware of the coup?" I asked.

"Yes—and they are undoubtedly serving as middlemen, relaying messages between Libya and whoever this Moroccan traitor is. Now about this message. Since it was intercepted yesterday, that could leave us nine days—we don't know for sure. Your job is to get this information to the King privately and quickly. The Embassy doesn't dare have one of its people received by the King. That would attract attention. Also, since the King always has a Moroccan official with him, and that very person could be part of the coup, the visit might tip off the plotters."

I told Jerry that it was almost impossible for me to see the King, much less alone, that the monarch's invitation to shoot did not mean he would be with us all the time. He might join us for one or two days, and there was no way for me to know exactly which days that might be. I also told him that the King's favorite brother, Prince Moulay Abdullah, would be acting as our host.

"If King Hassan doesn't plan to join the party until one of the last days, he could be dead by then. We'll keep trying to find other avenues on our side, but meanwhile you find a way to get that message to him personally." Having never been assigned to an Arab country, Jerry knew little of their protocol and customs. For a woman to have a private audience with an Arab chief of state was almost impossible. Nevertheless I had to try.

Hoping to be able to contact the King as soon as possible, I telephoned Fatima and asked her if she thought Hassan would be at the reception the night we arrived in Rabat.

"The King rarely goes to such affairs," she answered. "Why do you ask?"

"I hoped to be able to speak to him," I said.

"About what?"

Quickly, I made up a feeble excuse. I knew that a friend, Antonio Sainz de Montagut, had shipped a "Spanish horse" as a gift to the King's eldest son. Since we raised the same type of horse on our ranch in Extremadura, I explained to Fatima that I would like to tell the King how his eight-year-old son could transmit the commands needed to perform the intricate steps. The Spanish horse had originally been the mount of armored knights in the thirteenth century. Three hundred years later, the Spanish Consort, Phillip the Handsome, impressed by the magnificence of these horses, had sent some to his Austrian homeland, and they had become the famous Lippizan horses of today.

"I'll see what I can do," she said.

The next day Fatima called back. "The King will have his aide take you and Luis to the riding school, where the horse has already been delivered, and he said to tell you that the young prince was enraptured with the gift. But unfortunately His Majesty will not be in Rabat the one day you are there."

I would have to find some other means of contacting him.

Chapter 5

One of the women I most admired in Spain was Carmen Franco. She was one of the best shots in the country, which was no small accomplishment, since Spain had many crack women guns, and she was quite a beauty, with long-lashed dark eyes, shiny, thick, black hair and a figure that belied the fact that she was the mother of seven children. Cristobal, her handsome blue-eyed blond husband, who held the title of Marques of Villaverde, was also a top shot, and his impressive athletic build made him the object of female attention wherever he went. Both Carmen and Cristobal had been friends for many years.

Since our invitation had been from the King and was in honor of Carmen, our arrival in Casablanca this time was especially grand. The King's brother, Prince Moulay Abdullah, was there to greet us, with many Moroccan government officials as well as the Spanish Ambassador to Morocco. The colorful scene gave a festive air to the terminal—the men were dressed in their formal white djellabas with red fezzes, but there were no women in the official reception. We were whisked into a waiting room decorated in true Moroccan style, with colorful tiles, carved, hand-painted ceilings and round tables with glittering silver trays holding Oriental silver teapots and samovars. While our luggage was being taken care of and papers attended to, we sat on banquettes, eating cookies and drinking mint tea from pink gilt-etched glasses.

Soon we were on our way to Rabat, escorted by a line of black Mercedes. Sirens resounded from the lead cars, and with flags and lights, they cleared the route. The forty-five minutes from Casablanca to Rabat were an example of the power of King Hassan, and the awe in which his people held him: cyclists, donkeys, and vehicles scattered before us as if a giant windstorm were blowing them away. Entering Rabat, we whisked through traffic and red lights. Too bad for the natives, I thought, astounded at the rapidity with which the clogged highway had been converted into an empty road, but it was a nice feeling to be the guest of a head of state.

That night the dinner dance being given by the Prince was scheduled to begin at eight-thirty, but those of us who had come from Spain had received a special invitation to have cocktails beforehand with him and his wife, a beautiful blonde Lebanese girl.

Dressed as she was, in a rose silk brocade kaftan and sparkling jewels, no one would have guessed that this delicate, ultrafeminine Moroccan princess had attended French schools and held several university degrees. As for the Prince, he was handsome by anyone's standards: tall, slim, with harmonious features and large lively eyes—truly charismatic.

It occurred to me that since I had been unable to reach the King directly, the Prince would be the ideal person to inform about the intercepted message, but many guests were within hearing distance and I dared not mention such a delicate matter without privacy. Glancing about, I looked for the room where a pamphlet in our suite had stated that an exhibit of important Moroccan paintings was being held that week—I was quite certain that it had to be one of the rooms off this one. As soon as I was able to talk alone to the Prince, I told him I was anxious to see the collection.

"That's easy, Comtesse. You only have to take a few steps this way," he said, pointing to the room. "If you are interested, I'd be delighted to show them to you. They're the best we have." I was pleased that my ruse had worked with such ease.

Fortunately, when we entered the exhibit, no one else was there, and I quickly broached the matter of the intercepted Libyan cable. I explained that friends in the American Embassy who did not have access to the King had asked me to pass on a piece of extremely sensitive information. I knew I was risking blowing my cover, but considering whom I was speaking to and the importance of establishing a connection, I felt it warranted the chance.

At first the Prince seemed to give slight importance to my words. In fact, I had the feeling that he was humoring me. His glance was mischievously skeptical.

"Comtesse," he said, "I'm grateful for your interest in the welfare of our monarch, but frankly I don't think you should give any importance to such rumors. We receive tips like this frequently, but they never prove to have any basis. You shouldn't worry your lovely head about such things. You can tell your friends in the Embassy that we appreciate the well-meant intelligence, but that we don't think there is any danger from the Libyans or anyone else—for the time being at least. I doubt I can even mention this to my brother. Part of my job is to ward off rumors and persons that might worry him unnecessarily." The tassel on his red fez bounced as he shook his head.

Nevertheless, I told the Prince what Abdul had told Luis. Abruptly, his whole expression changed, as if a black cloud had come over his face. The handsome forehead creased, the dark eyes squinted. "Ah . . . uh . . ." For a moment the Prince did not know what to say. Obviously Abdul's message had given an entirely different light to my information about the intercepted message. It was undoubtedly the fact that Abdul had died that gave my information greater weight.

"Do you have any further information of this kind, Comtesse?" he asked.

"Right now, no," I answered. "But I may later on, and it would be an advantage if you could give me someone who has the King's confidence to advise if anything comes my way. Someone like yourself, or someone you are completely sure of."

Prince Moulay Abdullah frowned. "I would prefer not to handle this sort of thing myself, Comtesse. But this is obviously a delicate matter, and an important one. To worry the King about a threat which may be only a malicious rumor—and to instill in him a lack of confidence in one of his close aides, as Abdul's suspicions indicate—could be imprudent." He shook his head. "No. No. I know personally all those men and I would not want to damage their credibility with my brother." He remained thoughtful. "Nor would I like to risk my brother being unaware of a genuine threat." I could see that the Prince was profoundly distressed. "The only person for such a delicate task," he pronounced the words slowly, "would be Rachid Salloum. He's without doubt my brother's closest and most loyal aide. He's also extremely well informed, and very intelligent."

The Prince turned away nervously, and began to walk quickly around the room, the folds of his long, white djellaba making the only sound. He was looking for something, and when he pounced upon a card lying on a Louis XVI desk in the corner, I realized what it was. Bending over the table, he scribbled, while I waited in front of a painting of a street scene in Fez, with horses and mosques in the background. In case someone came into the room, I wanted to appear to be studying the exhibit.

Then the Prince returned to where I was standing and handed me the card. "Here—you have his name and this will serve as an introduction if I'm not able to do that personally."

Two people appeared in the wide double doorway to the next room. The Prince stretched out his arm toward the painting. "This work is not that of a national artist," he said. "It's by Eugène Flandin. But it has been included in the exposition because of the remarkable manner in which it depicts a typically Arab scene." The couple glanced our way and then passed on. As their footsteps receded, Moulay Abdullah returned to our topic.

"Rachid is a splendid fellow. His father was an important sheik in the Sahara, so Rachid was brought up in the desert. He came to the notice of my grandfather, Mohammed the Fifth, because of his extraordinary intelligence, and received his early education from the most learned men in the country. Later, my grandfather sent him to Paris for advanced studies, and it followed that Rachid eventually became my brother's tutor. There's no time to tell you more about this now, but I hope you'll get to know him on this trip. He's a good man, and no one knows better how to protect the King." The Prince touched my arm lightly and led me toward the large double doors. As we walked out of the room he added, "I'll advise Rachid of what you have told me. He'll be ready to receive any information you may want to pass on."

Perhaps I looked concerned, because he added hastily, "Don't worry. You'll find him easy to talk to. If I see him here tonight, I'll introduce you, but he rarely comes to these large parties." He tapped his handwritten note as I was placing it in my evening bag. "When you have the first opportunity, show him that paper and he'll know you're the person I will have mentioned to him. Since he'll be with us on the trip, you'll have no trouble reaching him."

As we walked back to the large salon, the luxurious carpet absorbed our steps. The Prince's silence made me aware that he was more upset than he wanted me to know. Just before we reached the others, he spoke again.

"I trust, Comtesse, that you will mention what you have told me to no one. This trip is most important for maintaining Morocco's good relations with Spain. My responsibilities oblige me to make certain that General Franco's daughter and her guests have an enjoyable visit and that nothing detracts from the impression that this country is under solid leadership. You have probably read in the press that Spain is now considering ceding the territories of the Spanish Sahara to Morocco. If it comes to pass, this would be extremely beneficial for my country, and the possibility of political unrest, if known, could be disastrous." He looked at me. "You realize, Comtesse, I am sure, that Morocco has had a tragic history. When the powerful European countries took control of African territories in the last century, Spain and France obtained territories in Morocco. Even as recently as 1921, when Abdul El Krim nearly succeeded in ousting Spain from its control of the Riff area, there was bitter warfare between our countries. This is a matter which, for you as well as for us, is of major significance. Our relationship with Spain is most important."

I also knew that General Franco had had a special relationship with Morocco, having been stationed in the Spanish-controlled areas of the country for thirteen years before, in 1936, leading Spanish and Moroccan troops across the Strait of Gibraltar to

Spain's mainland to defeat the Communist upheaval during that country's civil war.

I assured the Prince that I would not mention our conversation to anyone. A few moments later we joined the crowd, which contained many celebrities. Malcolm Forbes was just coming in, and behind him I recognized Brigitte Bardot, with Yves Saint Laurent. Yul Brynner, who had been filming something nearby, was also in the room. Everywhere I looked, familiar faces mixed with the glamorous Moroccans resplendent in their grandest kaftans and evening clothes. In no time the Prince was again chatting and joking with his guests, offering drinks and introducing people with such smooth, carefree charm that I wondered whether I'd overestimated the importance he'd given my information.

Fatima approached with a handsome man in tow. "Aline," she said, "I want you to meet General Medbouh, a friend of mine who will be on your tour. He's the head of the King's guard, one of our most important generals, and the youngest." They exchanged a warm glance as she spoke.

"Madame la Comtesse," he said with perfunctory courtesy, "I feel as if we've already met. Fatima has been telling me so much about you." He inclined his head in a courtly, genial bow, but he seemed distracted. He was in his forties, handsome in a crisp way, with a firm mouth, long black eyes, and black hair. His white djellaba hung like drapery over a muscled statue. Something in his demeanor, however, showed that his thoughts were elsewhere, and underlying his good looks and languid self-assurance, he seemed uncomfortable. Fatima disappeared into the crowd in a wave of perfumed air, and I tried to begin a conversation with this important Moroccan, though his attitude made me feel ill at ease.

"Your country . . ." I began, smiling formally.

"My country," he interrupted facetiously, "is indeed fortunate to have such a lovely guest."

I acknowledged his flattery with a weak smile and tried again. "I've always been so enchanted with Morocco's ancient customs and its hospitable people."

A look passed over his face, the kind of look that spreads over a man's face when he is bored and uttering social amenities. Medbouh was not interested in conversing with me, but made no attempt to move on. Nevertheless, he took a step closer and continued to speak. "Until now, you have not seen the real Morocco, Comtesse," he continued pompously, as his eyes scanned the room. "You will see ancient cities where these customs you appreciate had their inception."

"Yes, I hear we'll visit some famous souks and"—I noticed he was focusing on someone behind me, but I continued—"and the fortune-tellers."

"Oh, you've heard of the famous *kri-kri* of Marrakech. Do not take her predictions lightly. She has foreseen many tragedies in my country, like the death of my brother. Morocco is a country where superstition, religious faith, tradition, and plots brew together." He stopped talking, concentrating on someone behind my back. I turned slowly to follow his gaze; it was Fatima, engaged in conversation with Yul Brynner, but with her eyes on General Medbouh. When she saw that I had observed their glance, she quickly turned her head. What did this mean? Medbouh continued his conversation about the *kri-kri*. "I hope you have the opportunity to visit her."

"Oh, yes," I responded. "Fatima is arranging a séance." With the mention of Fatima, I captured the man's complete attention for the first time.

"You have known Fatima long?" General Medbouh asked.

"Yes—she's an old and dear friend." And, testing the General, I added politely, "We share all our secrets."

His eyes looked startled. He bowed, saying, "I do hope you enjoy your visit," and moved on.

Why did I say that? I said to myself. Of course the secret part was not true, but the General had reacted in such a curious fashion, as did Fatima when I caught them gazing at each other. I couldn't resist. I wanted to know more about this important general who was head of the palace guard and therefore influential with the King.

As guests continued to fill the room, I listened to the names and watched the Prince to see if he made any gesture that would indicate that my contact, Rachid Salloum, had arrived, but he did not; so I took for granted that the man had not come. Eventu-

ally, the interesting people and the general gaiety of the reception put the matter of the Prince's cutout in the back of my mind
for the time being.

The dinner took place in the grand ballroom of the hotel,
where the decor outdid any Arabian Nights fantasy. Tables for
eight were set European-style; a band from Paris was playing.
Probably because I was American, I had the good fortune to be
seated between Malcolm Forbes and Cary Grant. Mr. Forbes
turned out to be a fascinating dinner partner, with unlimited
interesting stories about Morocco, and Cary Grant was not only
handsome, but a great dancer. Across the table was my friend
from Madrid, the beautiful Ava Gardner, who certainly caught
the attention of Forbes, and by the time Luis came over to ask
me to dance, they did not notice our leaving the table.

While Luis and I danced, I couldn't help noticing how much
other women looked at him. I glanced at his eyes and marveled
how the stark black of his dinner jacket and white of his shirt,
and his tanned skin, made them seem greener than ever, and I
told him so.

"I doubt that," Luis said, shaking his head and smiling at me.
"You just think so because you see me so often." I nestled closer
into his arms. I love to dance, and Luis was superb. He led me
strongly but smoothly, his right arm tight around my waist,
pressing my body into his. It was exciting.

"But that would make me think your eyes were less green,"
I murmured. "The things one's used to always seem less remarkable."

The music ended and we walked arm in arm out into the
patio, where a three-tiered fountain splashed water from one
level to the next with a sound like millions of glass beads falling.
With Luis beside me, I mused for a moment on my marriage;
how, unlike so many things in life, it grew more absorbing and
engrossing with time. Then I thought of Salima, and her tragic
experience with the terrible American. But that was the key, the
partner; I thanked heaven and all the stars for leading me to such
a man as my husband.

As if she had read my thoughts, Salima suddenly appeared
before us, looking breathtakingly beautiful. It was not just the
superbly embroidered silk kaftan she wore, whose rich greens

and gold enhanced her striking coloring, nor her sumptuous jewels. It was a radiance that emanated from her whole being. There was no doubt that she was happy.

"Aline, I've been looking everywhere for you," she said. "I wanted to tell you my wonderful news. And to thank you. Michel de Bonville has hired me to work in his company. I'm in charge of advertising and public relations for all Morocco. It's a huge job, and I don't know how I'll possibly get it all done, but I couldn't be happier."

I was elated. "Nothing could please me more," I told her. "There's nothing so wasteful as a beautiful, intelligent girl languishing without something to occupy her mind. I think you'll find that everything else will now fall into place."

"I can already feel that," she said, looking around at the lovely room. "Everything about my country seems better suddenly."

"And is Michel de Bonville an agreeable boss?" Luis asked.

"He seems fine. I've hardly seen him, to tell you the truth. There's so much work to be done. The company has been very lax about publicity until now, and it really shows." She looked around the room, her long white neck beautiful in its circle of gems. "I think he's supposed to be here tonight," she said.

General Mohammed Medbouh was just passing by, with an officer resplendent in a white-and-red uniform and multiple decorations. Salima nodded toward him. "I saw you talking to General Medbouh. He's so attractive and charming. My family knows him quite well, because when I was a little girl he used to court Fatima."

I was more bemused by her answer after having seen the glances exchanged by her sister and the General. Salima went on. "The King considers him to be outstanding. And everyone likes Medbouh, although he's so busy we do not see him often. He's now married to one of the most beautiful girls in Morocco." She said goodbye and rushed away to greet a friend.

"She's certainly changed her tune," said Luis. "What a difference from before—you'd think she'd fallen in love."

"A woman can fall in love with more things than just men," I teased. "As you know, I was passionate about my career, too."

Luis scowled, then relaxed. "If you'd really considered your

work the most important thing in life, I don't think you would
have ended up with me," he said, giving me a sly smile.

I spotted Michel de Bonville across the room and, leaving
Luis, went over to talk to him.

"I'm so pleased that things worked out with Salima," I told
him.

"What a favor you've done me, Aline," he said, taking my
hand in both of his. "Salima is such an asset to the company—
exactly what we needed. It's better that she's Moroccan—she
knows the market, and what might affect it, better than a European would. She's more professional than I could have hoped,
and instead of my having to look for her, you've brought her to
me."

As he spoke, I noticed again what an extraordinarily good-
looking man he was—the gray eyes, the thick brown hair, and
the charismatic smile that reminded me of my son Alvaro, always concealing a sly grin over some plot he was brewing. I
wondered if Salima had been impressed by his good looks—if so,
she had not mentioned them. I hoped that it was work and a
career that interested Salima now, since no good could come of
her being involved with a Frenchman. Still, I had made a successful match—even though not one of the usual sort.

Before the party ended, Serge Lebedev, the Russian whom I'd
met at Fatima's sister's party during my last visit, asked me to
dance. At first I was inclined to refuse, but it seemed unnecessarily rude not to accept. Perhaps the fact that he was tall and
slim and had a Slavic attractiveness also had something to do
with my decision. As he put his arm around me and we started
to move to the beat of the music, I couldn't help enjoying his
rhythmic strong lead, similar to Luis's. He must have been as
aware as I that dancing close together was a superb way to
communicate, and so it was this evening. How lucky could I be,
first Luis, and then Serge. How he had learned to dance so well
in Russia I had no idea, but strangely enough the way he held
me reminded me of college years ago. I wondered if some of his
diplomatic career had been in the U.S.A., then I remembered
the terrible story about his wife and children and dared not ask
him anything personal.

As we left the dance floor, we bumped into a large, pleasant-faced man with sparse gray hair and a plump, nice-looking older woman in a long cotton paisley print gown with white collar and cuffs; I was not entirely surprised when Serge introduced them as the Soviet Ambassador and his wife. Over half the guests at the ball were diplomats, Rabat being a small city where social life depended mainly on foreign embassy personnel. We did not speak much as he took me back to my friends, but I had the impression that he had enjoyed the dance as much as I had. Despite his country's political system, I couldn't help liking him. He was quiet and distinguished in gestures and manner.

As soon as I was back at my table, Fatima came over and pointed out a short Arab with a round sallow face who was smoking a cigarette near the door. She took a compact from her bag and began to pat the shiny spots on either side of her nose. "That's the journalist Moustapha Benayad," she said softly, "who wrote those articles criticizing Luis." She continued to repair her makeup as if that were her only interest at the moment. "He's a dangerous man, known to be sympathetic to the Libyans. He's Algerian but he's lived here for many years," she went on. "He plays up to anyone with money or power. I wouldn't be surprised if he were a member of the radical left wing of the Istiqlal party. Look at him. He's probably standing there hoping to talk to General Oufkir, the Minister of the Interior, who in our country is the minister with the most responsibility and power. He's about to leave the party through that door. See how the General is heading that way. Of course Oufkir will have to say hello."

At that moment, to my surprise, Jupiter appeared. He sat down next to me and for a while we spoke about generalities with Fatima and Luis, but as soon as it seemed appropriate, he asked me to dance.

We had barely taken two steps when he said, "We're in a bit of luck. Do you know who is in town? Bill Casey, with his wife, Sophia. They were supposed to come to this party, but they have just arrived and were too tired. You remember Bill from your OSS days, don't you?"

I nodded. During World War II, tall, gangly Bill Casey had become a legend for the OSS agents operating in Europe. He'd been stationed in London as head of Secret Intelligence for Western Europe, in charge of the Jedbourgh groups that parachuted behind enemy lines in northern France. The Jeds were teams of three men: a radioman, a demolition expert specializing in bombing bridges and railroads, and an infiltration spy who eased into local life, absorbing valuable information about train schedules, troop movements, and fuel and ammunition storage depots. Bill had assisted in setting up a highly successful network headquartered in northern Europe; had helped sidetrack Nazi efforts to obtain supplies of heavy water, essential for the production of the atomic bomb; and had played a leading role in the grand deception of D-Day, leading Nazi generals to defend the wrong beaches. Though the Normandy landing had been costly, it could have been much worse except for his cunning deceit. Bill had also devised newsletters dropped behind enemy lines to demoralize German soldiers. His accomplishments were endless, and I was thrilled at the prospect of seeing him again. When the war had ended, Casey had been approached, as had I, by General Donovan, chief of the OSS, and Whitney Stevenson, who had served as chief of Secret Intelligence, to continue in an elite espionage cover called World Commerce, Inc. I had accepted and worked with them until I married in forty-seven, but Bill had returned to his position as a lawyer in New York.

"Of course I remember Bill," I said. "And I'm proud to have been a colleague. Finally, I'll meet his wife. He always talked so much about her. What is he doing here?"

"The King has invited him on this trip, too. Spanish economic relations aren't the only ones being pursued this week. Did you know he's been nominated as Director of the Securities and Exchange Commission in Washington?" John Derby's low voice was barely audible over the noise of the booming fourteen-piece band. We were waltzing under a ceiling carved with small geometric designs—like the inside of a lacy intricate beehive. Women whirled by in brilliant fuchsias and greens and piercing blues. The shimmer of satin and silk combined with the glitter of jewels produced a dazzling effect.

Before I forgot, I hastened to tell John about the cutout the Prince had given me.

"Good, Tiger. That was quick work. Every moment counts."
His waltz became less energetic. "Remember, the intercepted
message said ten days." The words emerged from the half-closed
mouth slowly, like water coming to a boil. "We assume that the
countdown began on April first. Tomorrow will be the fifth day;
today is already the fourth, so every moment counts. I've always
connected this assassination attempt with the King's invitation.
It's just too much of a coincidence. Make contact with that
cutout as soon as possible. It's fortunate that you now have a
means of getting information to the King. Though we're trying,
I don't think there's any way anyone from the Company could
contact him. The conspirators will be scrutinizing everyone
connected to the Embassy and the CIA. Any attempts to contact
the King by us at this moment would certainly attract their
attention."

While we danced we set up a system by which I could send
messages to him in Washington during the trip. I would call a
number in Madrid, which would be a special unregistered telephone in the COS's office there, but which would figure as my
private home telephone number. My conversation would be in
code, using sentences that referred to children and household
matters.

"Then Jerry will relay your messages to me. And don't worry,
our new man here will attend to your requests promptly, although it's better you do not have any contact with him, so as
not to arouse suspicion. It's too bad you went into that office in
Rabat. You know, local nationals working in American embas-
sies around the world make quite a profit selling information to
the Soviets and other governments. Certainly the Moroccan
intelligence service is aware of who goes in and out of our
offices."

By the time John Derby took me back to my table, our strategy for the next few weeks had been settled.

The next morning the hotel was a bustle of activity, everybody excited about the departure for the glamorous trip. While
Luis went outside to look for our driver to make certain our
luggage was taken care of, I went to the hotel cafeteria for
cigarettes. As I walked into the large empty room, there, seated

at a table in a corner, were Serge Lebedev and the radical journalist, Moustapha Benayad, in what appeared to be a heated
conversation. When they saw me, both men ceased speaking,
and Serge stood up. Despite the distance between us, he bowed
ceremoniously and smiled. Since the woman at the bar had no
cigarettes, I merely waved hurriedly in their direction and
rushed out before the Russian could come over to say hello. As
I ran down the steps, I wondered what Lebedev and Benayad
had been talking about. It annoyed me to see that attractive man
I'd enjoyed dancing with on such chummy terms with a rene-
gade like the journalist. Seeing them together reminded me that
Serge Lebedev was no friend, after all; he was an employee of
a government whose system was in direct opposition to my own.
I decided to ask Jupiter what position Lebedev held at the Soviet
Embassy. I also wondered if the newspaper man, Benayad,
knew that I was the wife of the Spaniard he had criticized in his
press columns and that I was American; although I realized that
being married to a Spaniard probably eliminated any significance my American background might have had for either of
them.

When I arrived at the entrance, guards and soldiers in brown-
and-green uniforms were directing cars and chauffeurs to their
places in a line of black automobiles. Prince Moulay Abdullah
was talking to Luis, and turned to face me, one arm on the sleeve
of a bright-looking young officer, whom he pulled toward me.

"This is Captain Omar Khalil, Comtesse. He will be your
guide and interpreter during the trip."

Captain Omar Khalil had a pleasant face, large black laughing
eyes, and a jaunty air, and he exuded the scent of some eau de
cologne unknown to me. He was obviously delighted to be part
of the excursion, and bobbed up and down in a series of stiff
bows.

"Omar also speaks Spanish," the Prince went on, "since his
mother is from Granada. He has a good knowledge of our national culture, and I'm sure he'll make your trip more interesting."

Before I could say anything, the Prince had moved on to
attend to other guests. The Captain mumbled a few polite words
about having to check everything with our driver and then

departed. Luis went off to look for Cristobal Villaverde, and I stayed, looking over the heads of the people at the foot of the stairs. Almost immediately I saw Bill Casey. Despite the fact that his back was toward me, there was no mistaking that tall, slightly stooped figure, the graying unruly hair. He was with an attractive blonde woman whom I assumed to be his wife. At that moment he turned my way. I waved frantically. When he saw me he waved back and smiled broadly. After directing a few words to the woman at his side, he bounded up the steps.

"Aline," he said, grabbing my hand enthusiastically. "It's good to see you. Washington's been so crazy, with the confirmation hearings—we just had to get away. I heard you were going to be on this excursion." His familiar slurred undertone brought back memories of the war and OSS. Whether he was telling a secret for my ears only, or simply conversing, he had always been difficult to understand; his mumble had always made me put my ear closer. Despite that, he was one of the wittiest and quickest men I'd ever listened to.

"I'm a great admirer of King Hassan," he said, "and delighted to be invited to go along." Casey gestured toward his wife, who appeared to be occupied in instructing where a certain blue suitcase was to be placed in their car. "You'll finally meet Sophia. She's a great girl. The trip will give you an opportunity to get acquainted. This should be an interesting excursion. I hear the King's entire cabinet is coming with us. That's special. Not easy for government business to stand still for ten days. The King is making a big effort."

"Yes." I wondered if Bill had suspicions that something was going on; he'd always been almost clairvoyant about such things. I realized I had not clarified with Jupiter whether I could discuss the plot with Bill, and now it was too late. I'd have to send Jupiter the request in a message. There was a disparity between Casey's gangly, almost awkward, bespectacled appearance and his sophisticated, razor-sharp mind. A pity, I reflected, that the CIA had lost the qualified skills of such an agent.

I changed the subject; I didn't want to mention the plot until I'd contacted Jupiter. "Bill, I didn't know you liked to shoot."

"I don't. Don't even know how. The only shooting I've done was back in a couple of days' briefing in Washington during the

war. They never even put me through the training program you
had at The Farm. Truth is, I don't even like shooting, but Sophia
and I want to see the beautiful villages and unusual sites I've
been hearing about. By the way, did you see our old friend John
Derby last night?" Leaning close to hear him, I had the unmistakable impression that we were now speaking as one "former"
spy to another.

"What's Jupiter doing in Morocco?" he asked. "We bumped
into each other at the concierge's desk and never had a chance
to talk." His keen gaze observed me. The thick glasses glinted
in the morning sun. I could sense he was still the consummate
observer, by habit missing nothing, through he seemed to be
paying little attention. I had no time to answer his question
about John Derby, because Bill casually gestured toward the
foot of the stairs. I looked and saw two men standing near the
hotel entrance, conversing as they watched the cars being loaded
for the trip. One was wearing a gray business suit; he was short
with long dank hair, but I couldn't see his face. The other, in
a black-and-white-striped djellaba, I recognized immediately as
the left-wing columnist, Benayad.

"I know that man," said Casey, quietly indicating Moustapha
Benayad. A cloud passed over his features and his voice became
hard. "That Arab means trouble. The last time I saw him was
in '43. I made the mistake of helping the guy out." Casey turned
back to me. "He might have been executed by the French officials in Algeria. He was a minor official in their military then."
Bill's eyes went back to Moustapha. "Now what is he doing
here?"

"He's an important journalist," I said, and then told Casey
about the anti-American articles Moustapha had published and
about his attacks on my husband.

"What you're saying doesn't surprise me. After I left Algiers,
it became clear he was actually a dangerous criminal. And I've
always regretted not giving him his due." There was a tinge of
irritation in Bill's voice. "In those days that fellow was young,
but he already had three kids. His family was starving, and he
needed money desperately. His wife came to see me and somehow convinced me that her husband was worth giving another
chance. According to her, he'd pulled his brothers out of the

gutter and used the money he got from us and from our enemies
to save them all from starvation." Casey shook his head. "I'm
always a sucker for young people's problems, especially when
they're poor. How do I know how I'd react if my family couldn't
eat?" My friend sighed heavily.

"I didn't know you were in Morocco during the war," I said.

"No, it wasn't Morocco. I was in Algiers, where we had the
problem with Ali Ryad. I'll never forget that name."

"That's not what he calls himself now. Maybe you're mistaken. That fellow down there is Moustapha Benayad."

"No mistake. He's one person who could never disguise himself. Notice those short arms and that tic of jerking his head
sideways. He always appears to be afraid someone may attack
him. Maybe that's the reason he usually kept two sharp-bladed
knives under his robe. He was an expert with those things. No,
no. No mistake. That's Ali."

"What were you doing in Algiers?" I asked. "I thought you
were in London all during the war."

"Yes, London was my base, but I was in Algiers for a few
days. You may remember that the OSS headquarters was moved
to Algiers when the Germans occupied southern France in '43.
Our people were operating out of a house called the Villa Mag-
nol." Bill looked down at the two men again. "Ali Ryad's not
going to be pleased when he sees me. He obviously wouldn't
want anyone around to know of his shady past. He also had a
reputation as a cold-blooded killer with those knives, but we had
no concrete evidence, another reason why I was against report-
ing him to the French authorities. He never showed any grati-
tude, though. Always arrogant and proud. A swaggering
pretentious sort." Casey moved down one step. "I'm going to
talk to him. There was something Ali did twenty years ago that
we now know about, that bastard. I also want to find out if he's
in the same old betrayal business. Usually I can tell. It's a world
you never forget once you've been in it. You should know."

I was astounded at what Bill was telling me. Glancing down,
I saw that Moustapha was walking away as fast as he could.
"Hurry," I said, "he's leaving. I think he saw you. You're going
to miss him."

Casey bolted down the steps, but Moustapha was gone when

he reached the bottom. I saw the black-and-white-robed figure dodging in and out between the Mercedes. Beyond the cars stretched a file of trucks and vans like a bumpy rope along the horseshoe driveway out into the street, where I lost sight of him.

While standing there alone I deliberated whether my friendship with Casey could lead Moustapha to wonder if I, too, might be involved in espionage. Right now this would be very inconvenient. However, I hoped to make use of Casey's experience along those lines during the trip; then I remembered again that I had forgotten to clear it with John Derby. I would have to do so at the first opportunity.

Our guide, Captain Omar Khalil, approached to inform us that the caravan was about to leave. I descended the steps and saw that Luis was just entering the car. Captain Omar rushed to open the other door for me, and stood stiffly at attention as I stepped in. "The Count and Countess's automobile will be number eleven in the convoy," he said, as he took his place in the front seat next to the driver. "There are twenty-one vehicles in the expedition." His voice took on the rhythm of a tourist guide. "The vans transport carpets, tents, and special foods, which are difficult to find in the isolated areas where we are going. There's also an ambulatory hospital with a doctor and a dentist. This trip will be a remarkable opportunity to see the most beautiful towns in the country and spend nights in some of the loveliest palaces." Our interpreter was obviously delighted to be on such an important trip. It was useful for me to know what languages Captain Omar spoke, so I could talk to Luis during our trip without being understood. "Do you speak English, Captain?" I asked.

"No. I only speak Arabic, French, and Spanish, Señora Condesa," he answered quite humbly.

Luis pointed to a stream of people filing into a large bus ahead. Our interpreter saw his gesture and explained, "Those are the cooks and extra menservants for the trip."

I was surprised to see that there were no women in the group. And then I realized that I hadn't seen any Moroccan women the whole morning. Our car had still not moved, and I looked around, trying to spot one of the wives of the ministers who were accompanying us, but not one of the Moroccan women I'd met the night before was on the steps or in any of the cars. Only Sophia Casey, Carmen Franco, the Spanish Ambassador's wife, and the wife of a Spanish businessman were in the group. When I asked Captain Omar Khalil where the Moroccan wives were, his eyebrows lifted in surprise.

"Oh, there will be no Moroccan women on this trip, Señora Condesa." The answer startled me. I might have asked him why, had he not jumped out at that moment to attend to some problem, but I continued to wonder for some time why Moroccan women wouldn't want to go on an excursion which promised to be delightful.

I observed Captain Khalil as he attended to some added luggage that was being loaded into the trunk of our Mercedes. As he did so, he chatted all the while with the fellow carrying the luggage. I could see that he was a forthright, pleasant fellow. He must have been around thirty-five, but he seemed younger than his face suggested. Captain Khalil was handsome in a soft, puppylike way, with a round face and cherubic black curls which wound over the rim of his officer's cap. His uniform encased a frame as small and frail as a teenager's, yet he had a devilish manner that didn't quite match his childlike demeanor. Since the departure of the caravan was being delayed for some unknown reason, others descended again from the cars to walk around, and Captain Omar remained talking happily to anyone who came near. He spotted Michel de Bonville lounging against a column of the porte cochere next to our car and, approaching him, began chatting in French. Through my open window I could hear Omar apparently trying to convince Michel that he had vast knowledge about the raw material employed in Michel's leather goods factory. He launched into a witty diatribe concerning the finer points of curing cowhide and how the truly rare leather could be selected from the mediocre; he spun a wild theory about feeding the animals fermented wheat and sunflower petals in order to nourish their skin. Michel looked puzzled, perplexed by Omar's ideas, not yet aware that the young officer was jesting, and unwilling to challenge the sweet-faced Moroccan. Then Omar went one step too far, something to do with rubbing brandy into the cows' flanks every night after they were milked. Finally Michel caught on, feigning great interest in the process, and asking increasingly detailed questions, until Omar was stumped. Soon, both men were laughing at the near-success of the joke.

Carmen Franco descended from her car, which was just in front of ours, and walked over to where I was. Before, while the caravan had been making the last preparations to leave, Carmen had fulfilled the obligations of the daughter of a chief of state by talking at length with the Moroccan officials who had come to see us off. She was always admirably patient in attending the countless meetings, ceremonies, and parties that her position required. She was very much like her father, unemotional and disciplined. "I wonder what the problem is. My driver thinks two of the ministers forgot their guns," she said.

"Don't think we're going to be shooting the first days," I responded. "I was told we'd be sightseeing. Maybe that's why none of the Moroccan wives are going along. They've probably seen these places over and over again."

Carmen chuckled. "I don't think that's the reason." She was about to say something more when General Mohammed Oufkir joined us. I had heard so many fascinating stories about him the night before that he was the one person, outside of Rachid, whom I most wanted to meet.

"Good morning, Señoras. We have a beautiful day for beginning our tour." He smiled. "His Majesty has asked me to see that you are well attended to." He bowed, just slightly. "Anything you need will be my command."

General Oufkir, I had learned, was Morocco's national military hero. After leading his class at the Moroccan Military Academy, the French government had offered to continue his military education at St. Cyr, the French military academy, where once again he had distinguished himself. He was a deadly shot with any firearm, from a revolver to a .50-caliber machine gun; his accuracy with a mortar was uncanny. His skills with knives and in hand-to-hand combat were legendary. One of the popular stories that circled about him was that when in Paris, while making the nighttime rounds of Paris bars with other junior officers, they rarely had to pay for their drinks, thanks to Oufkir. They had devised a trick. One of them would bet the patron that Oufkir could pin a playing card to a wall from ten meters, or thirty feet, with a knife. Drink bets would be ceremoniously placed, the card pinned to the wall, and the distance paced off, while Oufkir stood alone, squinting at the playing card, which was difficult to see through the haze of cigarette smoke. Then a patron would usually ask, "Where's the knife?" As quick as a striking cobra, Oufkir would reach behind his neck, where he concealed a small throwing knife. There would be a quick sound, like a hummingbird's, as the deadly weapon streaked the thirty feet to pierce the playing card, the slight blade vibrating dead center in the wall. Total silence would envelop the bar; the congenial atmosphere would be replaced by the unease caused by Oufkir's deadly performance. This lethal act earned him the nickname "Lieutenant la Mort," the Death Lieutenant.

I had also been told that the French military had later shipped Oufkir to their last bastion, Dien Bien Phu, in their losing, savage Vietnam war. Oufkir's reputation had preceded him, and he simply augmented it there, leading his troops into one vicious jungle skirmish after another. He took no prisoners, and the deadly hummingbird was very active. Though wounded several times, he seemed immortal and was awarded one decoration after another.

Remembering these stories, my eyes were attracted to the long, jagged scar on his left cheek. In the bright sunlight I saw that it must have been a deep wound, and wondered which of his many heroic feats in Vietnam had been responsible. As he walked away, both Carmen and I agreed that the ugly gash added allure to his appearance.

Luis had just joined us and laughed at our remarks. "There's no understanding women," he said. "Remember that day in your pool in the Pardo, Carmen, with our bullfighter friend, Dominguín? All the women were fascinated with his bullfight scars, but not one commented on the very visible war wounds most of us men had."

Carmen laughed. "Well, a wound from a bull on the number-one matador is more glamorous, but I don't intend to be impressed with General Oufkir's charm, because last night someone told me that not too long ago he had his wife's lover executed. She was supposedly his fourth wife, and only fifteen years old. Evidently Oufkir caught her in embarrassing circumstances with one of his subordinate officers. Nobody knows what happened to the young wife, but she disappeared."

Our conversation was interrupted by the return of Captain Omar. Carmen asked him if it was true that General Oufkir had many war decorations.

"More than any man in our nation, or in the French military, for that matter, Señora Marquesa." He cleared his throat. "General Oufkir has so many decorations that they cover the entire front of his uniform. Twelve gold-and-silver-palm emblems. It would take much time to recount only some of his famous exploits."

At that moment cars started to move. Carmen rushed to get into hers and Omar opened our car door again. "The tour begins," he announced formally.

The roads inside the city had been blocked off, and the twenty-one vehicles of the caravan proceeded to the main highway in file. The breeze cooled the sun-heated air inside the car, and through the open window wafted the scent of green grass and wild flowers. It was a perfect day to begin an adventure into the unknown.

Chapter 6

In the beginning Luis and I were alone in the car, with the driver and our guide, Captain Khalil. About two hours later, when we stopped for gasoline in the ancient Roman city of Meknès, General Medbouh approached the passenger side of our car and asked if he could join us. We assured him we'd be delighted, and he changed places with our guide, who jumped out and moved into another car. From the front seat, Medbouh turned around.

"Condesa, my pleasure to see you again." He spoke Spanish, ensuring that our conversation could not be understood by the driver. "Conde," he said, directing himself to Luis. "I was hoping to have a chance to speak with you. I've heard many good things about the operation of your mines."

"Certainly not from any Algerian newspaper columnist," began Luis a trifle bitterly, then caught himself. "Thank you," he amended. "My visits here are always interesting, and I trust that the mines help your economy."

Medbouh smiled at me. "Your wife seems to be enjoying herself."

"Oh, I am," I said. "I'm not interested in mining, though. I just want to see as much as I can of this beautiful country." I turned to point out the window at the city of Meknès. "Can you tell me something about that town, General?"

"That's one of the oldest towns in Morocco, built by the Romans in the second century. And those buildings near the wall are part of our military academy," he explained. I observed him carefully. There was not a hint of his stiffness of the night before. Instead, he was boyish and charming. "I'd been a cadet there, and General Oufkir, too, and many other officers you met at the ball last night."

"Tell me about Oufkir. I've heard he's the most decorated officer in either the French or the Moroccan Army. He's very impressive."

"He is all of that." Medbouh was now completely turned around, with one elbow and a hand leaning on the back of the seat. "You see, my duties are closely connected with General Oufkir, so I know him well." His pride at being associated with Oufkir was unfeigned. "General Oufkir is undoubtedly the best officer we've ever had," he added. "And he has reason to be. His father was also a famous leader, a sheik from the city of Tafraout, on the edge of the Sahara. Oufkir's ancestors were also brave warriors—in the desert. For generations they fought and controlled their part of the country. So you see, our General is also a nobleman." Then he recounted the same story I had already heard about Oufkir's dexterity with a knife.

As our trip progressed, General Medbouh went on to tell us about some of the cities we would see.

"Today we are on our way to Khenifra, a small city in the mountains, where we'll stay in a *parador,* which you know is a government-run hotel for tourists. Tomorrow we'll be at the Governor's palace near Midelt, a small city which is the door to the southeastern part of our country. And since there is no town nearby where we could lunch today, we'll be eating in the open country."

We passed great fields with tall gawky camels hitched to small donkeys, each pair pulling an ancient Roman-type plow guided by a farmer in bloomers with cloth wound into a turban on his head. I'd seen these same plows at our ranch in Spain until about ten years ago, when we had replaced them with mechanized farm machinery, but our plows had been pulled by oxen and our men wore long pants and a straw-brimmed hat. The countryside here was really not much different from southern Spain, but these sights had probably looked the same centuries ago.

When we arrived at our destination in the middle of open

country, we piled out of the car near a huge tent the size of an American circus tent, but completely different in appearance. The Oriental shape of the shallow curving tops, and the long fringe of the multicolored, richly embroidered material, gave it a romantic, exotic aspect. One of the ministers and Michel de Bonville descended from the car just behind ours. I was surprised to see the good-looking Frenchman still with us. At the hotel that morning, I had thought he was merely there to see the group off, and commented on this to Carmen.

"He's considering the construction of a new factory, which has pleased the Moroccans, so I've heard they invited him to see different parts of the country where he could establish the plant. This is an agricultural country, with practically no industry— without industry they can never climb out of their poverty." Carmen nodded. "You saw how our country changed when your American compatriots started to come in with their money and technology. That's what Morocco needs."

"That might explain the presence of so many members of Hassan's cabinet," I added.

Luis and Prince Moulay Abdullah, accompanied by a skinny man with a long, narrow, El Greco face, pointed gray beard, and haunted black eyes joined us at that moment.

"Madame la Marquise," said the Prince, introducing him to Carmen Franco. "May I introduce Monsieur Rachid Salloum."

The name brought me immediately to attention. Moulay Abdullah had pronounced it emphatically, so I would be aware that this was the man he had chosen to be my cutout with the King. While Rachid Salloum talked to Carmen about a recent meeting he had shared with her father, I observed him. His Spanish was flawless and he spoke in a strong voice, mellow and deep, similar to that of a news broadcaster. He was tall and gaunt; his shoulders had a spiny edge as straight and narrow as a clothes hanger, from which a brown cotton djellaba hung in empty folds to the tip of his pointy, worn leather babouches. The hood framing the narrow face, and the dark sunken eyes, gave him the aspect of a Spanish monk. The bone structure of his face appeared to have been chiseled from stone in a few sharp slices—one gash for the long thin nose, another for the protruding eyebrows, several vertical slashes for the deep wrinkles lining his cheeks. If it hadn't been for the vigorous voice, he would have seemed more spirit than man. So far, he was probably the oldest person I'd seen in the group, but when he turned to kiss my hand, the agility and grace of his movements made me realize he was younger than I'd thought. I wondered if he knew that I wanted to speak to him about the threat of a coup, and wondered, too, how I would go about this, with so many people always surrounding us. Would he initiate the conversation or would I have to look for a way to approach him?

Bill and Sophia Casey, who had just emerged from their car, joined us. In the bright sunlight, Sophia's blonde hair and clear blue eyes made a glamorous picture, and the Arab men stopped speaking to look at her. She was the only blonde in the entire group, and I understood immediately why Bill was so infatuated with her. Her warm smile and handshake made me feel I had known her for some time. Rachid, I thought, paid more attention to her than to Carmen and myself, and I even wondered if he had the mistaken impression that she was the woman Prince Moulay Abdullah had said would contact him.

About twenty paces in front of us was the enormous red, silver, and gold tent. It was supported on many poles, with a higher pole in the center, and its fancy fringes and the colorful designs woven into the intricate, thick, carpetlike fabric glistened in the midday sun. Flaps were tied back on several sides so people could enter. I stood looking at it, spellbound. In front of us, masses of carpets were being moved from the vans into the tent. Nearby, around an open wood fire, men in dark djellabas and turbans bent over steaming copper pots. Rachid Salloum led us toward them and pointed to the deep cauldrons, where partridge and quail were bubbling in a thick yellow sauce that exuded wafts of saffron and spicy herbs. Over other large open fires, the carcasses of whole lambs and goats were being turned on spits—the dripping juice spattered and hissed as it bounced off the flaming embers.

Rachid looked around. "We need something to quench our thirst. The drive was dusty." As he spoke he passed near me and in an undertone added, "Madame la Comtesse, I look forward to speaking with you."

So he did know! I felt a wave of relief. Monsieur Salloum

continued to gesture for a waiter until one appeared with a silver tray filled with rose-colored, embossed glasses. *"Voilà!"* Rachid made a flamboyant gesture and turned to us. "At last something to wash the dryness from our throats."

It was obvious that Rachid had easy social graces; he seemed so suave and self-assured. We sipped the hot mint tea and chatted while the finishing touches to the tent were completed. When word arrived that we could enter, Rachid Salloum took Sophia's arm and led her inside. The rest of our group followed.

The view inside looked like something from the Arabian Nights. From the delicately woven red-and-blue ceiling, literally hundreds of small, round, coin-shaped pieces of tin dangled above our heads, tinkling in the breeze that passed through the open flaps. The dirt floor had been covered with luxurious orange-and-red carpets, and filling the space were many low, round tables set in a blinding array of sparkling silver and snowy-white embroidered damask cloths. Already some guests, with legs crisscrossed in front of them, reclined against piles of rich satin pillows. I stood transfixed, enjoying the thought that this scene was probably not unlike the banquets of years past, when sultans, sheiks, and kings from remote countries met to enjoy a royal feast.

Rachid led Sophia to a table and next came to my assistance as I was trying to find my place. He picked up some pillows and showed me how and where to sit. I thought he was going to take the place next to me, and was pleased, thinking we could find a way to talk, but he saw Bill Casey wandering around nearby and called to him. To me he said, "This is my place, but I think I'll change with Mr. Casey, who may not speak French. Meanwhile, I will attend to his wife, who is also seated with people who do not speak her language. But I'll try to sit with you for a while later on." He continued to show me how to stretch out comfortably and still be able to eat. It was more difficult for me than for the men to find the right position, so that my skirt would not roll up over my knees, but eventually I was molded into a comfortable position, and Rachid went back to help Sophia.

Bill Casey took the place Rachid had offered him next to me, and, despite his long legs and arms, arranged his pillows with as much expertise as the Moroccans.

"It looks to me as if that fellow has taken a liking to my wife," grumbled Bill. "Can't say that I blame him, but having spent some time with Arabs during the war, I know these men are mesmerized by blonde women."

I joked with Bill about Sophia's instant success, while servants entered carrying silver trays with huge glistening pitchers, and with white linen towels on their arms. Although I knew I was supposed to wash my hands, I didn't know that it was supposed to be done with lots of soapy lather, and that after washing, the menservants would rinse them with water scented with orange blossoms. As soon as this ritual was over, two other waiters appeared, carrying between them a huge, round, glistening silver serving dish, which they placed in the center of the table; they lifted the pyramid-shaped cover, releasing a delicious aroma of thyme and rosemary.

"Baby kid," said Bill. My Moroccan neighbor, who did not speak English or French, reached into the huge serving dish and pulled off a choice piece, which he handed to me with a smile. There were no knives or forks, and soon I, too, was diving into the huge silver dish, pulling out my own pieces, copying the men, who were taking bread and dipping it into the sauce. Just as I was about to dive for the third time, my neighbor restrained me. "But it's so good," I said. "I really would like more."

"No, no," he said. Then, in halting French, he added: "Wait. Many more."

I looked in amazement as that huge serving dish was replaced by another containing a dozen small quail in a bed of rice and olives.

At the next table we could hear Rachid in animated conversation with Sophia Casey, and see him waving his bony hands with their long, pointed nails. Bill kept looking their way. "Something about that fellow makes me distrust him." His remark worried me, since I knew Bill had a special instinct for these things. Was the Prince absolutely certain Rachid Salloum was reliable? I wondered.

For a while during the fifth course, General Oufkir came to

sit at our table. "There are few tents as large as this one, Comtesse," he explained. "But what may surprise you still more is to learn that this one probably took several hundred men and women many years to make. Every thread comes from the wool of our sheep, the designs are taken from the Koran. Even the dyes were made by hand and will not run, no matter how much rain falls. The cloth is remarkably thick and protects us from the violent sandstorms that occur on the desert. I might sound immodest, but you'll never find tents as beautiful and as strong as these in any other country."

Rachid, hearing this from the next table, said to Oufkir, "General Oufkir, I wonder how much time you've spent in a tent." His tone was light and his expression pleasant, but his eyes were sharp. A bit surprised, I watched Oufkir closely for his reaction.

"In the army we spend whole summers in tents when on exercises, not to speak of battle tents, of course," Oufkir replied, unruffled, and turned back to us.

When the silver serving dish of pigeons in rosemary sauce appeared, General Oufkir excused himself, saying he would be taking the next course at another table. One after another, the huge, round, silver serving dishes were removed and another appeared—an entire roast lamb, then cous-cous with barley, and after that a towering almond cake filled with chopped dates and honey. But the luncheon was far from over. Now the festivities were about to begin.

Someone handed Rachid a guitar. Very slowly, he stood up, looking for a more central spot from which to play. He looked our way and then came to sit between Bill Casey and myself, squatting down cross-legged. He began to tune the instrument, but did not play until the applause became insistent. Finally, lifting the guitar in the air in sign of acquiescence, he began to pluck strange plaintive chords. After a few moments he lifted his head, closed his eyes, and began to sing. I wondered if this was a song of the desert people with whom he had lived for so long. As his warm deep voice wailed the eerie music, the silence in the tent was such that one could almost hear the breathing of the fifty or so people who listened. Like statues, the waiters in their blue djellabas and red fez caps stood motionless, and Rachid sang one song after another. Gradually, I too became hypnotized by the unusual melodies; Rachid Salloum's chants were full of nostalgia, solitude, and loneliness. They resembled somewhat the Spanish flamenco *cante jondo*, probably because the Gypsies who brought their music to Spain had come from Morocco centuries before after a slow migration from India through the Middle East and northern Africa. When Rachid Salloum laid the instrument down, a groan of disappointment, like a wave of heavy summer air, passed through the tent.

"Enough," he said, as he stood up and handed the guitar to an aide.

As he walked back to his place at the other table, the sound of metallic music and the ring of castanets caused everyone to look toward the entrance. At least fifty women, sparkling in long lamé djellabas and turbans, their faces covered by the sheerest of veils, moving and gyrating to the music of dozens of flutes and the loud boom of drums, danced to the center of the tent. The expressions of the Moroccan men told me in one brief second why they had left their wives at home. While we were being served mint tea, the dancing continued in frenzied movement around the center table, where Prince Moulay Abdullah was seated with my husband and Carmen Franco. Then I heard a sound overhead. As the dancers screamed, Bill gave me a violent shove which sprawled me facedown about a yard from where I had been. A loud crash burst in my eardrums and the weight of many pounds of heavy carpeting fell on my head. Only then did I realize that the huge wooden pole supporting our corner of the tent had collapsed almost on top of me. It crashed down exactly where, one moment before, both Casey and I had been leaning toward each other in conversation. I tried to sit up but couldn't, due to the heavy enveloping folds. The weight of the stuff was smothering. Someone lifted the heavy material from my body and I looked up. Shattered plates, glasses, and cakes were everywhere. A groan of pain rose above the pandemonium. My face brushed the thick, hand-woven carpet; one metal coin cut into my head. Someone helped me to my feet. Bill was still buried, but I could see his long legs struggling to get free. I moved my legs and shook my head. I seemed to be all right. When I looked again toward Bill Casey, he was standing, a bit dazed but apparently unharmed.

Luis appeared at my side, paler than I'd ever seen him. "Are you all right, darling?" he asked. "When I saw that thing come smashing down on you, I was sure you'd be killed." By this time, the Prince, Rachid, Oufkir, and other Moroccans were crowding around me. I continued to bend my knees and arms and turn my head from side to side to make certain I was in one piece.

General Medbouh added his voice to the others. "Countess, did the blow hit your head?"

"No. I'm just fine," I said.

Luis was still testing my arms and looking into my eyes. "If Casey hadn't shoved you aside . . ."

"You're right, Luis, Aline could have been killed." It was the Prince speaking now. "And Monsieur Casey as well."

Prince Moulay Abdullah and I looked at each other. I wondered if we were thinking the same thing. Had this apparent accident been planned? To frighten one of us? Who . . . ? Was someone accompanying us involved in the plot? I remembered Abdul's unexplained assassination, and I knew Prince Moulay Abdullah did, too.

"Rarely have I seen a pole cave in like that." Rachid's hood had fallen to his shoulders, revealing a shiny bald head. The creases in his forehead were now almost as deep as those in his cheeks, and I saw a bloody scratch across the long bony fingers when he rubbed his head. Sophia was standing with Bill at her side; she was unharmed. It seemed that a few pieces of broken porcelain had hit their table, but nothing more.

Raising his voice to no one in particular, Rachid boomed, *"Who is responsible for raising this tent?"* A racket of Arabic raged back at him. For the next ten minutes, servants, officers, and soldiers were embroiled in heated conversations. Meanwhile Luis and I separated ourselves from the commotion and walked outside. We took a turn around the half-collapsed tent and stopped when we saw Prince Moulay Abdullah on his knees, absorbed in examining the spot where the pole had broken. We knelt down beside him and watched as he sifted sand through his fingers. He shook his head in puzzlement. "It seems this pole was jammed carelessly into the ground. Where there are customarily four support ropes, there were only two. I've never heard of this happening before, but don't worry, things will be all right from now on." He sat back on his haunches, looking at me. "Aline, I would appreciate your making certain Carmen is not upset or frightened." We had become "Aline" and "Carmen"—evidently sharing the experience of an almost fatal accident had brought us closer to the Prince.

"Oh, that will not be a problem, sir. She's very unspoiled. It takes much more than this to ruffle Carmen." Rachid Salloum was approaching with two officers and General Medbouh. Bill Casey was just behind them. I knew he wanted to study the spot and the pole that had nearly finished us off. Luis and I walked with the Prince, who kept repeating that in his lifetime or his ancestors' lifetime, such an accident had never occurred. He was deeply upset.

Later, as we returned to the cars, Casey walked with me. "I took a look at that pole. Guess I was born suspicious, or maybe the habits of the trade are hard to break. I did check the two support ropes. One of the heavy wooden spikes that secures the ropes to the ground had pulled loose . . . or had been pulled loose. God," he continued, "to secure a portion of such a huge and heavy tent with only two ropes is absurd. Any kind of wind would collapse it. These tents must be falling on their heads all the time. . . . Ridiculous." When I told Bill that there were normally four bracing lines, he stopped dead in his tracks. "Do you know of anyone around here who harbors a dislike for Americans?"

"That newspaper man, Moustapha?"

"But he's not here, as far as I can see." He lowered his voice. "In my opinion that Rachid's a slimy character. I'm keeping my eye on Sophia from now on." He chuckled. "Maybe he just wanted to remove the competition." Casey's chauffeur was leaning against our car, chatting with our driver. Bill nodded to him, indicating he was on his way to his own car, and the two walked away together. Obviously, Bill was not seriously worried, I gathered, but I was left with the preoccupation that perhaps someone involved in the plot had learned about my visit to the CIA office in Rabat, and that the pole might have been a deliberate act. How long would it take to contact Jupiter and get his permission to make Casey aware of the suspected coup? That he would be an asset to our cause, I had no doubt.

The Prince and Rachid, who had been walking behind us, stopped next to our car. The Prince's forehead was still creased with worry. Rachid, his hands clasped behind his back, said nothing, but the expression on his long, gaunt face was not happy.

"I am so sorry, Aline," the Prince said. "If that tent had been smaller, the accident would not have occurred, but with such a large tent, there's enormous weight on the poles. You and Mr. Casey were lucky, but that poor waiter has a broken shoulder." Rachid was shaking his head. "If the pole had hit anyone's head, the skull would have been crushed."

Luis and I climbed into the car, our mood subdued. Once the caravan was moving, we spoke softly and in English, so Omar Khalil, who had now retaken his seat, would not understand.

"Look, this is no joke." Luis was leaning close. "That accident could have been planned. Those fellows didn't explain anything to me, but Rachid Salloum and the Prince look pretty worried. I bet they're thinking the same thing we are."

"At least if that's the case they may take my warnings more seriously," I answered. "I haven't been able to talk to Monsieur Salloum yet, and it worries me, because according to the intercepted message, this could be the fifth day of the countdown. The King should know about the danger he's in."

"Especially if Abdul was right." Luis sighed. "Now I'm sorry that I let you get mixed up in this."

Both Luis and I knew there was little I could do if I could not consult with Rachid or the Prince. I knew Jupiter was trying to contact the King through other channels, but I had little hope for his success. The Moroccans were a proud, formal people, and protocol was difficult to break. They resented foreigners intruding into their internal affairs, even if their sovereign was threatened. For my part, there was no way I could speak to the King directly if Rachid did not initiate the contact.

Chapter 7

We arrived in Khenifra, where we spent the night in the *parador*, an ancient palace recently refurbished by the Moroccan government. Luis took my arm when I got out of the car and led me up the steps of the lovely old palace as if I were an invalid. I was frankly less bothered by the danger itself than by Luis's reaction to it. He now regarded everyone who was not an old trusted friend with suspicion. That night he tasted my dinner before he would let me eat it—quite embarrassing. When we went to our room, he entered first and checked behind the doors and curtains. I protested that this kind of behavior took away the fun of our vacation, but Luis merely replied with his usual calm that if I would refrain from mixing espionage with our social life, we would have a better time. As usual, his quiet logic left me without a reply.

The next day we traversed the Atlas Mountains, where the pure dry air made my nose tingle. The colors were eye-wateringly bright, the green seemingly more green because of the contrast with the dry land around us. We arrived at Midelt at one o'clock and drove to the palace of the Governor, where we would be spending the night. After centuries of wind and rain, the color of its thick stone walls was almost pure gold-yellow against the cloudless blue sky. I figured that here, the dangers, if there were any, would be minimal, and I anxiously hoped Rachid Salloum would find a moment to talk to me.

As we filed into the luxurious entry hall, I was astounded to find Fatima and Salima there to greet us. Laughingly, Fatima said, "I guess you didn't know that the Governor is our uncle. Coming here was Salima's idea. She wanted to surprise you, and our uncle has been begging us for months to come visit him. When we were children, we came often, and he's always been fond of us. Today he has arranged a luncheon just for you, Luis, and ourselves. The Villaverdes and your other Spanish friends are being entertained, along with the rest of the party, by the mayor of Midelt." Fatima seemed happy, and I surmised that her worries about Salima had passed.

The prospect of a cozy lunch with the Governor was delightful. Luis and I were shown to our rooms, which, much to Luis's displeasure, were on opposite sides of the palace. I discovered that we women guests would be sleeping in the Governor's harem. Although polygamy was no longer practiced among the upper classes, the harem was still maintained as it had been for centuries. It consisted of a cluster of rooms surrounding a large bath called the *hammon,* which looked like a smallish round swimming pool; many of the rooms opened onto a spacious walled-in tropical garden. Originally the bath had been the harem's most important feature, the place where the Governor's young wives were bathed, and where the adjoining rooms were used for rubbing their skin with powders, polishing them with henna, and perfuming them before going to the Governor's quarters. The pool-like *hammon* was lined with tiny, iridescent tiles of turquoise and dark blue, which gave the impression of an undersea grotto. Fatima had told me that the size of the harem depended on the wealth of the man. Some harems housed over one hundred women while others might have had only twenty. I remembered Fatima telling me years before that the harem was ruled over by an older woman who was capable of maintaining peace and order and enforcing the many strict customs; she ruled the harem like a sergeant. Harem women were not allowed to leave the enclosure of their part of the palace except for special occasions, and then in groups, chaperoned by the matron, and they were obliged to be covered in white veils and voluminous white togas, called *haiks,* which concealed their shape and age. Eunuchs, she said, were never employed to maintain order in Moroccan harems as they were in some Arab countries. Fatima also told me that the Mohammedan religion assured that Moroccans were extremely clean; they washed meticulously before each of their five daily prayers, before eating, and before and after every sexual encounter. She said that their extreme cleanliness contributed to their being especially sensuous people.

I refreshed my makeup, using some of the kohl Fatima had given me, rather than my usual eye liner. The Moroccan women claimed that kohl was actually good for the eyes, which would have been hard to believe except that their eyes were so strikingly beautiful—the whites always stark and clear—that I thought it might be true. I noticed that kohl never stung or itched, the way normal eye liner could. When I was ready, a maid led me to the Governor's apartments. Luis was already there and comfortably reclining on red cushions, talking to the Governor. Naturally, both stood as I entered. I was amused, remembering that Luis's only complaint about sitting on the floor in Morocco was that getting up when ladies came in was a lot more effort. As the Governor kissed my hand, his two nieces appeared, and we all sat down on the thick carpets and soft pillows.

"So tell me, Salima," Luis said as the food began to arrive. "What about your new job? Michel de Bonville tells me that sales have actually picked up since you joined the company."

Salima beamed. "They have improved, although I really don't know if I can claim any credit. Michel is such a brilliant businessman, I think everything would have improved anyway."

"My niece is modest," the Governor said. "My brother's daughters are not only beautiful, but clever and gifted at everything they do. I remember them as little girls, pelting each other with oranges in the garden. I knew even then that they would both achieve great things."

Turning to me, he asked if I liked my living quarters. "As you probably have learned, that part of this old palace used to be the harem," he said. "Only fifteen years ago there were over fifty women housed here, and before that over one hundred."

Luis was astounded that any one man could have so many women, and said so. The Governor chuckled. "The very rich had even more."

"But how did they keep those women from killing each other from jealousy?" I asked.

The Governor laughed again. "Oh, they have killed each other now and then. Human nature being what it is, of course, it happened. The most popular method was poison."

"Really?" said Fatima. "What kind of poison?"

"Well, there's a flower called *bsibisa* which grows in this part of the country. That was popular. Also, a green flower called the *gouza,* which is easy to find. It's similar to a calla lily, with a long center stem. All you have to do is to put a bit of water in the center and let it become concentrated. It's deadly and tasteless. A few drops into some drink or food, and your victim is dead within minutes. Then there's *kif,* our hashish plant . . . any of these flowers can also be dried and pounded into a powder, and there you are. Nowadays, the way women are becoming liberated, I suppose soon they'll start using these poisonous herbs on their husbands."

"If our husbands tried to install harems in our houses, perhaps we would," quipped Fatima. "None of us would put up with that."

"But the country people still do," piped up Salima. "A man can have four wives."

"But you can't call four wives a harem, Salima," remonstrated her uncle.

"I could if I were one of them," she answered. "Share my husband with three women? Never!"

The Governor turned to me. "I hear you had a close call in one of our large tents. Not a common experience. But sometimes the men are lazy and don't drive the stakes deep enough into the ground, especially those big heavy tents."

Pleased at the Governor's suggestion that the incident might have been an accident after all, I shot a look at Luis. However, Luis's skeptically raised eyebrow made it clear that he was unconvinced.

It was almost five when we finished lunch and decided to go to our rooms for a short siesta. About seven, Fatima came to my room and suggested we take a walk in the harem gardens. As we wandered among dark-leaved fruit trees, where small, brightly colored birds were hopping from branch to branch, she turned to me. "Aline," she said after a bit of chitchat, "I wanted a moment alone with you to mention something which has been worrying me."

"What?" I asked, thinking of the tent accident.

"I have a suspicion that Salima may be falling in love with that Michel de Bonville," she said. "First that terrible American, and now a Frenchman."

"What makes you think so?"

"You've never heard anyone talk so much about a company. I just can't believe it's the work alone that excites her to this degree. Not only that, but recently she's begun attending business dinners with him."

"But if they're business dinners, wouldn't it be logical that she be included?"

"Maybe." Fatima seemed uncertain. "But she was so insistent that we come here to Midelt. 'I'm dying to see Aline,' she kept saying, and her face would grow red. I couldn't help but wonder if it was Michel she wanted to see."

"It's possible," I said. "One can hardly blame her—the man is good-looking."

"Yes," Fatima agreed. "He certainly is. But what worries me is that nothing but trouble will come of her falling in love with him. Either he won't reciprocate her feelings, then she'll become depressed and miserable again, or she'll want to marry him, which would be even worse."

"It's hard to imagine anyone resisting a girl as beautiful as Salima."

"Well, I don't think that Michel is as taken with her as she would like. But can you imagine my father's reaction? I shudder just thinking about it. Salima's already on shaky ground with him, although I'm not sure she realizes it. She's a bit of a spoiled brat, as I told you. Being the youngest, we all made a fuss over her. She thinks she can get away with anything. She's headstrong—always has been."

"Well, if she's falling for him, there's very little anyone can do about it. But I'll try to talk to her about him next time I'm alone with her, just to get a sense of what's on her mind. I can't promise anything, but I'll try."

Fatima looked relieved. "Thank you, Aline. We must keep her

from doing anything foolish. I don't know why, but I worry about her more than about my own children. I suppose it's because she's so much younger, and I always felt responsible for her."

Strangely enough, I had the feeling that there was more to Fatima's concern about Salima and Michel than she wanted me to know. Nevertheless, I continued our conversation as if nothing unusual had crossed my mind. "I also felt sorry for her when I first met her at your exhibit," I said. "But she'll learn how to take care of herself with time. We all do." I remembered my own challenges when I was young, especially that first night years ago in Portugal at the Casino—my terror at seeing a dead body on the floor, with blood pouring out of a knife wound in the back. Little did I know then that that corpse was hardly to be my last. "We were all young once," I added, and Fatima, perhaps thinking of her own lost youth, smiled and nodded.

There was a spicy smell of oranges and cloves in the air, which cleared the memories of death from my mind. "Is it true that you and Salima used to pelt each other with oranges?" I asked.

"As I remember, it was usually our older brothers pelting us, and we were always running away."

We were now walking through rose gardens. Each bud or full-blown flower was so perfect and richly hued that it looked like wax or silk.

"Do you know Rachid Salloum well?" I asked, as we were nearing the house. We passed through a pocket of cooling air, and I shivered and pulled my jacket close. It was almost dusk, and around sunset in those high altitudes, the temperature dropped quickly with the sun.

"Of course I know Rachid. Quite well." Fatima looked at the maids removing the terrace furniture and lowered her voice. "He's a very controversial figure, but extremely close to the King. Only Oufkir has as much influence with His Majesty." Fatima's face lit up when she mentioned Oufkir. "Now that's a really fascinating man," she said. "Oufkir, I mean. That special expression in his eyes. Have you noticed?" She turned to look at me.

I shook my head.

"It's a sort of cold glaze," she went on. "He was burned by

a flame-thrower in Vietnam, not seriously, but it did something to the color of his eyes. Look next time." The sky was getting darker. Fatima glanced at her watch. "Speaking of time . . . Oh, it's almost eight-thirty."

"Uh oh, we're late. We hardly have time to dress," I said, quickening my steps toward the house. Inside, the palace was bustling with servants preparing for the evening celebrations.

"Don't forget," she whispered, "if you hear anything about Salima and Michel, tell me."

As the harem doors closed behind us, I saw Carmen Franco changing in the communal dressing-room, the Spanish Ambassador's wife having her nails manicured, Sophia Casey wrapped in a white towel, having just emerged from the sauna. Two hairdressers stood at the door, waiting to assist us. A long table faced a mirror which stretched across one wall, giving us plenty of room to put on our makeup. The scene reminded me of the models' dressing room at Hattie Carnegie years ago.

When we emerged from the harem and moved to the central patio, Bill Casey greeted us. After speaking for a moment with his wife, he murmured to me, "Aline, I've been thinking about that tent accident yesterday. I wasn't especially worried at first, but . . ." He broke off and looked swiftly around the room. "These things don't happen. The Prince was shocked, and something tells me there's more to it than a careless mistake."

I sipped a fruit drink, wishing I could tell him the whole story. "I know, Bill," was all I said, "but unfortunately, there's really very little we can do about it now."

"If there had been anything fishy about that, all the evidence has been destroyed, of course," he said with a slight smile. "That's the problem with a tent as opposed to a building. But seriously, Aline, seeing that Algerian again has brought back those days, when every word or gesture could mean something entirely different. During that entire lunch I felt something was afoot, and it wasn't just because that cad Rachid was paying so much attention to my wife, either. What do you suppose was up between Rachid and Oufkir, in that small exchange of insults during the lunch?"

I regretted not being able to take advantage of his perceptive judgment, but all I dared say was, "I've no idea. I would think two leaders in high positions of command would experience some measure of friction."

He shot me a quizzical glance as if to berate me for my lack of curiosity, but didn't press the matter. Perhaps his intuition told him that I might have a good reason for not discussing it, because he said ironically, "I know, I know, this is a trip for relaxation and scenery, and just because there's a little mishap, I get all fired up. Let's go find our charming spouses, shall we?" We joined Luis and Sophia, who were in a group nearby.

Several newly arrived guests who were joining our tour were being introduced. For the most part, they were foreign diplomats from Rabat whose schedules had prevented their leaving the city until today. All were strangers to me except for Serge Lebedev. He greeted me enthusiastically. "Countess, I thought you would be on this trip. That was one of the reasons I wanted to come." He kissed my hand. I had thought that Soviets didn't kiss ladies' hands, so his gesture surprised me. His exaggerated pleasantness also put me on guard, but then I calculated that he, like myself, thought useful information might be gathered by fraternizing with the enemy. Besides, it would be difficult and impolite not to be courteous to all the members of the group. These considerations soothed my conscience because the truth was that Serge's charisma would have made it difficult for me to ignore him under any circumstances. "Thank you," I replied. "It's good to see you again, Mr. Lebedev."

"This seems like a dream, doesn't it?" Serge said to me, apparently unaware of the machinations my mind had just gone through in order to prepare myself for our friendly exchange. He breathed in the spicy night air and glanced up at the starry sky and around at the lovely columns and arches. "For you, this may be less impressive, but until I came to Morocco, I'd never seen anything to compare to the languid sensuality of Arabic living. You see, I was an orphan and educated by the State in large, modern, impersonal schools. I can't complain about my intellectual preparation there, but none of us had an awareness of how sweet and soothing life could be in a country like this. . . ." There was a sadness in his voice as it drifted off.

"I've always wondered about schools in Russia. What are they like?"

He looked at me, his smile turning the slanted, pale-blue eyes into sparkling slits. The flickering orange light of the torches around the patio made his tanned skin golden, highlighting the white, sun-bleached streaks in his sandy hair. "Now you've brought me back to reality." His masculine voice was soft and calm. "If you really want to know, it wasn't all bad. We were young. That helps. Five years at the Moscow State Institute for International Relations and then another in special training, then . . . Oh, why talk of such things when we have all this to enjoy?" His hand swept in an arc around us.

Determined to take advantage of the moment, I persisted, "But you don't even know where your parents came from, or if you had brothers and sisters?"

"Yes, I was able to determine later on, when I was about fifteen, that I had been brought to Moscow from Lithuania when I was two years old. But there's no record of my family at all. Even my name, I suspect, was changed."

"And doesn't that bother you? Not to know . . . ?"

"Not really. You see, when I was a child, many of the students in my school were in the same situation, and it seemed quite natural to us. Our teachers were kind and affectionate, and we looked upon them as our family."

"But never to have known your own . . ." As soon as I'd said the words, I regretted it.

His face become a stiff mask, and his voice, when he spoke, was as somber as stone. "I did have a family once, my own family," he said quietly. "And it was the best family in the world. But these wonderful things don't always last. I've learned not to expect too much from life."

I didn't know how to change the subject. I didn't have to. Lifting his head, he began to speak again. "Why am I wasting all this?" he asked. "A beautiful woman." The pale-blue cloud of his glance descended on me. "A romantic setting." His head turned to the columns, the tables set up in the center of the patio, sparkling in white damask and silver, then up to the sky. "Look how those stars are winking at us."

I wasn't sure how to respond to this sudden courtly flirtation. He was being polite, of course, trying to return the conversation to a lighter vein. At that moment others joined us, and we drifted apart, but as the evening wore on, I became aware that Serge Lebedev was observing me . . . too much. His previous short spell of gloom had not completely passed, however. My old fear that I'd somehow blown my cover made me worry that he was studying me because he suspected me. There's no doubt, I mused, that being on opposite political poles makes us more aware of each other; it was like a cat-and-mouse game. I was glad to see when dinner was announced that Serge was at another table.

Before sitting down I went to Luis for a moment and squeezed his hand. "About time you paid some attention to your husband," he said. "I wondered what happened to you after lunch."

I told him that I'd taken a nap and then Fatima and I had gone for a walk in the garden, where we had again discussed her preoccupations about her sister.

"I can help with that," Luis said. "I know very well what a woman looks like when she's in love."

"Oh, really?" I said, looking into his teasing eyes. "And what makes you so sure about that?"

"I knew you were in love with me right from the beginning. You didn't fool me for a minute."

"You most certainly did not know!" I cried. "I concealed it perfectly. And you were terrified that I was going to leave Spain and that you'd never see me again."

"That's what I wanted you to think."

"Luis," I cried, laughing in exasperation. "Listen to me. If you think—"

But Luis was already moving away. With a sly wave in my direction, he went to his table. What a husband!

Still marveling at his ability to win any argument, even a playful one, I went to my own place and settled down on the thick carpet, placing the pillows and cushions comfortably behind me. By now I was becoming an expert. Conveniently, I was once more seated beside Michel de Bonville, who began to tell me about ideas Salima had put to use in his company.

"Salima has already become indispensable," he said. "Americans are way ahead of Europe when it comes to marketing."

"That's why I recommended her to you, Michel."

"And I'm certainly grateful to you for that," he said as he

wiped his lips with a napkin. "She's caught on so quickly that I feel she's been with us for months. She also has such an attractive family. Her sister Fatima is so impressive. She's bright, knowledgeable, she seems to know everyone in Casablanca and Rabat."

His words about Fatima were innocent enough, but since Fatima had made no mention of having spent any time with Michel, I was surprised. Since he continued to mention Fatima off and on during the lavish dinner, I concluded that his interest in Salima was merely a matter of business, and that he found Fatima the more interesting of the two. Then it hit me all of a sudden. Could Fatima be attracted to Michel herself? Could she be jealous of her sister? But almost as soon as the idea occurred to me, I dispelled it. It was impossible that Fatima, the perfect wife, the conservative law-abiding matron, would flirt with another man and risk scandal. Yet it had never seemed to me that her husband was attractive enough to maintain Fatima's interest. I shook my head. It was a silly thought.

After dinner, Rachid Salloum came to sit beside me. I was about to talk to him about the King when a group of women dancers swept into the patio in swirls of gold lamé, wearing jangling bracelets and beating a contagious rhythm on their castanets. Tables disappeared and guests moved back to make room: suddenly we were squeezed in with others and I dared not mention such confidential matters. Most of the dancers directed their greater efforts toward the Prince and General Oufkir, who sat cross-legged on the other side of the patio. Oufkir was delighted, smiling his enigmatic smile. Rachid saw me looking at Oufkir.

"Madame la Comtesse," he said in an undertone, "do not get taken in by the General. He has a way with women, but if they knew what a bloodthirsty fellow he was, they might not be so infatuated."

"Why, what do you mean?"

"To give you an idea, once in Vietnam, he was surrounded by the enemy, outnumbered, and out of ammunition. He had his men cover themselves under the earth, then, as the enemy came closer, he stood unarmed with a white flag in his hand, followed by a few of his men, their hands clasped over their heads as if they were the sole survivors. The Viet Cong, convinced he was surrendering, relaxed their guard. At the last second, he and his men pounced on the enemy; his other troops jumped up and scrambled forward, disarmed the enemy, lined them up, and killed the poor devils with their own rifles . . . completely unethical conduct according to military code." Rachid Salloum's long, narrow face squeezed into a grimace of disgust. "And that's how the cad won his medals."

I felt I had to defend a man who had been polite to me. Besides, I suspected Rachid's story might be biased. "At least he saved the lives of his own men," I blurted.

Rachid turned a skeptical glance at me and then laughed. "Oh, women are all the same, no matter what their nationality. They're always taken in by the villains."

The evening's activities became more and more spectacular. After the first dancers retired, ten more in bright red-and-orange silk danced into the patio. Their specialty was the *danse du ventre*, their voluptuous movements and sultry glances bringing groans of pleasure from the men. Again, I was reminded of why the Moroccan men had not brought their wives. When the glittering women swirled out of the patio, the Governor stood up. He looked toward the table where Fatima was seated. "Fatima—Fatima," he clamored. "Dance for us." Despite his pleading and that of others—it seemed to be well known that Fatima was a good dancer—she did not comply until her husband went to her table, took her hand, and proudly led her to the center of the patio. The guitarists began to play soft, plaintive, centuries-old music, and Fatima began to sway slowly to the languorous rhythm. At first her movements were hardly discernible, yet I could hear the tinkle of the little gold bells hanging from her belt tassel. But as the music became louder and the tempo increased, the dance began to blossom like a flower. Her hips gyrated, at first slowly, then more quickly, but always in time to the music. She threw back her head and slowly raised her arms in a suggestive caress of her breasts and shoulders, then moved them above her head like twin cobras to the beat of the music. Her entire body moved with sensual fluidity and control; her torso moved independently of the rest of her body, keeping up its rhythmic motion as her arms swayed in graceful, slow arcs. There was none of the wild exhibition of the girls we had just seen. Fatima's entire body was twisting, her breasts arching high and her pelvis moving seductively, each gesture transmitting a sensual thrill. On her face was an expression of languorous abandon; her almond-shaped eyes were half-closed but held a sultry fire, and her full lips pouted, slightly open. Her intoxicating dance held everyone spellbound, men and women alike, and I glanced at Luis who, like every man in the room, was obsessed, but General Medbouh, sitting beside him, was smiling! A look of smug satisfaction crossed his face. I was startled, not only by the General's unusual reaction, but also by this facet of Fatima's personality that I'd never seen before. Never could I have imagined that she was capable of such sensuality in public, but she had actually done nothing wrong. She had not stripped off her clothes nor touched any man in the room.

Now Fatima sank to her knees, then arched her back with her long dark hair almost touching the floor. She gathered that massive mane of black hair in her hands and let it tumble over her face as she slid onto her back with a final soft chord from the guitars. For a moment, she lay motionless on the floor. There was not a sound, no one wished to break the spell created by Fatima's sensual dance. Finally, she rose to her feet to wild applause. I would never forget it, nor would anyone who was there that night. She twisted her hair back into its chignon and resumed her position at the table. She was flushed and breathing hard, and I saw her husband give her a long, lingering look of appreciation.

The dancing girls reappeared and the Moroccan men in their white djellabas, the women in their kaftans, remained stretched out on the thick carpets, reclining on the pillows, enjoying the exotic night. The guitars and flutes continued to play while the shimmering girls danced. The show ended and we were told that it would be a few minutes before other numbers would follow, and we all rose to stretch our legs. The Governor charged across the room to ask me how I had liked the dancing, and then jokingly asked me if I would like to learn. I laughed and started rather clumsily to imitate what I had just seen. In Western dress, I felt uncomfortable amidst the graceful Islamic arches, the intricately designed walls, and told him so.

"Ah," he replied courteously, "but you have a natural talent for our native dance. You should take lessons from Fatima." Abruptly, he took my hand. "Now let me show you how I do your dancing." He whirled me around in a few awkward steps, humming as he bounced, as delighted as a little boy.

"All the foreigners here tonight are charming," he went on. "For example, who is that young man right now talking to my niece Salima?"

He twirled me so I could take a look.

"That's Michel de Bonville," I said. "The Frenchman we were talking about at lunch."

"The leather-goods man?"

"Yes, that's him."

The Governor was troubled. "Well, well. Prince Moulay Abdullah just told me that Fatima had interceded in de Bonville's favor—asking that the Frenchman be invited on this shooting excursion—that he was going to develop a large business in Morocco which would entail the construction of more factories and employ many people. That Frenchman has certainly started out on the right foot, enlisting the aid of my influential nieces." What little grace the Governor's steps had possessed quickly evaporated as he kept his eyes fixed on Salima and Michel.

"A Frenchman?" the Governor said again. "Humph. Let's hope she hasn't taken a fancy to him."

The words about Fatima having arranged Michel's invitation surprised me. She had told me Salima had asked for him to be invited. I tried to be rational. Had Fatima had Michel invited to separate him from her sister? But she had appeared unexpectedly at her uncle's with Salima, knowing full well that Salima would see Michel. . . . Her interest in Michel, her erotic dance, General Medbouh's reaction . . . my old friend Fatima was becoming an Arabic conundrum.

I glanced at Michel and Salima. What I saw struck me as nothing out of the ordinary. Michel was speaking and Salima was listening, like any young impressionable girl overawed by her boss. As for Michel, even as he spoke to Salima, his eyes flicked restlessly around the room, as if his thoughts were somewhere else. Was it my imagination or was he exchanging a glance with Fatima? Not once did his glance wander down to

Salima's pale, upturned face or her river of blonde hair. I had the distinct impression that their conversation was of scant interest to him. Michel and Salima parted and he promptly went over to speak to Fatima. Whatever Fatima thought of him, in my opinion it appeared that Michel found her more interesting than her younger sister.

Chapter 8

I walked around the room, looking for Rachid. I was desperate to talk to him about the King, but Serge Lebedev appeared again and, taking my arm, propelled me outside, toward a deserted terrace opening onto the garden surrounding the palace. "I can't," I sputtered, caught completely off-guard. "I'm on my way to refresh my makeup—" But his arm transmitted such urgency that my curiosity took over. He led me to the terrace, where we sat on a bench. He immediately started talking in a low intimate voice with an ease and grace of manner that put me on just the intimate relationship with him that I wanted to avoid. "I wanted to add something to our earlier conversation," he said. "I'm sorry to remove you so forcibly from the party, but what I have to say is urgent and cannot wait. Forgive my impatience."

"I don't know whether you're aware of this," I said determinedly, before he could speak another word, "but I'm American by birth, and although I've lived in Spain ever since my marriage, I'm still a citizen of the United States." I watched his face closely to gauge his reaction. By his look of impassive calm, I could see immediately that he already knew. I wondered, however, whether he would feign surprise.

"Yes, I know that," he said.

Though his honest reply came as a relief, I began to speculate about how he had learned this. I remembered seeing Moustapha and Serge talking in the hotel cafeteria in Rabat. Could the information have been from Moustapha, who had written those vindictive articles about Luis? I remembered what Casey had told me about the journalist's background. My mind raced on. . . . I wondered if the charwoman in the American Embassy in Rabat had informed someone about my visit to the Chief of Station's office.

"In fact," Serge continued, "it is of great interest to me that you are American." His voice was lower than ever and he moved closer. There was something threateningly intimate in his proximity. I moved away, and he put a hand on my arm to restrain me.

"And why is that?" I asked, forcing my voice to sound calm.

"America interests me," he said a trifle vaguely, as if my question were irrelevant.

"That's hardly unique," I said, hoping to gain insight into his intent by pressing the matter. "My impression is that America is usually of interest to your government, just as the Soviet Union is interesting to us. Enemies are concerned with one another." I hoped to dispel any suspicions he might have about my connections to the CIA by speaking freely.

"I am a great admirer of your country of birth." His hand on my arm tightened its hold for emphasis.

What on earth was he getting at? Was this a trap of some kind? I looked blankly at him and remained silent.

"Needless to say," Serge continued in the same whisper, "this is a dangerous revelation for me to make. I have never spoken to anyone of this before."

I took a deep breath and looked at him directly. I could hardly believe the significance of what he was telling me. Did he want to work for us? If so, Jupiter would be ecstatic. As I looked at Serge Lebedev, I couldn't help noticing, even in these circumstances, how Scandinavian he was in appearance—the gold eyebrows and lashes, the incredible blue of the eyes, the firm mouth. His narrow cat's eyes were intense. He held my gaze, and it was I who was forced to look away first. "I can't explain why, Aline, but I trust you," he said. "Please don't betray me. Do not repeat to anyone what I have told you. It would mean my life."

I heard myself murmur a promise not to repeat his words. He

wants to work for us . . . the thought kept running triumphantly through my head. What a coup for the U.S., and what personal satisfaction—especially considering how I'd been treated in Rabat by that Henry Rice.

"Not even to your husband," he insisted. The blue eyes held mine with their unrelenting focus.

"Not even my husband," I repeated. I decided I could tell Luis once Serge had defected. At this stage, I knew I had to move with extreme delicacy; I would need to know what conditions and what payment the Company would make before I proceeded. This was information I had to obtain from Jupiter.

"I know how hard it is to promise something like that," he went on. "I've been married and I was very much in love with my wife. But I trust you, Aline. You're an exceptional woman."

"Serge, you can relax. I will not repeat your words to anyone," I said, aware that this might be a scheme. The KGB often resorted to planting attractive agents in strategic situations to compromise the enemy and then use blackmail. I determined to take no chances with this man; Jupiter would make the ultimate decision. "I promise this will be our secret," I said, "at least until—"

I heard laughter and conversation; people were coming. I knew that with his help, our chances of uncovering those behind the coup would improve enormously. We knew through the dead drop that the Soviets had direct contact with those involved in the coup. Time was of the essence. If *El Hadj*'s message had been properly interpreted, only four days remained before the move on "Mecca." I had to transmit the possibility of recruiting Serge Lebedev to Jupiter immediately.

Serge's face relaxed for the first time since he had led me out to the patio. His eyes shone and his cheeks were red, and it was clear that what had been said between us had affected him deeply. I stood up. He did the same, but for an instant he held on to my arm tightly. I liked this man. If he truly wanted to change sides and work for us, it would be easy to trust him.

"Thank you, Aline," he whispered. He smiled and was gone. The Governor and others were crowding onto the terrace and I moved back into the patio. As I watched the brightly colored silk robes of the dancers, I saw Luis, red-faced, pushing his way toward me. Immediately, I realized that he was in a rage. Something awful must have happened.

"Luis, what's the matter?" I cried, rushing to him.

"That's what I came to ask you," he retorted, leading me brusquely aside where no one could overhear. "Don't think you can fool me, my dear. I can see right through you."

"Right through what?" I asked, astonished.

"I saw you with that Russian," he said, so angry his voice shook. "I, and everyone else in the place. You might try to be a bit more subtle next time."

Luis was always calm and in control except when he was jealous. This emotion had led to the only disagreeable moments in all the years of our marriage. Usually I took pains to avoid this problem, but the Soviet diplomat's presence had made me careless.

"Luis, you're wrong," I cried.

"Oh?" he said, crossing his arms. "Then please enlighten me. And don't tell me you were discussing the economic implications of the cold war."

His sarcasm made me blush. "Of course not. You'd never believe it, but he was telling me—"

I stopped in midsentence, suddenly stricken by the promise I had made to Serge. Luis regarded me with tense impatience, waiting for my reply.

"I mean . . ." I fumbled, unable to recover myself. Every thought of how I might finish the sentence, every possible excuse, had fled from my mind. I shook my head and sat down heavily on the banquette.

"Look at you!" Luis cried. "You can't even think of an excuse, you're so guilty. Well, it's better that you don't, because I can see for myself what's going on. He never took his eyes from your face, except to get a better hold on your hand."

"He never held my hand," I answered indignantly. "He merely touched my arm now and then to emphasize his point. People do that in conversation. You're imagining things."

Luis ignored my words. "Have you already forgotten our discussion earlier this evening? As I told you then, I know perfectly well what a woman looks like when she's falling in love. And a man, too."

While Luis was unleashing this diatribe I became angry, and by the time he stopped speaking, I, too, was indignant.

"On the contrary, what you've proved is that you haven't the slightest idea," I said coldly. "I'm offended by your accusations and your tone of voice and I refuse to defend myself."

"Oh," said Luis sarcastically, "do you?" And with that he turned and walked away.

For a few seconds I stood there, wondering what I could do. Then I ran after him. I knew he would take longer to forget than I could bear. He was already on the terrace when I caught up with him; I took his arm. "Luis, I'm sorry," I said. "Please believe me. My only interest in Serge Lebedev is to gain information from an enemy. Luis darling, I'm in love with you, and there's no way I could be attracted to another man."

He tried to loosen his arm, but I gripped stronger. "Please forgive me," I pleaded. "I just cannot stand your being mad at me. Ever since that tent pole almost killed me, I've been nervous and frightened."

Luis stood in silence for a moment, and I held my breath. "Please, Luis," I said as I put my arms around him. "Please."

"All right . . ." He smiled, regaining some of his cool, unruffled demeanor. "Now that we've settled that," he said reasonably, as he took me to join the others on the dance floor, "why not tell me what you and the Russian were talking about and clear the air?"

"Horses," I said, smiling ingenuously at him. "Horses from start to finish. I tell you, I don't think the man thinks of anything else."

Of course Luis didn't believe me, but he didn't press the matter. Instead, he took my arm in a gesture of reconciliation. "I had no idea that racehorses were of such interest to you. I have a hard enough time getting you to come to the racetrack even when you are supposed to present a cup."

"That's racing horses, Luis," I answered hastily. "You know how I love my saddle horse." I hoped my words had sounded convincing.

He said slyly, "We'll have to discuss horses more often."

The band stopped playing; the party dispersed soon after, and we women left for the restricted confines of the old harem. I had not been able to talk to Rachid confidentially, and we were now on the brink of the seventh day. I had to get Jupiter's advice about recruiting Serge. As soon as I could, I left the harem for a small office just off the palace entrance, where earlier in the evening I'd spotted a telephone. By a miracle, or perhaps because of the Governor's position, I immediately reached Jerry's man in Madrid. Our conversation rambled on, as we had previously planned, about home affairs and children, but in all that family chatter was my coded message—"Suspect Soviet Embassy official Lebedev willing to work for us stop Give instructions how to proceed stop Also request permission to disclose plot to Casey." How long would it take to get Jupiter's answer? I wondered. They had my itinerary: I hoped that it would be tomorrow. But I was uneasy as I went to my bed. We would be leaving early in the morning, at an hour which would be the middle of the night in the U.S., making it difficult for me to receive a quick answer. Nevertheless, the elation created by the prospect of being able to offer Jupiter such a prize as a Soviet defector made it difficult for me to sleep. This was the first gratifying result of my efforts, yet I knew King Hassan's life was still as much in danger as ever.

The next morning I wanted to go to breakfast with Luis, but since he could not come into the harem, I dressed early and asked the maid to inform him that I would meet him in the patio. He was already waiting when I went into the sunlit center of the house, where we had dined the night before. Two maids, their ankle-length cotton djellabas covered by long white aprons with crocheted borders, were rolling a round table into a shady corner. The table was filled with enticing comestibles—at least six different-colored juices in tall, graceful glass goblets, various silver platters containing almond bread, small honey-and-almond cakes, little kernels of something sweet and hard, and a wicker basket of exotic fruit. Luis seemed to have forgotten Serge Lebedev and chatted enthusiastically while we devoured the feast. I wanted to know what had happened the night before, after the women had been shepherded into the harem.

"It was quite amusing and somewhat uncomfortable." Luis grinned. "As soon as you girls had gone to your quarters, our host took us to a large patio at the other side of the palace and brought the belly dancers back. They had practically nothing on, and their dancing was quite erotic and crude. When they had finished, the Governor invited us to take our pick. 'They're untouched,' he said." Luis broke out into a hearty laugh. "I was dying to tell him that I certainly believed him. Who would touch any of them? Some smelled bad, others had no teeth, and many were fat. Not even those long, shimmering gowns could hide all their sins." Luis continued to chuckle. "Cristobal and I had a terrible time refusing without hurting our host's feelings. Of course, the Governor thought he was offering us a great treat, and that's why you girls were all placed at the other side of the house. We were assured that you were locked in."

Luis and I spent so much time over breakfast that when I returned to the harem, I barely had time to finish packing before the servants were carrying my luggage to our car.

Chapter 9

Aﬁter all the hurry, we had to wait: a mechanical problem
had developed in one of the cars. Salima and I walked
back into the patio and then out to the garden, where we
sat on a bench facing a fountain surrounded by calla lilies.

"What did you think of your sister's dance last night, Salima?"
I asked. "I never knew she was such a wonderful dancer."

"I didn't like it much, frankly. That kind of exaggeratedly
sensual dance is fairly dated among people my age. Fatima's
generation has a different code from mine—that dance is an
example."

Amused, I said, "She's only ten years older than you, Salima.
Why do you find her so different?"

"Don't you see? She belongs to the old ways, the generations
of women who depended on their sexual allure to attract their
men; they are totally dependent on the opposite sex. The same
was true in Europe when women were less educated than men.
They had no preparation for careers in business or politics, or
anything serious. And since women did not earn a living, they
needed inherited money or husbands to support them, so they
concentrated their minds and bodies on sexual attractiveness."
Her full lips pressed together. "It's sad," she went on. "Frankly,
I feel sorry for Fatima. She's so out of step with the times."

I didn't understand at all and told Salima so. "First of all,
Salima, Fatima is better educated than most men, and she has

a husband who loves her. Why should she have to worry about such things?"

"But she adheres to tradition and believes that the old ways are best in spite of her modern education. So of course she thinks that sensuality is the only means of attracting a man."

This seemed highly unlikely to me, and far from anything I could surmise from my long friendship with Fatima. But I held my tongue.

Salima continued. "I would never do a dance like the one my sister performed. It represents a display of sexuality and availability. I thought it demeaned her." She turned her blue eyes to me. "Did you notice the way Medbouh looked at her? I think he still likes her, and maybe they see each other now and then. She's too old to be flirting with men. She's aging so fast she looks twenty years older than me, not ten."

"Salima," I said softly, "don't harbor such animosity against your sister. She loves you very much."

"No matter how I may feel about Fatima," she answered, "I suppose I shouldn't say those things. Please, Aline, don't take any of it seriously. I forget sometimes that I owe my sister a measure of loyalty."

I noticed that she said nothing about loving her sister.

With a smirk, she added, "But still, Fatima's not the saint you think she is."

A voice rang out, calling us to the cars. I stumbled out of the garden, my mind in chaos. I had just learned that Salima was extremely jealous of her sister. Perhaps it was even more than that. And her hint about Fatima's having an affair with Medbouh . . . how well did I know my old friend? Or perhaps it wasn't even true. If Salima disliked her sister as much as it seemed, she might be capable of inventing any story against her. Ten years could be an enormous gulf separating two sisters. But I knew that it was more than that. For all Salima's independence and rebelliousness, she was very much in the shadow of her successful, glamorous older sister, and for a moment, I had had a glimpse of a vulnerability in Salima that wasn't always apparent.

Again we bid goodbye to the Governor and each of us ran to

our respective cars. The Governor remained on the steps of the palace, waving at our departing caravan, and the trip from Midelt to Tinerhir began. It had been decided that on our way to Tinerhir we would make a detour to explore the Todra Gorges. These were known to be spectacular, something like the Grand Canyon, but very narrow and deep. The roads were notoriously difficult and would normally be impossible to traverse outside the dry season, but this winter had been dry. The rivers were low, the roads passable, and of course our cars and drivers were of the highest quality.

In a few hours the long line of sleek black Mercedes was winding its way along the bottom of the Dades Gorges—a gigantic fault in the plateau which separates the High Atlas Mountains from the Jbel Sarhro range. The dirt road followed the river along the bottom of the crack between gigantic slabs of rockface, and as we proceeded, the cliffs on either side became higher until the sky was reduced to a narrow slit. Huge black birds flew in lazy arcs overhead, and through my open window I could hear their high-pitched cries, like the squeaking of large bats. Down the sides of the gorge, from high above, small streams of water tumbled like pulsing silver veins in the black rock. A misty rain covered the car, forcing our driver to turn on his windshield wipers and headlights. Luis, who had been taking pictures through the open window, closed it. Even with the windows closed, the air inside the car became cool and damp. The mood was gloomy, and I moved closer to my husband. I felt as if the bright, cheerful morning had slipped away forever. I held Luis's hand and we both sat quietly during the rest of the dramatic, breathtaking drive. The entire experience was imposing and unforgettable.

Finally, the road began to climb, and soon we were nearing the town of Ait Hani, which, according to the map, marked the end of the Gorges. Our route was zigzagging and backtracking to include the most picturesque spots. Our driver marveled repeatedly over our good fortune that the drought had made this impressive route possible. When I asked whether the ride through the second gorge would be as somber, he was quick to assure me that it would be completely different. "That road is high, on the top of the canyon. It goes up and around, up and around," he repeated. By now I was looking forward to the sun and sky again, and greeted his news with relief.

The situation between the two sisters continued to fascinate me. What could I do to help? I said nothing to Luis about my conversation with Salima. There was no sense in spoiling his opinion of her, and he sincerely admired both girls. As the car continued to climb the mountain, my spirits rose, and soon Luis and I were laughing and joking. But before long the road became treacherous, full of hairpin turns and steep inclines. Nevertheless, after the desolation of the Dades Gorges, I enjoyed the view and the feeling of open space and blue sky. On our left was a drop of at least two hundred and fifty meters. Rising sharply on our right, like a wall, were mountains composed of rough, buckled stone which looked as if it had been wrenched violently from the earth. Amethyst and quartz crystals glittered here and there from the knuckles of dark rock. At our request the driver stopped and Luis used his pocketknife to chisel away a small piece for me. Others behind us did the same.

The route suddenly passed through a startlingly green oasis sprinkled with olive and pomegranate trees which spread out on either side, glistening in the sunshine. Then we were looking at rustling fields of wheat and barley, and more palm trees.

At the town of Msemrir, we stopped for lunch. The vans had been sent directly there that morning and the tent was already up when we arrived. As we got out of the car, there was a waft of fragrant food, and walking toward us were Fatima and Salima, both smiling and chatting happily together, evidently in the best of spirits. As I watched them, I was more puzzled than ever—these sisters were, after all, very similar—but by now I felt convinced that it was a love/hate relationship. They even looked alike as they walked side by side; despite Salima's blonde hair and blue eyes, they were both tall and slim, the cheekbones, the mouths, even the gaits were the same.

"But what will be the fate of the company without either you or Michel?" Luis teased Salima as we met. "Surely it will fall to pieces."

"Oh, but Michel said I should come along for the entire trip since I was invited," she explained. "Don't think I would take the chance of losing such a wonderful job."

The sun cut like a hot knife at this hour, and the cool tent was inviting. We relaxed against cushions while servants went through the previous day's ritual of towels and silver kettles of perfumed water until all hands were clean. Afterward an entire roasted lamb was brought to the table. The Prince said, *"Bism Allah"*—"In the name of God"—inviting us to begin. Fatima was at my table, and told a story about her brother's best friend who had attempted to drive through the Todra Gorges shortly after a rainfall and had slid off the road, plunging to his death.

As she spoke, I glanced across the tent and saw Serge Lebedev looking at me. My eyes locked with his pale blue stare, and for a moment I had difficulty looking away. Our conversation of the night before seemed dreamlike now, yet a lingering impression of intimacy remained. His request for secrecy had created a confidence between us out of all proportion to our brief acquaintance. The sensation was uncomfortable, and not having mentioned anything to Luis about Serge's possible defection weighed on me. Yet, even after reconsidering it, I still dared not tell my husband. He was not good at maintaining a false front, and Serge might notice a change in Luis's attitude which could make him lose confidence in me. If there was a chance of the Russian working for us I would not risk losing it.

Just then I happened to glance at Luis, and found him watching me, a wry smile on his lips. I smiled as innocently as possible and turned to my neighbor, afraid to look any longer at either Luis or Serge. Yet Serge's stare remained ever present. It was obvious he wanted to talk further, but I would have to be patient and wait for Jupiter's answer before I could broach the possibility of his working for us.

When the last course was served, I decided to stretch my legs, which felt cramped after sitting so long, legs crisscrossed on the floor. While most of the group was still having coffee and mint tea, I left the tent and wandered out into the sunlight, which reflected so fiercely off the crystalline rocks that I almost staggered. The inhabitants of Msemrir, a sleepy little village, squinted at me from their doorways, some through veils of white cloth. Obviously our arrival was the most activity they had seen in years.

After passing along a dusty dirt lane, I reached the edge of the town. The view was stunning—mountains everywhere, dazzling in the bright light with their snow-capped tips. All of a sudden I became aware of vaguely familiar voices on the path just below. Instinctively I began to descend the steep dirt trail; others from our group had probably come here to enjoy the spectacular scenery. But a moment later, after only a few paces, I paused, startled to recognize Salima's voice and that of a man. Quickly, I looked down, and despite the thick branches that separated us, I could see parts of her frilly white blouse. Since she was only yards away, I was about to call out when I realized that the man had his arms around her. I could just see his dark, curly head next to her face. She was leaning against a tree and he was holding her in a tight embrace with one hand inside her blouse caressing her breasts. With a sinking feeling, I realized it was Michel de Bonville. Sprinting silently up the path like a mountain goat, in seconds I was on the dusty street again. As I paused to catch my breath in front of an array of silver trinkets, Salima appeared alone at my side. She was deeply flushed and her hair hung around her face in sweaty ringlets.

"Look at all this gorgeous jewelry," she cried, her enthusiasm far outweighing the common baubles she hastily grabbed. "Aren't they absolutely wonderful?"

Deciding that this was not the moment to discuss what I had just witnessed, I struggled to match her high spirits. By the time we had made our way back to the group, Michel had managed to get there through some other route and was already immersed in conversation with Rachid Salloum.

Since I wasn't sure what to do about these developments between the two young people, I said nothing to Fatima, but I decided to ask Luis's opinion during our afternoon drive, since he was apt to be more objective. We were underway shortly thereafter, since Prince Moulay and General Oufkir were both anxious that we make this next, difficult part of the trip through the Todra Gorges while the sun was still high.

As the car began to climb a steep incline, its engine whining with the effort, I understood their precautions. Captain Omar

Khalil pointed upwards, and Luis and I craned our necks to see out the window. High above us soared the mountains, and our route through them twisted and turned, dipping suddenly and then shooting up again, doubling back over itself without warning. The view below was staggeringly beautiful once we had climbed higher—the land opened like a pair of jaws to expose the plunging gorge hundreds of feet below, where the Dades River cut a steep narrow valley through the limestone, forming dizzying cliffs. The river unraveled far below along the valley like a tiny silver thread.

I noticed that Captain Khalil was caught up in his admiration of the view, so I said to Luis in English, "I've just discovered something."

He inclined his head. "What's that?"

"Salima and that Frenchman are having an affair. I discovered them quite by accident, and what I saw left no doubt in my mind that they're intimately involved."

He burst out laughing. "So, my dear, quite by accident you stumble on this interesting development! Is it the same 'accident' by which you come by a lot of your other information?"

"Luis," I said, smiling, "I wasn't spying on them. I came across them on a path after lunch today. Now what should I do? Should I tell Fatima? This affair can only lead to grief and trouble, just like the one with the American did."

"What good will telling Fatima do? Before you do anything, talk to Salima herself. Maybe what you saw wasn't what you thought it was."

I had a brief flash of memory, of Michel's hand caressing Salima's breast under her shirt, and of her look of rapture. "I know exactly what's happening between them, but you don't have to believe me," I said, a little annoyed.

"You can't blame her," he said. "After the terrible time she had with that American, and Michel seems to be a very nice fellow. I wouldn't let Fatima's worries upset me too much if I were you." He added somberly, in an undertone, "But much more important, if you can't talk to Rachid, you should discuss the countdown with the Prince. Time is getting short. Think about that, and stop worrying about those two women. It's not your problem."

Omar chose this moment to turn to us, saying, "While looking out at all this rock I have been thinking about your mines, Señor Conde." He looked at both of us when he spoke, not just at Luis, and I liked him very much for that. "I am glad to see that our resources are being developed and used. There is much possibility here, and so much potential. I hope you are favorably impressed with our country, now that you have seen so much more of it."

Luis nodded his head slightly, acknowledging first the compliment and then the question. "Yes, I am," he answered in his usual deliberate manner. "And I recognize the value of mining here, a great resource for your country."

"And you, Señora Condesa," Omar said solicitously, "even though you had the unfortunate accident, which was a terrible thing, are you still able to enjoy yourself?"

"Of course," I answered, amused and touched by his careful politeness and the interest he was taking in our welfare. "I can't wait to see the wild-boar shoot, though—I hear they're very different here from the ones in Spain."

"My wife is an avid hunter," Luis explained. "Many Spanish women are good shots and she's no exception."

He braced his hands on the back of Omar's seat as he spoke, because the car was accelerating rapidly. The driver barked something to Omar in Arabic, and I noticed that his knuckles were clenched white on the steering wheel. Luis and I exchanged a worried glance. The road was far too dangerous for such speed. "Why so fast?" shouted Luis. The red clay of the mountainside streamed by like blood outside the window, and the black cliffs towered above us like thunderclouds. A few feet to the left the road dropped sharply off the barren rock cliff into empty space; there was no guardrail. Fifteen hundred feet below, the river winked and beckoned.

"I'm having trouble with the brakes, sir," cried the driver. "I checked the car, especially the brakes, before we left this morning, just so this would not happen and—" he shouted. The rest of his words were swallowed by the wind that engulfed the speeding car. He said the words almost like a prayer, as if by saying them we would all be reassured that this was not happening. We were now speeding down the winding road, and the

driver wrestled with the car to keep it from flying off into space.
The car ahead of us had been half a mile away, but was now
looming just in front. We were in danger of running into it after
the next curve. On this narrow road, there was no room to pass.
For several seconds the driver had been pounding the brakes to
the floorboards, with no reaction. I watched his shiny black shoe
pump the pedal, my mind strangely calm and empty, noticing
only the flawless black leather and the thumping of the brake
pedal.

When he screamed, "I have no brakes at all," my mind absorbed his remark as if from a great distance.

"Try the emergency brake!" shouted Luis.

The driver quickly grabbed the handle and pulled. The heavy
car slowed slightly, the back wheels skidding, then gained mo-
mentum once again.

I felt Luis's grip on my hand only dimly. Later I would discover a bruise on my wrist from the strength of it. I raised my
gaze to the rearview mirror and saw the driver's ashen face,
white-lipped and hollow-eyed. The car continued to accelerate,
and our driver seemed to keep the heavy Mercedes on the road
through sheer force of will. I do recall admiring the luxurious
leather interior of the car, and thinking what a shame that it
would soon be reduced to smashed junk, just like our bodies.

"Drive into the mountain!" screamed Luis. "The mountain—
the mountain—otherwise we'll go over the cliff—"

Luis and I gripped the back of the front seat as we slid violently from side to side. On the next turn, it was certain that we
would either shoot over the cliff or smash into the car in front
of us. We were descending a straight section that banked sharply
down to the left in a quarter of a mile or so. "Into the mountain!"
Luis screamed.

Just as the road dipped away to the left, the driver swung the
heavy Mercedes into the cliffside. There was a wrenching im-
pact of metal on rock and the sound of shrieking tires and
breaking glass. The whole world descended around our ears in
a cacophony of turmoil, and as I was flung over Luis, I smashed
my head against the rear window on his side. My head almost
broke the window. We felt the car turn on its side, and as it
ground itself to death against the cliffside, two wheels spinning

in the air, the piercing shriek and acrid smell of crumpling metal assaulted us. Inside, we were a tangle of limbs and confusion. The smashed wreck of the car finally slowed, ground across the road, and came to a stop, the two front wheels hanging over the sheer drop.

Dazed, I raised my bruised head and looked at Luis. Blood was pouring into his eyes from a long gash in his forehead; for an instant I was certain that he was dead. The red, thick blood washed across his face and made his features liquid and unrecognizable. My veins froze like winter streams, and a screen of black began to close over my vision. Before I passed out, however, his lashes moved and his eyes opened, and he looked right at me, conscious and very much alive. His green eyes squinted through his own blood and he struggled to sit up.

The driver was slumped over the steering wheel, the back of his head and uniform littered with shards of glass from the windshield, which gaped in jagged icicles. His back rose and fell, so I could see that he was still breathing. A piece of glass fell from the frame to the road with a tiny clinking sound, the first noise since the silence had fallen over us except for the steady moan of the mountain wind through the broken windows. Omar, who had been stoically silent during the whole insane race down the mountain, now sat holding his head, groaning quietly, picking bits of glass off his uniform. "Can we really all be alive?" I wondered, amazed at our luck. "How is the driver?"

Omar reached out a hand and shook him gently. He came to with a start. He sputtered some words in Arabic.

Omar turned around to look at Luis and me. He had a purpling goose egg on his forehead, and his mouth was bleeding slightly. "Señor Conde, Señora Condesa, you are all right?" His lip was cut so badly he could hardly speak, but his concern for us was evident. His eyes were warm and worried, as he searched our faces for any sign of damage. When he looked at Luis his eyes widened. "Señor Conde, you're badly cut!" he exclaimed. "Let me give you something to stanch the flow." He reached into his pocket and pulled out his handkerchief. Luis put it to his forehead.

"Thank you, Omar," he said in a surprisingly steady voice. "And," he added to the driver, "you should be commended for saving our lives. You did the only possible thing to keep us all from being killed."

The four of us sat for another moment, regaining our composure. Then we gingerly climbed through the twisted window frames and stood, surveying the wreckage of the car that an hour earlier had been a fine, stalwart black Mercedes and was now a scrap heap of scratched metal.

A car pulled up behind us. Michel de Bonville leaped out and came running, his face a study of incredulous horror. "My God," he shouted. "Are you all right?" We nodded dumbly. "It's a miracle that you did not go over the cliff. When I saw your car pick up speed, I thought you were all goners."

The remaining cars of the caravan were stopped in a long line behind us, visible only on the points of the curving road. Bill Casey appeared with his driver. I will never forget the flood of relief that passed over his face when he saw that we were unhurt.

Omar Khalil, Bill's driver, and ours struggled to lift the hood, which finally rose with a metallic groan. Omar, turning to Luis and gesturing toward Bill's driver, said, "Abdel is probably one of the best mechanics in Morocco."

Along with our driver and Omar, Abdel leaned over the engine. With expert fingers he touched different parts of the engine. It was so hot that he withdrew his hand several times before he could withstand the hot metal. Eventually he stood up, shaking his head, conversing with Omar. "What did he find?" asked Luis.

"There's a tiny hole in the brake hydraulic line near the master cylinder, through which the fluid escaped," Omar said. "With a leak like that, there would be some braking possible until the cylinder was empty and all the fluid had escaped; then no matter how much the brake pedal was pressed to the floor, nothing would happen. Our driver," continued Omar, "checked the brake system this morning and found nothing wrong. In fact, all the drivers have specific orders to check their brake systems every day."

Moments later General Oufkir came striding up. Usually he rode in the last car, acting as "sweeper," so in case of a mishap nobody would be left behind. Since Rachid was today accompanying the Prince, who led the caravan, as yet neither man was aware of the accident. I realized how upset Moulay Abdullah would be when he learned of the second near-tragic accident. This time it seemed pretty clear that if this had been planned, it was Luis or me, or perhaps both of us, they wanted out of the way.

The General confronted the driver. "What has happened here?"

"Sir—there's a hole in the line feeding hydraulic fluid to the brakes," the man stammered. "I cannot understand, sir. I checked everything thoroughly before we left Midelt."

Luis gestured toward our driver. "General, if we had not had such an expert chauffeur, we would be at the bottom of the gorge."

The driver looked at Luis with deep appreciation.

Oufkir inspected the engine himself, looked up, pointed to our driver, and said, "The fault lies with this man. He did not check the brakes properly."

Our driver sputtered and turned red. Luis quickly realized the man's position and once again said, "Well, one thing is certain, General, this man saved our lives by his superb driving. I think he should be complimented for that alone."

Oufkir looked at Luis approvingly. "Well, Count, I am most pleased that you feel that way. It's certainly kind of you after the blow you've received. And he looked at me. "Countess, are you all right?"

I assured him I was fine.

"My apologies to you both. I'll get you out of here right away." He turned around, glancing impatiently at his watch. "We must get off this mountain road before the sun goes down."

By now the doctor had cleaned the blood from Luis's face, disinfected the wound, and placed two neat butterfly adhesive patches over it. Oufkir made a gesture, inviting us to follow, and at the same time he gave our driver a pat on the back. Our chauffeur, looking very worried—probably, I feared, in danger of losing his job—went to the trunk to remove our luggage. Everyone piled back into their respective automobiles. We crammed in with the General and waved to our despondent driver as we passed.

Slowly, the other cars also began to circle our wrecked Mercedes, which had been pushed against the mountain, and we moved carefully over the ragged, twisting road. The General complained about the difficulty of finding reliable drivers. "Lazy!" he confided to Luis. "We have very intelligent people, but once you take these men out of Rabat or the big cities they become less responsible. I do apologize for your disagreeable experience."

Luis again interceded on behalf of our chauffeur, then he took my hand and looked into my eyes with concern. Realizing his anxiety, I nodded slightly to signify I was fine, questioning him the same way. He nodded and squeezed my hand firmly. What a husband!

In the General's car, we began to relax, and I concentrated on the scenery once more. Even after we had passed through Boulmalne, which marked the end of the Gorges, the terrain remained spectacularly beautiful. Again the General addressed me. "Some of our most romantic villages are in this area, and dozens of beautiful kasbahs—they're the ancient walled-in sections of the town." We were passing through a vast desert plateau, where a fortified city appeared perched high on a hill, dramatic and beautiful—its crenellated walls outlined against the blue sky, pocked as if they had survived a machine-gun battle.

General Oufkir noticed our fascination. "That's a town noted for its famous kasbahs." He told us that many people inhabited these castlelike buildings. The golden city with adobe walls blended in with the surrounding barren dirt terrain, which was the same color. A short time later the landscape changed again and we found ourselves entering an avenue of palms.

The General looked at his watch. "We're arriving at our destination, Tinerhir. The accident did not make us lose much time after all."

Chapter 10

In Tinerhir the caravan followed an avenue of palms which led to the government hotel. From the outside the building looked modern, but inside, the decor resembled ancient Moroccan homes, with latticework on the windows, colorful tiles, many arches, and intricate plaster-of-Paris carvings on the walls.

It was near sunset when Luis and I walked onto the terrace and stood together, watching the sun smolder in its last red-and-orange rays. Behind us was the sound of servants carrying luggage up a stairway, and from below, out of the palm trees, came the loud chattering of birds. Such a wondrous beautiful country, and yet the strange accidents of the last days had marred our enjoyment of it.

Cristobal Villaverde, Carmen Franco's husband, came out and suggested that Luis join him in the bar for a whiskey, but I remained there, transfixed by the view, enjoying the aroma of the orange blossoms wafting up from the lush garden below.

I must have been there alone for several minutes—everybody else seemed to be occupied finding their rooms—when I heard a step behind me. A moment later Serge Lebedev was at my side. I prayed that Luis would stay in the bar until I could get rid of Serge.

Forcing a smile, I turned to face him and commented on the lovely view. However, as soon as I looked at him, his dismal expression made me realize he had serious matters on his mind.

"How unfortunate about your car," he began, shaking his head. He looked out over the open expanse, his hands clasped behind his back.

"Yes," I murmured in agreement. "Well, I think it's time I went upstairs to—"

"Wait," he said, placing his hand on my arm. "There's something I want to tell you."

I paused. As we stood there, the sun dropped below the line of the horizon and a slight chill entered the air.

"Aline, I don't know what led me to say what I told you last night," he began.

"Let's not discuss it, Serge," I pleaded, growing more and more uncomfortable. "You can trust me. I told you that."

He smiled. "Whether I can trust you or not is irrelevant," he said. "I'm not so innocent as not to realize that if you want to betray me, there would be nothing I could do about it."

His words left me perplexed. What was he trying to tell me? I waited for him to continue.

"However, right or wrong, I do trust you."

Was he worried that I would tell Luis about our recent conversation? I decided to be frank with him. "I must tell you," I said, "that it does make me uncomfortable to discuss with you something I've kept secret from my husband."

"I understand," he said. "But right now I would like to say something that your husband would thank me for, and would prove my goodwill toward you both."

"What is it?" I asked warily.

Looking me straight in the eye, he said soberly, "Someone is trying to kill you. Please," he cautioned as I began to speak, "don't ask me how I know. Just believe me. My advice is that you both leave this party and go back to Spain as quickly as possible."

I was stunned. "Serge, a warning like that does me no good unless you tell me—"

"I can't say more—but I urge you to go."

His voice had become increasingly nervous. Dusk was falling quickly, and the big palm trees below were one huge greenish blur of swaying leaves, which made a sound like falling rain.

"I'm going inside now," he said. "Stay here a few minutes longer, please."

In the thick bluish dusk, we stood for one moment looking at each other. His face was less distinct in this light, and I wondered how much I could trust the staring blue eyes. Was this a clever strategy to fool me? No, it was further proof that he had decided to help me and my country. There was something in his every glance that inspired confidence—that made me feel he was an honorable man. More than ever, I needed Jupiter's answer to my message. There was no way I could follow his advice and leave the party with the countdown getting so close—tomorrow would be the eighth day.

"For your sake I hope this is the last time I see you here," Serge said sadly. "Though nothing could make me more unhappy." He lifted my hand to his lips; then, in an almost military about-face, he walked toward the lighted entrance of the hotel. His graceful gait seemed ill-matched with the awkwardness of our conversation.

I remained on the terrace for a while, wondering about what moral difficulties an honorable man must go through to reach the monumental decision to help the enemy.

As I stood musing about Serge, enveloped in the shadows, I heard the crackle of a step on the gravel path below in the garden. Someone was walking down there. At first, in the heavy, shadowed light, I couldn't see who it was. Then the person passed by a window, and in the brief arc of light I recognized Bill Casey's chauffeur, Abdel. Since he'd spent most of his time chatting with our chauffeur whenever we stopped, I knew him quite well by now as a polite, well-mannered man with a kind face. He was smoking a cigarette as he walked along, and the smell of the black tobacco wafted up to me. He continued on in the semidarkness, his path marked by the orange glow of the cigarette tip.

I was about to turn to go to my room when a figure jumped out from behind some bushes and grabbed the chauffeur by the arm. Embers flew and the glowing tip skittered to the ground. Whoever had accosted Abdel must have been hiding there, and it occurred to me that he could have overheard Serge's warning. I didn't like the idea. Fortunately, I was wrapped in shadows and could lean over the railing without being seen. I looked for Casey's chauffeur and the man who had attacked him, but could see neither, until voices in strident Arabic indicated where they were. They were quarreling. The voices became louder, and Casey's driver let out a yelp as the other hit him and I heard him fall with a thud to the ground.

At the same time I was aware of the echo of a man's footsteps on the tile floor of the hallway behind me. I turned and recognized Bill Casey's stooped figure and ambling gait. Running across the terrace, I called to him, "Bill, come look—I think your chauffeur's in trouble."

My friend came in a flash and rushed with me to the edge of the terrace. Leaning over the stone railing, he peered down into the dark garden through his thick glasses. The altercation was still going on; now there were groans. Before I realized it, Bill leaped like a cat silently down the steps. His movements were quick. There was a scuffle, then a cry of pain. Bill must have struck the attacker, because I heard his voice: "Drop that knife."

I leaned forward, determined to miss nothing, squinting to get a glimpse of the dark shapes amid the bushes and flowering shrubs.

"So, Ali Ryad," Bill's voice boomed out. "What did you have in mind with my chauffeur?"

For the first time I saw the man's face. It was the journalist Moustapha. It was a shock to recognize the man I had most suspected since arriving in Rabat.

"None of your business." Moustapha's gruff voice in broken English was that of a man in pain.

Abdel was still on the ground.

"How are your starving children these days, Ali—and your loyal wife?" Casey, towering over him, had twisted Ali's arm behind his back. The hold was so severe that Moustapha was on his toes in agony.

A muffled curse was the answer.

"It seems you are not anxious to converse with me, Ali," said Casey menacingly, still calling him by the other name. "You're afraid, because I know what you did twenty years ago. And you damned well should be."

Moustapha, out of breath from the struggle, his arm still

twisted behind his back, fired back in staccato bursts. "I did not need your help then and I'm not afraid of you now, you cursed American. To hell with you, you damned imperialist, we're going to kick all your white asses out of Africa." The palm trees gave a dry rasping sound in the rising breeze. The atmosphere was ominous, and remembering what I'd heard about Moustapha's violence, I had a sense of foreboding.

"Your wife," said Bill in a deadly calm tone, "was indeed loyal. But I fear not well-founded in her loyalty. Now, Ali, there's a small matter we have to discuss, a twenty-year-old matter. You know damn well what I'm talking about." And Bill shoved the man's arm even higher behind his back.

There was a guttural moan of pain as Ali replied, "To hell with you. You can't prove a damn thing."

"Maybe it will be easier for you to remember if I tell a few people on this trip of your real identity and a bit about your past. They tell me that justice in Morocco is deadly swift with traitors."

Moustapha cried out in agony as Bill yanked his arm so high that I thought that he might break it. The menace in Bill's voice made me shiver. "Why, my dear Ali, this is nothing compared to what the Moroccan secret police will do to you. Get the hell away from this party. If I see you again, you're a dead man." He gave Moustapha a violent shove that sprawled the man onto his face; he lay there, weeping. In that sound were pain and rage, but even more, I suspected, the humiliation of being so humbly subjugated.

Bill turned and began to climb the stairs to the terrace where I'd been watching, but then I saw Moustapha jump up and go after Bill. I screamed, "Look out, Bill!" Instinctively, Casey dropped to his knees and a knife blade sang harmlessly over his bent figure. Moustapha quickly melted into the darkness of the garden. Bill rose, dusted off his knees, and looked up at me on the terrace. "Boy, I'm getting old," he said to me with a wry grin. "Thanks for the yell. Imagine turning my back on that snake. I forgot about that damn second knife he always carries."

Bill leaned over and assisted his frightened driver, Abdel, to his feet; the man was almost hysterical, babbling his thanks in three intermixed languages. Bill helped Abdel up to the terrace and led him to better light. Checking him out closely, he said, "You're lucky Ali didn't get that first knife into you. Well, you're going to have a black eye and a puffy lip. How do you feel?"

Abdel nodded in the affirmative and once again started a torrent of thanks. Bill patted him on the back, saying, "Go get yourself cleaned up and lie down for a bit. We'll talk later."

When the man left, Bill turned to me. "My driver will be all right once his fright has passed. That Ali brings problems wherever he is. Since seeing him, I fear the accident on the road could have been planned. Aline, be careful. Observe everything. I have to get back to Sophia; she'll be worried. I don't want her to know about this. Ali is bad news."

I didn't say anything to Bill, but I knew that if I'd had my old Beretta in my purse, seeing Bill in danger, Ali might no longer be with us. The fact that I was a Spanish housewife and mother faded from my mind in moments of crisis, but I realized how badly out of practice I was—I might have shot the wrong man. Nevertheless, it would have been comforting to have the firearm, which was now in my bedside table in Madrid, handy here. But how could I have possibly known that this glamorous invitation could become such a deadly human game?

Bill went back to the lighted front hall and I made my own way inside and up the stairs, my mind spinning with the effort of interpreting the day's events.

Luis was in our room waiting for me. In grim silence he shut the door behind me and strode to the window. Fortunately, our suite looked out upon a view of the mountains instead of the valley. For a moment I had feared that Luis's austere manner was due to his having observed me talking with Serge, but from this room he could not have seen us. Something else had occurred.

"Our chauffeur finally arrived from Tinerhir and he has just left this room," he began. "He used the excuse of bringing back a briefcase which had been left in the car, to warn me." Luis's voice had none of the fury of his comments about Serge the night before. On the contrary, now he was calm and thoughtful. "This has gone too far," he said.

"What are you talking about?"

Luis continued in that quiet, determined voice he used when he was seriously upset. "The driver showed me the brake hydraulic tubing with the hole through which the brake fluid escaped. He had cleaned the metal tubing thoroughly. If you looked closely you could see an indentation, as if the hole had been made with a sharp centerpunch."

"But," I replied, "our driver used the brakes before we entered the steep part of the road and they were fine."

"Let me show you something else," Luis responded, placing the tubing in front of my eyes. "Covering the surface of the tubing near the hole was a substance like glue."

I looked up, perplexed.

"I think that's epoxy glue. Say someone wanted to close that hole temporarily. They could mix more resin than epoxy and close the hole, though it would not harden. It would hold enough for easy braking," he continued, "but when you started braking heavily, the pressure would blow the epoxy off the hole, and after several pumps of the brake pedal, all the brake fluid would be gone—and no brakes."

"But what about the emergency brake?" I asked.

"That's a mechanical system and works on a cable," Luis replied. "Our driver checked that, too. Someone had loosened the nut."

"How could the driver tell?" I asked.

"The driver could see the shiny part of the cable where the nut used to be. It was backed off some twelve turns. Somebody tried to make damn sure we were killed," he concluded.

"There's no doubt in my mind that someone tried to eliminate us today. Add that to the pole collapsing almost on top of you, and we have two serious incidents." Luis's forehead creased in a deep frown. "This is probably due to your blasted spying." He shook his head. "Aline, I want you to give it up." He moved toward me. "Tonight you are going to call off the mission by telephone, using whatever codes or subterfuges you've set up with John Derby . . . I don't care what you have to do, but this stops right now."

"Luis," I answered, struggling to remain calm, "calling off the mission is not going to remove the danger. How will the enemy—whoever that may be—know I am no longer helping the Agency? Either we invent a logical excuse to leave and go back to Spain or we take greater precautions and stay here and help prevent the King's assassination."

I dared not tell Luis that Serge had advised me to leave the country. The mission had suddenly become more dangerously intriguing than ever, and I had no intention of giving up. Realizing that my husband was an extremely honorable man, I hoped my words about the danger to the King's life would touch him.

For a few moments he was pensive. "You're right about one thing. If the King's life is in jeopardy, we do have a responsibility to assist in any way we can. What really upsets me, though, is that we don't know whether the King has been informed about the plot."

"That's also a constant worry to me," I said. "According to that intercepted message, tomorrow will be the eighth day. Only two days left. You know, every day there's a rumor that the King will be joining the group the following day. What if we leave and the King arrives tomorrow? We have to stay to warn him. What excuse would be good enough to leave?"

"You know I don't believe in inventing false excuses," Luis said while walking to the table, where he took a glass, filled it with ice, and added whiskey. "We'll give it another try. I wouldn't want the King's death on my shoulders. But from now on, we must be on guard!" He paused. "And there's another morbid side to all this." Luis sat down with his drink in hand, looked up at me, and said solemnly, "I'm wondering if whoever it is, is more interested in getting you or me. Perhaps there's nothing involving the King after all. Remember those newspaper articles?" He put the glass on the table and shrugged. "Who knows? Just in case we're targets, I'm going to find some weapons we can keep handy. We'll just have to keep our eyes open and be on guard at all times." This was just what Bill Casey had said.

I didn't want to worry him about the recent incident involving Casey and the radical journalist. And thank heavens Luis had not seen Serge talking to me! I was going to be careful, yes—but I was going to find out who was plotting this coup and what Serge's intentions were. I turned around and began to look through my luggage to choose a dress for dinner. After all, I considered, with so many officers and almost half the King's cabinet present, everyone will be taking care that another accident does not occur. We are all forewarned by now, I mused. Who would dare try again?

At cocktails before dinner, General Medbouh invited Luis and me to join him for dinner. In the midst of another remarkable meal, addressing us both, he said, "It's regrettable that you've had those two unfortunate incidents. However, since we're spending tomorrow here, I have a special distraction for each of you. Count, perhaps you would join me in a hunt nearby. Only ten miles away is the best pigeon shoot in Morocco." And turning to me, smiling, he said, "There's a special souk here in Tinerhir. It is of course much smaller than the souk in Rabat, but in each region there are handicrafts indigenous to that area. Fatima, who is always eager to find new ideas and designs for her jewelry, has offered to take you and the Marquesa de Villaverde." Luis and I glanced at each other, reflecting the same thought. Was Medbouh trying to separate us? And since Fatima was such a good friend, why had she not asked me directly instead of going to Medbouh?

After dinner, back in our room, Luis told me that he did not want to leave me for the whole day, therefore he was not going to accept the General's invitation.

"Oh, darling, that's silly. I'll be with people all day. I won't even use the car, because the souk is within walking distance. Please go," I urged. "You know how much you enjoy shooting. It will do you good to go, and I'll be perfectly safe. I'm sure that Carmen will join us."

"Well, if you really think so," he answered. I surmised that his willingness might also stem from the conversation we had had the night before, when I had told him that his unwarranted jealousy about Serge was putting more of a damper on our vacation than did the possible threat to our lives.

The next day, after breakfast, I was in the lobby of the hotel, praying that the call from Madrid would come through before we left on the shopping trip, when a bellboy appeared, announcing that I did indeed have a call. Hoping this would be Jupiter's answer, I picked up the receiver, deciding to be cautious; others could be listening. Jerry played his role well, speaking as if he were my butler. The message he transmitted was exciting. Jupiter was enthusiastic and congratulated me for my success with Serge. Full permission to incorporate the Soviet had been given, but I was reminded not to jeopardize blowing my cover. However, the line cut off before I could ask about bringing Bill Casey into the affair, and try as I might, I could not get the connection to Madrid back.

Fatima came into the lobby and I had to hang up. We walked together to the souk; Carmen had decided to sleep late that morning. We walked through the wide main street of the town, and I was surprised to see many men standing near the arched entrance of the souk, looking as bored as their camels, which were tied to trees or lying on the ground.

Fatima explained. "This particular *zoco* is different from others. Here, only women can enter and the men have to wait outside. You see, we women do have some privileges in certain areas after all."

We passed through the arched entrance into several small streets bordered by little stalls selling every product one could imagine—carpets, flowers, foodstuffs, ceramics, makeup, children's toys, fabrics, chairs, kitchen utensils—everything the larger souks carried. Fatima talked to me as we ambled along.

"My worries about Salima increase every day," she said, holding a silver pendant by its chain so that it turned gently in the sunlight. The woman who had made the pendant smiled shyly and adjusted the corners of the cloth on which her wares were displayed. Her fingers were bent and stubbed from years of hard work.

"What's happened?" I asked.

"Well, shortly after dinner last night she disappeared, telling me she wasn't feeling well and wanted to lie down. But when I passed by her room later and knocked at the door, there was no answer."

For a moment I said nothing, though I knew this was the moment I should tell Fatima about the amorous scene I had witnessed between her sister and Michel. However, since Salima's vicious criticism of her sister's dance, I was reluctant to say anything that might add to the antagonism already existing between these two sisters. The memory also flashed through my mind of what it had been like for Luis and myself when we had decided to get married. Neither of our families had been pleased with our match: his, because Luis was the primogeniture of one of Europe's great families and he had been expected to marry one of his own; and mine, simply because it meant my being so far away from home. Yet in the end it had all worked out for the best. My family adored Luis, and since the "Abuelo," Luis's famous and formidable grandfather, had liked me, the rest of his family had received me with kindness and affection. My own marriage had proved to me that differences in background do not necessarily mean that two people will not be happy together. And I remembered my anxiety, when, on our honeymoon, Luis had gone to visit my parents in Pearl River. It had worried me that his having been brought up in a gigantic palace with sixty servants was too far removed from how I had lived. On the contrary, when he had seen my parents' house, he had been charmed. "It must have been wonderful to live so close to your parents," he had commented that first night in Pearl River. "Do you know, I only saw mine when the governess took me down to their quarters in the mornings to say, 'Good morning, Papa, and good morning, Mama.' The same performance in the evening. And those governesses! They tyrannized my two sisters and me. There were three of them living with us at the same time, one German, one French, and one English. Oh," he sighed, "you were lucky."

And when the next day he saw the red brick schoolhouse I had attended, he just stood there for a few moments. Then he said, "Now I realize how underprivileged I've been. What I wouldn't have given to go to a school like this! I've always been ashamed to tell you that I've never been to a school. My parents thought that tutors at home would give me a better education and more time to learn sports."

No, I thought, I won't mention anything about Salima and Michel to Fatima. They may end up being as happy and lucky as Luis and me, and nobody's background could be more different. Instead, I said, "Perhaps Salima was asleep."

Fatima gave me a droll glance. "To my knowledge the girl survives on three hours' sleep every night," she said. "Particularly since she began working for Michel."

I watched my friend pay for the pendant, her long, pale fingers and polished nails contrasting grotesquely with the blunt, twisted ones of the peasant woman. I felt guilty concealing anything from Fatima, especially since she had asked me to help, but nevertheless I restricted myself to saying that sometimes love affairs can turn out better than the families expect.

When she looked at me, her gaze was full of indignation. "Not in this case. That girl is doing all she can to encourage Michel, and he's not in love with her—I'm certain of that. Salima's not as meek as she appears. If I told you some of the things she did when she was in her teens! There would be no problem if she wasn't throwing herself at him." Noticing my surprise at her vehemence, she tempered her voice. "I don't know what to do. If I tell my father that I suspect Salima is sleeping with Michel, he'll certainly fly into a rage, but at the same time he'd put a stop to something which can only lead to misery for her."

"Wait," I urged her. "Before you tell your father, let's talk to Salima and give her a chance. Lord knows what she might do if she's pulled away from her job and from this man—the only things that have made her want to remain in Morocco."

"You're right," Fatima said. "We should talk to her together. Above all I want to avoid scandal. And Salima knows how to do that too well."

"By the way"—I had suddenly remembered an unfinished conversation we had had two days before—"you were going to tell me about Rachid."

"He's the one really powerful man in the country, outside of the King. Oufkir hates him, because Rachid knows everything—everybody's secrets. He discovers Oufkir's affairs—and he has plenty. Some rather macabre—like that young officer he had killed, and the wife who has disappeared. There are no secrets for Rachid. Oufkir might not mind so much, if it weren't for the fact that Rachid is such a prude. Rachid never has girls or boys or anything like that. And Oufkir is always looking for a complaint that he can take to the King about Rachid. Conversely, Rachid plagues the King with criticisms of Oufkir. Neither will succeed. Rachid was the King's tutor from the time His Majesty was eight years old and he trusts him completely. But the King respects Oufkir, too. He knows he's the best officer the army has, and he'll never get rid of him."

"Why does Rachid know so much about everyone's secrets?" I asked.

Fatima eyes widened. "Didn't you know? He's the unofficial head of our DST, our Secret Intelligence. Rachid knows everything that goes on. He has spies all over."

Fortunately Fatima had no idea how her information affected me. Did Rachid suspect my collaboration with the CIA? That was certainly possible. Now I realized that being director of Moroccan intelligence was undoubtedly the reason Prince Moulay Abdullah had chosen Rachid as my contact. But Fatima, unaware of the havoc she had created in my emotions, went on.

"Rachid was locked in my uncle's study after lunch for hours the afternoon we arrived. I suspect my uncle is Rachid's source of information in that province. They say Rachid's memory for names and faces was sharpened by the years in the desert when he kept track of the Bedouin tribes under his father's control. You told me our ministers never tell you anything about the history of our country. Well, try asking Rachid."

As we roamed through the little shops, Fatima continued to talk about Rachid. "According to stories my father told me," she said, "Rachid was the youngest of many sons of a desert sheik who moved from oasis to oasis, and therefore he was brought up to live off the animals they fattened or the wild ones they trapped. His father's fierce band of nomads had to defend their rights to each oasis from rival tribes, because this was their only source of food and pasture for their animals. The tribe would live on some of the oases for weeks only, on others for months, and the rivalries between one tribe and another often lasted centuries. Although quiet and serious, Rachid was clever and ruthlessly cunning, even merciless, with anyone who threatened his father's tribe's livelihood and right to encamp."

Such stories always fascinated me, and I listened eagerly.

"One night," she went on, "it is said that Rachid's family and followers were sleeping in their tents at an oasis in the southern desert. He was only twelve at the time, but he was given the night watch. When Rachid heard the camels snorting and pawing, he quietly stole over to where they were tethered. He knew that the camels, being obedient beasts and not fussy about which masters they followed as long as they were fed, could be easily stolen. As Rachid came closer, he saw thieves feeding delicacies to the camels to lure them away. You must understand, Aline," Fatima interrupted her story, "without camels, the desert nomads would perish. They depend on their camels as on nothing else. To get back to Rachid," she said, "he had to defend the only life he'd ever known. His bare feet made no sound, his small child's body no shadow. There were two men leading the camels away; he surprised them, his blade slashed twice through the air, the robbers were dead before they knew who had killed them."

"Rachid appears so saintly, so monklike," I said. "I can hardly imagine him capable of such a thing."

"Gentle people are often surprisingly fierce when threatened," said Fatima.

Fatima and I wandered a while longer among the stalls, watching the women weaving carpets with lovely geometric and symbolic designs, until the sunlight became so intense that it was uncomfortable. I suggested that we head back to the hotel. Walking down the street after leaving the *zoco,* a tremendous racket broke out just behind us. We both jumped in fright. Turning around, we found three robed figures looming over us. All wore crude masks and were making threatening sounds and gestures. Accustomed in moments of danger to have a weapon handy, my instinct led me to reach inside my bag, but of course there was nothing there. Fatima started to laugh, and I realized there was no danger.

"I would know that voice anywhere," she said, reaching out and pulling the absurd mask from the face of a handsome young man. The fellow was grinning and reached out to kiss her hand. "You can't fool me, Ahmed," she went on. "After all, we've known each other since childhood."

With that, she introduced me to Ahmed Faradi, whose mischievous eyes and charming manner won me immediately.

"You never stop joking, Ahmed," Fatima continued. I smiled, though my heart was still racing. How jumpy I'd become!

Ahmed's two cohorts removed their masks. Captain Omar Khalil smiled sheepishly at us. "We had the Countess really startled—I could see it in her eyes. Do forgive me," he said.

My attention was riveted on the fellow Fatima had just introduced. Both Luis and I had noticed him during the trip, probably because of his stature and good looks, but also because he carried himself with a poise and dignity that made him stand out. We all remained in the street having a good laugh about their ruse. Ahmed Faradi explained. "We found the masks at a stall over there." He pointed to the opposite side of the street. "And I couldn't resist. Fatima and her sister Salima have been my favorite girls as far back as I can remember." Then he turned to Captain Omar. "And my friend Omar was dying to do some prank with these masks, too. You ladies were just the first friends who happened to pass by."

When the three men had moved on, I asked Fatima about Ahmed. Her face opened in a look of pleasure. "That's the boy I would like Salima to marry," she said. "He's perfect—his family has been friendly with ours for generations. He's intelligent, kind, and good-hearted, and was top of his class in the military academy, which impressed my father. However, he has hardly seen Salima since she was in school in America." Fatima looked in the direction of the disappearing officers and sighed. "If it weren't for that Michel de Bonville being on this trip, this would have been the ideal occasion for Salima and Ahmed to get to know each other again."

Chapter 11

The next morning the hotel was in a whirl of preparation. An hour or so from now we were scheduled to leave Tinerhir and head into the wild countryside, climbing the Atlas Mountains once again, this time to the City of Roses. A rumor was circulating that the King might join us, and the possibility had sent tremors of excitement through the Moroccans and the guests. Servants were running around at a dizzying speed loading cars and trucks. An extra van had pulled up in front of the *parador* and was being packed with a new assortment of colorful carpets, just delivered by local merchants. I was perhaps more nervous than anyone, but I'm sure for different reasons, because today was the ninth day of the countdown, and so far I had not been able to talk to Rachid, or to the Prince, or to find any other means of warning the King about the impending threat. There had also been no answer as yet from Jupiter about my speaking of the coup to Bill Casey. And after Serge Lebedev's warning, the awareness that I had an unknown enemy who could strike again increased my necessity for obtaining his help, but as yet I'd had no opportunity to ascertain whether his carefully worded admiration for my country indicated he was willing to work for us.

As I went past the concierge's desk, he handed me a message. "A telephone call just came in for you, Madame la Comtesse, and we could not locate you. It was a gentleman but he declined to give his name, insisting instead that I write down his message and give it to the Comtesse personally."

Opening the paper, I read, "Answer to second request is yes." I knew that was Jupiter's permission to discuss the coup with Bill Casey. I gave a sigh of relief and immediately started looking for Bill. Most of our group was milling around nearby or on their way out to the cars. Sophia was standing near the door, and I rushed to her. She told me that Bill was upstairs in his room having his hair cut, that the Prince had sent his personal barber, manicurist, and masseur. She laughed. "Bill never does such things, but he didn't want to seem unappreciative of the Prince's kindness, so he's suffering through it. I'm afraid he's going to be late." It was irritating to have to wait to talk to Bill, but I remembered the journalist, Moustapha, and decided to find out if he would be with us today. Outside, I did a turn around the cars and the garden, but I didn't see him. After his run-in with Casey, I calculated, he would probably stay out of sight. I went back upstairs, where Luis was in our room, putting a variety of things he had bought into a briefcase. His mood seemed to have improved.

"The Minister has suggested riding in our car this afternoon. He wants to discuss the Riff Mines and the possibility of expansion."

"Hmm," I said, less than thrilled by the idea of listening to the two men talk about the mining business for several hours. At the same time I had another idea. I had already changed my mind and finally told Luis about Salima and Michel, and now I suggested that Fatima and I could ride with Salima in our car and discuss the problem, while he proceeded in the Minister's car.

"Perfect," Luis said. "But if I were you, I would ask Salima only. She'll resent her sister being included, and two against one is never fair."

As usual he was right.

"And another thing," Luis said. "Our driver wasn't canned. General Oufkir decided to give him another chance."

"Thanks to you," I said. "You're the one who stuck up for the fellow."

"No, it's the General," Luis said modestly. "Apparently he

learned that the driver had twelve children back in Rabat and just didn't have the heart."

Or could it be that since the accident General Oufkir had realized that someone had definitely tampered with our brakes? I wondered. I wanted to ask Bill Casey if he had learned from his driver why Moustapha had attacked him.

The cars were waiting in line outside the hotel. I spotted Bill and together we strolled over to a bench in the shade under a tree.

"Bill," I said, "there's something important I've been wanting to talk to you about ever since you arrived in Rabat, but I had to receive approval from John Derby. It's just come through and I'm desperate to fill you in and ask your advice." Quickly, I told him about the suspected coup and assassination, and gave him a rundown. "According to one particular intercepted message," I said, in finishing my account, "the coup, we think, is scheduled to take place on the tenth day. This is already the ninth day, and to date I don't know whether anyone has advised the King of the danger. Jupiter says he's been trying, but time's almost up and I haven't uncovered any clues as to who is behind this plot."

As I spoke, a smile spread over his face. "I knew it," he interrupted triumphantly, his eyes agleam. "I knew something was fishy. The tent pole, the car accident—you know these things don't normally occur. Then that criminal Ali . . ." I knew he was referring to Moustapha. "That fellow could very well be involved."

"I wanted to ask you about him," I said.

"He's completely crooked." Bill frowned. "He'll do anything, no matter how nefarious, as long as the price is right. As for his convictions, political or moral, he has none. He operates out of pure self-interest. Which is not to say that he's not cunning enough to plan and direct on a higher level. He's slippery and wily."

"Why did he attack your chauffeur?" I asked.

"Because Abdel had uncovered why your brakes had failed— that was clever, the epoxy and all. Ali told Abdel to keep his mechanical expertise to himself or he would be killed."

"Then you think Ali knows about the plot?" I asked.

"Oh, it's possible," responded Casey. "But he wouldn't be an important part of the group. He's not that bright or influential."

The relief of being able to have Bill's assessment gave me a surge of hope, and a torrent of questions occurred to me. "What do you think about the two accidents, the tent crashing down and the car?"

"When I put those two together with the information you have just given me, I realize they were carefully planned. But what stymies me is the purpose. So far the intended victim seems both times to have been you, and that does not make sense. Not unless the plotters are pretty sure you know their identities, which you do not. And then, they could fear that you would denounce them to the King. All that is difficult for them to ascertain, or so it seems to me. At any rate I'd recommend a crash helmet at all times." His eye-crinkling smile flashed and disappeared. "Your Moroccan friend's death, what was that name you told me . . . ?"

"Abdul."

"Well, Abdul's death and these two attempts make it clear that these fellows mean business, whoever they may be." Casey was pensive. "But I just can't understand why you and Luis have been the targets."

"If I really am the intended victim, or Luis is, they haven't done a very good job."

"On the contrary," he said soberly. "So far the attempts have been very professional. You've been damn lucky." He looked out at the file of palm trees lining the driveway, waving in the breeze. "The best advice I can give you is to be on guard, rely on those good instincts of yours, and tell me immediately of any suspicions you might have. This is a volatile situation and anything could happen. Ever since I began this trip, I've experienced premonitions of something unforeseen occurring; I even thought perhaps it was the climate, or maybe something in the air."

I laughed. "Based on what I've told you, who do you advise keeping an eye on?"

"Listen, Aline, you know how I feel about that Rachid, but my opinion may not be professional, since it may very well stem from a husband's possessiveness after seeing him so attentive to my wife."

I thought of Luis's dislike of Serge and nodded.

"But for what it's worth," he continued, "my instincts sometimes pay off. At this point, though, it seems pretty obscure. The leader of the plot could be anyone, but he has to be damn important to pull this off."

I agreed with him and said so. Omar appeared and told me that the caravan was about to leave.

"Rest assured," Bill murmured, as we both stood up, "we'll stay close."

I looked for Salima, but she was nowhere to be found. General Oufkir stood with Luis, watching the first vehicles move up the long drive; the vans with the food and carpets, as usual, were leaving earlier.

"Surely you've heard of the region we're going to visit today," the General said as I approached them. "Kelaa M'Gouna is the famous rose-growing area of Morocco. The perfume water which our ladies are so fond of is produced there, and the extract is exported to Grasse in France, where all the great perfumes of the world are made. The roses come into bloom when the almond trees have finished, and they have a festival every year during the month of May."

I wanted to ask him more about the City of Roses, but Luis asked a question about the shooting for tomorrow. General Oufkir began to tell him about the game they would see, and the two men, both avid hunters, became absorbed in their favorite subject. Eventually the Minister appeared to take Luis to his car.

Salima passed by at that moment. "Salima," I called, waving to her. "Come ride with me. I'm going to be alone. You and I've hardly had a chance to talk since you arrived."

Instantly I saw that she didn't like the idea, though she struggled to conceal it. "Oh, I wouldn't want to inconvenience you," she said.

"You'll be keeping me company," I assured her. "Luis is riding with one of the ministers to discuss mining. I'm alone."

She laughed politely. "Really, Aline, I just can't . . ." She was at a loss for an excuse, and I presumed that she was reluctant because she supposed I would inquire about Michel.

"Salima," I said, coaxingly, "you told me that the purpose of joining this trip was to see more of me."

Having no option, Salima gave in. "But of course I want to be with you, Aline," she said with a smile as the chauffeur opened the door.

Soon we left Tinerhir, heading northwest into the more mountainous area. Now and then, we passed another small fortified town, its walls and towers seemingly carved from the golden earth of the barren hills. The view out the window kept me spellbound, and neither Salima nor I said a word for a while. After we had passed the third little storybook town, I turned to her.

"Oh, I wish we could go skiing," she said quickly. "Do you know, the best skiing in Morocco is nearby. Of course it isn't like the Alps—the snow at this time of year is icier—but the slopes are very steep and there are less people in your way."

I was somewhat taken aback by this outburst, coming just as I was about to broach my delicate subject. "I'm not a skier," I told her. "I'd love to try, but I'd probably break my neck and Luis doesn't like the snow."

"But you could come with me and I'd teach you," she babbled. "You're athletic, you'd learn in a hurry . . ." She was speaking frantically, staving off any other topic I might wish to touch upon. "The best skiing in Morocco is in Khenifra, where General Oufkir has a home." The torrent of words continued. "In Oukaimeden, too—that's on the way to Marrakech. There are ski-lifts—"

"Salima," I interrupted her, "what is it you're afraid I'm going to talk to you about?"

"I have no idea," she said ingenuously.

"I think you do."

She said with resignation, "Why don't you just say it instead of making me guess?"

"You know perfectly well that it's about you and Michel. Fatima and I have both realized you are falling in love with him, and I'm sure we're not the only ones."

To my surprise, my words seemed to cause Salima immediate relief. "Well, then, you know," she said, shrugging her shoulders and smiling—her old self again. "I suspected you'd seen us on the path. Michel loves me and I couldn't be happier."

"But, Salima, you must be worried or you wouldn't try to

keep it secret. This creates a problem, as you know. Not a simple one for you."

"I've never been in love before," she said, growing serious. "I thought I had been once, but now I realize it was not really love. But what I've learned with Michel is that love is the most important thing in life. Our love has made me want to live again. You didn't know it, but I was very desperate when we first met several months ago. Michel loves me and I love him. It's that simple, and it's all that counts."

I found myself confounded by this logic. "But, Salima, there are other factors here. Your father—"

Her face darkened. "Let's not talk about him," she said.

"Not talking about him won't make the problem disappear, and you know he won't take the news lightly. He's certain to hear about it from someone on the trip."

"Then let him hear," she said. "Not even he can stop us."

"Salima, this isn't a fairy tale," I said, growing more stern. "This is probably the most important decision of your life, and you can create a serious problem. Your father most certainly can stop you from marrying Michel. For example, with his power in this country, he can easily terminate Michel's visa and therefore his job, which could affect the man's whole career. What chance would your relationship have then? Not to mention how all this would affect your family."

Salima was silent, clearly chastened by my suggestions. "What can I do?" she cried. "I've never felt this way about anyone—nor has he. It's the strangest thing, I can sit and just look at him for hours. Just look at him sitting there! Can you imagine?"

"I can," I said. "Believe me, Salima." And it was only then, thinking of myself and Luis, and how in love we were, that I was overcome with sadness for her.

"Do yourself a favor," I said. "Try to separate yourself from Michel now, before it's too late. I know that sounds callous and impossible, but believe me, it won't be nearly as difficult as the consequences."

Salima's already pale skin was even whiter now. "I can't," she said. "I just can't. Michel would be so miserable. He doesn't deserve such treatment. How could I do such a thing?"

I opened my mouth to speak but stopped. What use was it to try to convince anyone to abandon the one he or she's in love with? Actually, I felt sorry for the girl—and for Michel. How ridiculous, I thought, that until now I suspected Michel of being interested in Fatima instead of Salima. I leaned back in my seat and exhaled slowly. "I don't know how to help you," I said. "But there is one thing I do know. Sometimes one falls in love and it doesn't work out. For whatever reason. And even though it may seem impossible, one falls in love again. You will fall in love again if you give up Michel." I was remembering the man who had swept me off my feet when I'd first worked for the OSS, a man who had turned out later to be a double agent—and who had nearly cost me my life. But of course I couldn't tell Salima that.

"Did Fatima ask you to talk to me?" she said. "Did she tell you to ask me to call it off?"

I nodded.

"Don't think my dear sister is only worried about me. She's also worried about her husband losing his government job if I bring disgrace on the family. I love Fatima, but she's an ambitious and proud woman." She sighed, as if this was a cross she had to bear. "Well," she went on, "the best I can do is to tell you that I will think about it." She shook her head. "I feel that it's not possible for us to give each other up, but I will talk to Michel."

I looked at her skeptically.

"I promise," she said. "There, you've done your job and what happens will happen. It's the most you can do. Michel and I will make our own decision. Above all I don't want to hurt his career."

As I looked back at the snowy peaks in the distance, I realized that Salima was right—there was nothing more I could do. I had given her my advice. Now the decision was hers.

"You can tell Fatima I promised to think about it and I'll make an effort," she said. "Or I'll tell her myself."

"All right," I said uneasily. "Just keep in mind, Salima, our preoccupations are for your own good." Resignedly, I turned back to the view, troubled by the sense that I had failed in my efforts to help.

Salima's voice broke the silence. "Have you known those Americans, the Caseys, very long?"

The abrupt change of her thinking and her questions about Casey jarred me. Why would Salima want to know such a thing?

"Yes, I've known them quite a long time. Why do you ask?"

"All the other foreigners on the trip are people interested in shooting, but he said he doesn't shoot. I was just wondering if they're enjoying the trip, that's all."

Her remark was strange and too vague. I suspected there was more to her mentioning the Caseys than she was saying. I justified Bill's and Sophia's presence with the suggestion that they would enjoy the beautiful places included in the tour, whether they liked shooting or not, then I let the matter drop. I certainly didn't want to become involved with Casey's background. Salima's musings could be innocent, I realized, but they could just as well conceal a meaningful intent.

When the caravan stopped to refuel, Salima jumped out. In a few minutes she was back, excitedly saying that Michel and one of the ministers had invited her to continue the trip with them. Happily, she gave me a kiss and ran off. Carmen Villaverde was stretching her legs, overheard her and, seeing that I was alone, joined me. By now we were high in the Atlas Mountains, and two hours later we entered the City of Roses. Omar could hardly contain his excitement. "Here we are," he said dramatically. "We are entering the city of the most beautiful women in Morocco. And it is here that I will take another wife."

Astonished, I asked, "How many wives do you have now?"

"Señora Condesa," he answered, "I have only two, but eventually I hope to have four. That is what the law permits." We spoke in Spanish as usual—this seemed to have the added attraction, for him, of impressing the driver, because the driver, of course, spoke only Arabic and some French.

"Don't tell me that a young man like you can support four wives?" I said. Behind Captain Khalil's back, Carmen Villaverde and I exchanged glances. She was shaking her head in amusement.

"The Señora Condesa doesn't understand our customs," he said with wounded dignity, as politely as he could. "Four wives are necessary for a working man. You see, they help each other. One does the cooking, one takes care of the children. . . ."

"I still think that many wives would be expensive." I was pulling his leg now, because I realized that these extra wives were like servants he did not have to pay.

"I never take on another wife until I can afford her."

"But don't they get jealous of each other?"

"Why? They know I'm not marrying each one to take her out into society. This next one will be useful to take care of the children."

Carmen entered the conversation. "Perhaps you are unaware, Aline, that the laws here favor the men only. If they tire of a wife, all they have to do is to announce out loud, 'I divorce you' three times, and then clap their hands three times and the marriage is dissolved."

"Ah, but the law forces the man to return the woman to her family with her dowry," Omar interrupted. "She can't be left on the streets."

As we were speaking, the caravan was rolling slowly up an incline to a village perched on the top of a hill. We came around a turn in the road and saw hundreds of women lined up on either side of the narrow highway, dressed in a completely different manner from those we had seen in other provinces. Many held baskets of flowers, and tossed rose petals of various colors in our path. Others, the younger ones, hid their faces behind their hands and, at first, peeped at us through their opened fingers. They wore multicolored skirts, white blouses, fancy aprons, and sleeveless boleros—much like our regional costumes in Spain. Many of the young girls had placed gorgeous yellow roses in their jet-black hair or had entwined them into their braids. Captain Omar explained that the women in this city were unaccustomed to having strangers see their faces, that for them, showing their visage was like being naked, and that usually their faces were covered. But today, in view of the visit of His Royal Highness Prince Moulay Abdullah and such distinguished foreign visitors, they had probably been asked to remove the veils.

In any event they saw few visitors; curiosity soon overcame their shyness and they stared at us. And it was true—the girls were extremely beautiful: they had extremely white skin and light blue eyes, and their faces were tattooed, but it was very flattering. At the far corner of the eyes were tiny green or blue dots which augmented the size of the eyes and exaggerated their color; little round orange-and-red-dots accentuated the cheekbones. Omar was enraptured and turned his head from one side of the road to the other, trying to pick out the girl he would marry, I imagined. The cars in front of us had slowed down so their passengers too could get a better look at the famous beauties of the City of Roses.

All the way into the town, Omar feasted his eyes, like a hungry man in a bakery. "I've seen many beautiful girls," he exclaimed, "and I've already made my choice!" It amazed me that he could simply arrive in an unknown town and expect within the period of one day to have a new wife.

"How are you going to get married here when we're only going to be in the City of Roses for one night?" I asked.

"That's where I need your help, Countess."

"What can I possibly do?"

"Ask the Prince's permission for me to have another wife. He'll have to marry me."

"That's complicated for him, isn't it?"

"Oh, no. No trouble at all. It will only take a minute of his time."

I had already heard from Fatima that everyone she knew had to ask the King's permission to marry, so I supposed that since the Prince was the only relative of the King on this trip, it was logical that he could give his consent. But I still could not understand how a wedding could be arranged so quickly.

When we descended from the car, a violent windstorm swept through the village, filling the air with the rose petals from the road. Next to a rambling old building of limestone and adobe, where Omar informed us we would spend the night, was another huge tent. We ran inside to escape the cold wind. Once everyone had entered, the flaps were dropped and the unique tinkling music of the thousands of tin coins hanging from the ceiling ceased. Course after course of delicacies was served, and it wasn't until almost two hours later that we finally finished with pastry and mint tea.

Throughout the luncheon, I had been aware of Rachid's intense activity, as his slim, robed figure flew first to where the
Prince was seated at the head of the largest of the low round
tables, near the entrance of the huge tent, then to General Oufkir, who was not eating and who stood at the back of the tent,
watching all of us with a dark, silent stare. He nodded curtly as
Rachid appeared, and the two men spoke in undertones; I was
watching them covertly, and sensed that a problem had arisen.
After a while Rachid hurried back to the Prince again, his long,
pale face drawn and intent above the gray beard. There was
clearly something upsetting him.

After a brief conference with the Prince, Rachid made his
way back toward Oufkir. When he reached the General, a torrent of rapid Arabic passed between them, and although they
were openly polite, I sensed an undercurrent of tension. I
couldn't hear, nor could anyone else, but the two men were
standing just above where Fatima was seated, and I wondered
if she had noticed the commotion. The deep scar on General
Oufkir's face whitened against his skin, which was suddenly
brick-red and almost radiant. Rachid, on the other hand, was
paler than ever, and although they maintained a perfectly civil
exterior, it seemed to me they were fencing with scimitars.
Rachid's slight body seemed to hover above the ground, while
Oufkir stood erect, motionless, arms clasped behind his solid
back, as if hundreds of soldiers awaited his command. They
were a study in contrasts, and I was reminded of medieval figures, Soldier and Monk, painted on a fresco.

Suddenly they began to move together toward the tent exit.
As they passed my table, the soft melody of the Arabic sounds
fell on my ears like gusts of wind in a storm. Shortly after,
Fatima came to my table with a glass of mint tea in her hand.
Her black hair was swept back from her face into a sleek chignon, and in a long-sleeved white sheath she looked especially
cool and unruffled. Immediately, I asked her if she had noticed
the heated conversations which had taken place during our
luncheon between the Prince, Rachid Salloum, and General
Oufkir.

"Certainly. Rachid and Oufkir are probably of different opin-
ions about something. According to my father, although they're

both too distinguished to show it in public, they're really in competition with each other for the King's favor. They're both so interesting and powerful, and brilliant, but in different ways." The two men were just coming back from the light outside to the shade inside the tent. "You know," she said, watching them, "it's common for people of equal stature and ambition to be either bitter enemies or closer than brothers."

"Fatima, I wish I understood Arabic. Did you hear what they were saying when they were standing behind your table?"

"Something to do with changing plans about staying here for the night. Evidently Rachid wants to move on, and in a hurry. I don't know why. And the General thought it would be more comfortable for everyone to stay here."

"I hope we stay. This town must be lovely. And my guide wants to pick up a bride here, his third." Despite my anxiety I smiled, remembering Omar Khalil's determined excitement.

"If Rachid wants to go, you can be sure the order will be to move on. He wields the power on this trip. Oufkir pretends that he's the one who has the last word, but it will be Rachid whose decision is followed. Just wait and see."

"So they really aren't equally powerful. There is an imbalance of favor with the King, and Oufkir can't admit it or overcome it? Is that the way it is?" I asked.

"Not quite. Rachid is frightened that Oufkir might become more influential than he. This situation has repeated itself so much in history—you know, who is the King's favorite? Fortunately, the King is well aware of their rivalry, but he needs them both. He really is a master diplomat in keeping everyone's personal animosities at bay, so they can work together and serve him well. It's a serious diplomatic game."

"Rachid appears so kind and magnanimous," I said. "It's hard to believe he is jealous of the General."

"There may be an explanation for their enmity. Something to do with their ancestors," said Fatima. "Once I heard my grandfather say that Rachid's father's tribe was the archenemy of Oufkir's ancestors. It may sound strange, but in our country, family feuds can be passed on from one generation to another. Remember that story I told you about Rachid's incredible feat killing those men when he was just a young boy? Well, perhaps

Oufkir comes from the same tribe that was robbing Rachid's father's camels. Who knows? Whatever the reasons, one always seems to be at the other's throat. Usually they try to conceal their personal feelings in public. I've never seen anything like this before. It must be very serious. After all, Oufkir's the most important minister, but Rachid has dedicated his life to our King, and although he lives like a monk, the truth is he uses all his wiles to persuade the King to follow his advice. Did I tell you that Rachid never went to school or learned to read or write until he was fifteen? He had many brothers and was not the eldest, but he was recognized as the most intelligent. He's not only highly cultured and has an incredible voice, as you've heard, he's also a great poet. There you see him, so gaunt and thin with that gray beard. Well, once he was the most skilled hunter with a falcon and also the finest tracker in the desert."

"A fascinating man, there's no doubt about that," I said. "And I've found him to be one of the nicest of the group. Many of your countrymen, although they are polite, are bored when I ask a question about their country's history, but when I ask Rachid, he always takes time out to explain."

"Yes, Rachid has a lot of charm. But he has his phobias, too. Like many of us, just as our ancestors did, Rachid takes the fortune-tellers of Marrakech very seriously. He's terrified of airplanes and tries to convince the King to fly as seldom as possible. Also, although he likes to hunt with the falcon, he can't stand firearms. I don't know what he'll do when we're shooting, but you can be sure he won't be taking part."

"Doesn't he have children?"

"Not one. He's never been married. I told you yesterday, he's very chaste. Rachid is consumed by religious zeal. He's made the pilgrimage to Mecca more times than anyone I know. As you can see, Oufkir is very attractive to women, and he scorns Rachid's celibacy as well as his consulting the *kri-kri*. These—"

All of a sudden the intercepted message about moving on Mecca in ten days flashed in my mind, but of course I could not mention that to Fatima. Instead, I said, "What strikes me as odd are those long, long fingernails."

Fatima threw her head back and laughed. "We're all used to that. Rachid claims his fingernails are necessary for the stringed instruments he plays. He really is incredible. There's no one quite like him."

At that time word passed from table to table that a change in plans had occurred. We were not going to spend the night in the City of Roses but would continue on almost immediately to our next destination. Fatima gave me an "I-told-you-so" glance. Everybody was disappointed.

My eyes lit on Bill Casey, two tables away; he was watching me and indicated that he had something to tell me. I turned to Fatima. "I'm going out for some air," I said and sauntered over to the tent entrance and stepped quickly outside. A moment later Bill followed and we strolled together down a path. When we were out of earshot he said, "Have you known those two men very long?" He pointed to Rachid Salloum and Oufkir, who were again in conversation near the tent.

"No. I met both on this visit," I said. "Evidently they're extremely important in the Moroccan government. My friend Fatima just told me a lot about their history." I filled him in briefly. "And furthermore, it's interesting that the two men closest to the King are sort of rivals. They had a disagreement during lunch about whether we should stay here for the night or move on. According to Fatima they dislike each other and disagree on almost everything."

"So," he said musingly, "what do you make of that?"

"It could simply be a personality conflict, having no further implications," I suggested. "Or it could indicate a broader dispute between factions of the government."

"We've never talked about that Russian. What is he doing here? How does he know Ali, or Moustapha, as you call him? Did you know that last night the Russian and Ali were talking together in front of the *parador* a short time before I found Ali beating my chauffeur?"

Bill's news worried me. "I don't know how to interpret that," I said. "Especially since the Russian has hinted that he would like to work for us."

"Well, all I can say is, be careful. These Soviets are clever at the game of espionage. And some Soviet involvement in the plot has already been determined. If they're providing services for transmitting messages, they may be doing much more. Overthrowing Hassan would be to their advantage in several ways, principally because it would open the door for leftist groups to bring a Communist government into the country."

Hearing voices behind us, we turned around and saw that the cars were preparing to leave. "Let's talk again as soon as either of us notices anything."

"Just give the sign," Bill said with his characteristic joviality as we separated.

Before I had taken a step, Omar Khalil came running toward me.

"Countess," he cried. "Please help me. I've found my next wife. I must marry her. Only you can arrange that."

I threw my hands in the air. "Me? Of all people. I can't imagine how. I haven't had the chance to speak to the Prince about your marriage, and now we are leaving almost immediately. . . ." I looked at him. "Omar, it's no longer possible."

"Oh, yes. It can still be done." He looked at me imploringly. I remembered all the amusing little favors he had done to make our trip more enjoyable. If possible I had to help him. "If the Señora Condesa will ask the Prince, I'm sure he'll say yes," he insisted.

"But what about the wedding?" I continued. "There's just no time."

"The wedding only takes one minute, Señora Condesa." His voice was pleading. "My bride and her parents are waiting."

I looked for General Medbouh to ask his opinion before bothering the Prince, but no one had seen him for the last hour. I gave up, and with Omar Khalil at my side, we looked for the Prince, whom we found giving orders for the trip to the next city. Around us, everybody was running helter-skelter from one place to the other; there seemed to be an unusual haste to leave. People rushed to the bathrooms inside the building; servants piled carpets back into the trucks and luggage into the automobiles. As I squeezed into the group near the Prince, Omar remained close by. Such a hubbub was going on, and the wind still blowing, that I had to raise my voice to make myself heard.

"Sir, please forgive me for asking such a silly thing," I began uncomfortably. By now I was convinced that Omar had lost his mind. "But Captain Omar Khalil has the crazy idea that he can marry a girl from this city if Your Highness gives his permission. I know that's impossible, but he won't leave me in peace."

"No, that request is not impossible, Aline." Prince Moulay Abdullah smiled. "Would you like me to arrange it?"

"Yes, sir. He's been so nice and he's such an excellent guide and interpreter . . ."

My reasons for assuring the Prince that I would like Omar's marriage to take place sounded ridiculously inadequate for something so monumental, but with the confusion of the moment and time pressing, nothing better occurred to me.

The Prince moved out of the group. "No trouble at all, no trouble," he said. "Where's that Omar Khalil?"

"Here, Your Royal Highness," said Omar, popping in front of him.

"And where is your proposed bride, Omar?" asked the Prince.

"She's right here, Your Royal Highness." From behind Omar, as if by magic, stepped a lovely little girl who could not have been more than fourteen or fifteen. Accompanying her were a man and a woman, obviously her parents. The beautiful child had very white skin, and her black hair was entwined around her head and adorned with small yellow roses. Her cheeks were very pink, and when I looked closer, I saw that she, like the other women in her village, already had little pink points of tattoo marks over her cheekbones and that her pale blue eyes were enhanced with tiny points of blue strategically placed at the corners and above the eyebrow. The effect was ravishing. The little girl looked up at us for a moment and then, embarrassed by our glances, covered her face with her hands.

The Prince moved closer and placed the hand of the father on the hand of the girl, then the mother's hand on theirs, and then Omar's hand on top. He mumbled a few words and then turned to me. "Well, Aline, your request has been granted. Omar and this young girl are now man and wife."

I was astounded. So this was considered a legal wedding in Morocco! Omar had been right. The parents of the girl appeared delighted—they were smiling when it seemed to me they should have been weeping to lose such a sweet young daughter. The girl stared shyly at the ground, acquiescing gracefully to the wishes of her elders, not even stealing a glance at her new husband. My heart went out to her; she was so young and beautiful, and now she was a third wife of a complete stranger. But since this custom did not seem to upset them, I tried to look as though I, too, were pleased with the marriage. I said a few words of congratulation, but the girl's parents did not understand French, so I resorted to shaking their hands, and then I rushed to my car. Omar ran to the car also, without even kissing his brand-new wife. As soon as he shut my door, he took his usual seat next to the driver. Almost immediately, the caravan started to move.

"Captain Khalil," I said, "how is your new bride going to get to Rabat where you live?"

He turned around and looked at me in surprise. "Oh, that's no problem. She's in the truck with the carpets, Señora Condesa."

Just by chance, at that moment our car was passing one of the vans. Omar pointed. "See. There she is." In the back of the truck, standing, hanging on to the tailgate, was the little girl, looking wistfully at her village as it disappeared in the distance. Her forlorn expression did not discourage Omar. He was delighted. "She'll be just perfect in my house," he said. "And since I'm still young, I can wait a bit before taking a fourth wife."

"She looks too young to be married," I said, thinking out loud.

"Oh, that makes no difference, Countess. She's not the one I will take to social events."

So this was marriage Moroccan-style, the most unusual wedding I ever expected to attend.

Chapter 12

I'd slept poorly, twisting and turning, worrying about what the following day would bring. We had quickly left the City of Roses and it was dark when our caravan finally arrived at another government *parador* in Ouarzazate, where we spent the night. I rose early and opened the shutters to the beautiful dawn of the day that had had me worried since I arrived in Morocco. If Jupiter's interpretation of the intercepted Libyan message was correct, this was the tenth day, Thursday, April 10, assassination day. As Bill Casey speculated, "It's only natural that the conspirators would pick a day when the King is present and their allies have been infiltrated into the groups of soldiers and multitudes of unknown beaters. An assassination could be made to look like an accident—a gun going off unexpectedly, a stray bullet—whatever."

Today we'd be high in the mountain, isolated from help. During that sleepless night, my thoughts had turned like an out-of-control merry-go-round, spinning to other things that bothered me as well: Luis's predictions that one day my espionage would bring disaster to us and to our children, that my cover would be blown. "Spies are looked down upon in Spain. Spying sounds dishonest. Even the family would think you are being disloyal to my country—your country—our children's country."

Though I had never involved myself in anything that could be detrimental to Spain, I was aware that Luis was right. My mind kept jumping from one disagreeable reflection to another. Perhaps I had endangered Luis. If the plotters knew I was working for the CIA, which already seemed the case, they might think my husband was an agent, too. And not least of my concerns was that despite my efforts the coup could occur without my being able to uncover any useful detail in time to help, and my reputation among my colleagues of twenty years would be seriously diminished. What if Serge Lebedev were trying to fool me about his intentions and I had done something that had led him to identify me with the CIA? No matter how I looked at it, my immediate future appeared fraught with calamities and failure.

When I saw that my husband had long since been awake and seemed unusually solemn, I presumed that some of the same concerns had been going through his head. But I determined not to add to his discomfort by talking about my own. Looking in the mirror, I saw my face was haggard. I had to be careful—my anxiety might become obvious to the others.

These preoccupations had bothered me other mornings, but never so forcefully. Often I'd awakened wondering what we would do if an uprising did break out all of a sudden, but the beautiful Moroccan sunlight usually made me more optimistic. Today I looked out at the green fields, at the snow-covered mountains glistening in the sun, and again it seemed impossible that anything sinister could be brewing. At first the view, as on other days, lifted my spirits.

Under my window, chauffeurs, gun-loaders, servants, and soldiers moved more quickly than usual. The military personnel had multiplied. Again my uneasiness returned. This was a bad sign unless it meant that Oufkir was taking greater precautions. But hidden in the extra troops could be enemies as well. I wanted to talk to Luis about it all, but continued to resist the temptation. Why get him angry with me again for involving us in such a risky situation?

Inside the *parador* doors banged, footsteps resounded in the hallway, bells rang, breakfast tables rolled by. We ate in our rooms almost in silence, both aware that this could be the fatal day, and not wanting to upset the other by talking about it. As

I was buttering my croissant, Luis unzipped his briefcase, which was on the chair next to him.

"Here—I want to show you how this works." A black handgun, shiny as a wet fish, glistened in his hand. "It's quite different from your Beretta." He handed me a German .380 Walther automatic.

"Where am I going to hide that?" I exclaimed. "It's so big!"

"Look, I couldn't find anything else. Our chauffeur had one, and I talked him into selling it to me. He was delighted to make the money." Luis shrugged. "It would be foolish not to be prepared. Put it in the ammunition bag which you hang around your waist. Nobody will know it's there." Luis went across the room, picked up the square leather pouch, and opened it. Dumping out the makeup, chocolates and other paraphernalia it usually contained, he slipped the automatic weapon inside. "See, it fits easily and you still have room for this stuff." He threw my makeup back in. "Now stand up and put this thing around your waist and let me show you how to use it."

The waiter came to remove the breakfast table and glanced at me, confounded by the worn leather strap and cartridge pouch hanging on my hips over my long peach satin dressing gown. When he left, Luis locked the door and I practiced taking the weapon out of the bag, inserting the loaded clip into the magazine, drawing the slide back, taking off the safety, cocking the gun, putting my finger on the trigger, and aiming. Manipulating the heavy automatic was not easy, drawing the slide back was hard for me, and the whole process took too long. The small Beretta had been so much simpler.

"I'll have a shotgun with me most of the time," I said. "Why bother with this bulky thing?"

"A shotgun takes longer to lift and aim. And what about all the time you're not in the shooting stand and far from the shotgun anyhow? No, no. You have to be ready. At every moment. And a concealed weapon is better. If you take care not to kill yourself or someone else by accident, you can simplify matters and save time by keeping it loaded, the hammer cocked and locked, that is, with the hammer drawn back to the full-cock position and the safety lever moved to 'safe.' Then the pistol can be ready for immediate firing by simply thumbing off the safety. The chauffeur managed to find another for me also, and I'll keep my eyes on you. So try to stay close to me."

Not sleeping well was beginning to show—my nerves were frayed. Luis said I was not pulling back the hammer fast enough, so I practiced for a while. Then I began to dress, and instead of concentrating on what I would be wearing and attending to my hairdo and makeup, I found myself looking out the window every few minutes to see what was going on down below around the vans and cars. I opened the door now and then and looked down the hall whenever I heard footsteps. As I laced my knee-length leather leggings, I thought, This is the day, Aline, so be ready. You've been on this mission all this time and haven't uncovered a thing, so you better be sure the King isn't murdered in front of your eyes and you've done nothing to prevent it. I felt better about the heavy automatic.

An hour later everyone was in the hotel lobby for the ride from the *parador* in Ouarzazate to the mountain. We'd been asked to be especially punctual, since the King would be shooting with us. I took my place in the Land-Rover assigned to us for the day, and watched as guns and leather ammunition bags were stored in back. This equipment was the plotters' delight, I mused; so many firearms—weapons available to all—could make the success of a coup almost certain, especially if the particular military personnel accompanying us turned traitor. My thoughts became gloomier by the minute. We would be farther from civilization than ever, deep in the wilderness of another remote province in the mountains.

Those coming in and out of the *parador* were dressed in costumes as different as the many nationalities they represented. Today, the Prince had surpassed himself. He strode out, absolutely smashing in a beige, ankle-length snakeskin coat which swung open with each step, revealing a beige mink lining. On his head, tied in his own special jaunty manner, was a soft cotton turban, a bit darker in hue, and instead of the ordinary footgear, he wore beige boots of the same skin as his magnificent coat. Despite the luxury and glamour, his appearance was as attractive and manly as the officers in their military uniforms.

I looked down at my best brown-and-olive-green tweed shooting suit with its wrap-around skirt covering my knee-length breeches, at my custom-made leather leggings, my hand-embroidered leather chaps, and my Austrian shooting hat, covered with trophies I had picked up over the years, which until now I had been very proud of. I had dolled myself up in my best shooting garb, but in comparison to the exotic Prince, I felt run-of-the-mill.

The Prince and Rachid had reappeared and were in front of the *parador* when I emerged. Moustapha Benayad, making no effort to hide, strode by. After the altercation in the garden and Bill's death threat, I had assumed that we had seen the last of him, but there he was, wrapping a belt of cartridges around his waist; I wondered why; he was certainly not going to be on the shooting line. It would be unlikely that a journalist often critical of the regime would be given a post. I watched him approach one of the officers and strike up a conversation. Were they plotting as I sat there looking on? Neither man inspired my confidence; they both had narrow black moustaches curving down over their mouth. Moustapha's nose was a large lump of sallow bread-dough down the center of his dark, gloom-ridden face; a shaggy brown turban sat on his bony skull like a bird's nest. Now he was glancing from right to left, observing those around the caravan with a hawk's eye. I shivered. After Bill's deadly warning, for Moustapha to parade around so openly, even armed, he must have a connection to someone very high in the government. It showed what confidence the traitors possessed that their attempt against their King would be successful. A few seconds later he mounted a motorcycle and, gunning the motor, sped off to the head of the caravan. I became more depressed.

General Oufkir emerged from a mass of officers and came to talk to me. "Well," he said. "Good morning. I see you're going to be shooting, too, today. The Prince tells me you're an excellent shot." In my unhappy frame of mind I could not think of a bright response, so I reached into my ammunition bag for a chocolate bar; I usually carried several for energy. In my haste to pull one out, the Walther automatic almost came with it. Offering him a piece of chocolate which he surprisingly accepted, I asked, "When does the King arrive?"

"Oh, he'll join us on the mountain. We never know at exactly what moment, but you can be sure the shoot will not begin until His Majesty is there." To my amusement the General munched on the candy with obvious enjoyment. "Now, Countess, you Spanish ladies may have been to many wild-boar shoots in your country, but this one will be totally different." He continued to chew on the chocolate. "And also the view today will be worth everything." His smile turned the scar on his cheek into a deep crease. "After the hunt is over, I would like to hear your impressions." His words were carefree, but I sensed a note of anxiety in his voice—or was my imagination leading me again to exaggerate? The General made a few more friendly remarks and then went on to speak to other guests.

Soon the caravan was starting to wend its way through the curving dusty road, and within an hour we were climbing up into the Atlas Mountains. Despite the pressure of the coup attempt, my thoughts wandered to Serge. I speculated how I could negotiate his crossover to our side. It was going to be difficult. Luis was still wary of him, no matter how he pretended to the contrary, and the Russian had maintained his distance ever since our meeting the other day. I counted on our COS in Rabat continuing to intercept messages to Libya, and hoped Jerry would have more information for me when next we spoke, but all these thoughts were inconsequential should His Majesty be murdered.

The terrain looked like southern Spain. In the foothills, the meadows were an Oriental carpet of color—scarlet poppies next to fields of deep purple wild flowers, and there was the smell of lavender and rosemary. The caravan of jeeps climbed through entire slopes covered with the white flowers of the *jara*, rock-rose, and stopped halfway up the mountain near a smallish tent. Everyone piled out and I looked up the steep incline, where a thick underbrush of retama bushes, like a green prickly blanket, provided cover for the game we would shoot today. Silhouetted against the blue sky, a few stray cork trees jutted up above the greenery. Inside the tent, hot mint tea and cookies were being served while we awaited the King's arrival. On the mountain it was colder, and windy too, but the tent was cozy, and as time stretched on, servants brought trays of delicious cheeses and bread.

Rachid appeared and I relaxed. Somehow, when he was around, I always felt safer. He came directly to where I was standing.

"Countess," he murmured, "may we sit over here?" He placed one hand on my arm and directed me to a mound of red velvet pillows in a corner of the tent where we would be alone. I looked warily at the pole next to us. "Don't worry." He smiled. "That will not happen again." He indicated for me to sit down, while speaking in a soft voice. "Your warning has been confirmed in one of our reports. I'm obliged to admit, Comtesse, that there is a possibility of a leftist faction plotting a strike against us." He sighed. "These threats have occurred before and are not usually serious, but nevertheless we must be on guard." I was surprised to see the monastic Rachid reach under the folds of his djellaba for a cigarette. I'd never noticed him smoking before, and wondered if this meant he was more preoccupied than he wanted me to know. "It could be that"—he stopped speaking to light the cigarette—"that the Libyan government, and the underground Communist Party in Morocco, with Soviet encouragement, are planning to launch an attack against us." His left hand dived into a pocket and removed a white, typewritten paper, which he unfolded. "We tolerate the Soviets inside our country but we watch them closely. So far Communism in Morocco has not been a problem. But our recent information will oblige us to give more importance to these activities." He looked around for a place to toss the cigarette ashes. "However," he went on, "it's hard to believe, as Abdul seemed to think, that one of the King's close associates could be a traitor. We are more inclined to think that our enemies come from outside, from people not interested in democracy. Often these radicals are only looking out for their own gain. Our King has been building the economy and strength of our country with the assistance of a freely elected parliament. In poor countries, without much industrialization, this is not easy and takes time. The international socialists know this and strike when the country is weak. They would have little success in a prosperous country such as the United States, but in ours . . ." His thin lips pressed into a fine line. "However, I don't want your trip spoiled with such preoccupations. I want you to rest assured that precautions are now being taken."

I looked at the paper. It was in code and in Arabic. Lines of five-letter blocks, just like those we used to do during the war. "Rachid," I said, "what worries me is that the report our people intercepted referred to the coup taking place on the tenth day. We are not certain when this countdown began, but if it started the date of the report, today is the tenth day. What about the safety of the King and everyone else who's here on this shoot? Does the King know about the threat?"

"Now, now," said Rachid. "You must not worry excessively about these things. The King has taken much interest in the organization of this shoot. It's most important for him that General Franco's daughter and her friends enjoy it. Spain is a close neighbor and it's important that good relations be maintained between our two countries. I wanted you to know that your warning has been verified, but that does not mean that the conspirators are strong enough to do any real damage."

"But does the King know his life is in danger?" I repeated. "It seems logical—"

Before I could say more, the Belgian Ambassador and one of the ministers were standing in front of us, inquiring about their shooting positions. My plans to ask Rachid if I could warn the King myself would now have to wait until a better moment. But when? Would there be another opportunity to talk privately to Rachid? The King was expected momentarily. Time was short.

Rachid replaced the paper in his pocket and stood up, addressing the two men. "Good morning, gentlemen. I'm pleased to see you again," he said, smiling. "Let's see your positions on this sketch of the posts, which I should have handy." He waved to an aide, who seemed to understand immediately what he wanted and brought Rachid a bulky briefcase. Rachid took out a large sheet of paper and spread it on the rug at our feet. The three men knelt down to see the sketch of the day's shooting positions. With one long fingernail Rachid pointed to the line of guns. "The Spaniards are here." He tapped a bony finger on the paper. "In the middle of the line on one side of His Majesty. And the Ambassador is here." His finger continued to tap the map. "On the other side."

The diagram indicated all the posts, with the names of those occupying each one. I tried to scan the names quickly. Carmen

and Cristobal were to the right of the King, Prince Moulay
Abdullah beside them. Members of the King's cabinet were
interspaced with the other guests. Luis was on the opposite side
from me, and next to him was Serge Lebedev. That frightened
me; I didn't know why exactly. After all, I had a certain confidence in the Russian, but still, what if he were fooling me?
"Never underestimate the enemy" was a phrase, learned in the
spy school, which I'd never forgotten.

Moustapha's name, of course, was not there. He was allowed
to accompany the shoot, I surmised, in the role of newspaper
columnist, but having seen him that morning, and knowing he
would be present, was worrisome. As a reporter, he could perhaps pick for himself some strategic spot for an easy killing shot.
There were over fourteen posts in all. I surmised that Rachid's
purpose in showing the sketch was to let me see where everyone
was. If I had suspicions which I had not mentioned to him, I
would now know from what direction the danger might come.
I wondered if Rachid suspected any one person in particular,
like Serge. If so, he was not sharing his information with me.

"Where do the people who are not shooting remain during the
drive?" I asked. The Belgian Ambassador and the Minister nodded, also indicating their curiosity.

"Some guests will be located in a second line behind the main
line of guns, to shoot the animals that escape. Of course we can't
make a line large enough for everyone, and fortunately some
guests here today don't practice this sport, but the onslaught of
wild boar, once the drive begins, is really enormous." Rachid
regarded me intently while the Belgian Ambassador and the
Minister were still looking at the diagram. The message—loud
and clear—was, "Watch for a possible sniper behind you."

"Where will you be?" I asked.

"I can't stand the noise of the guns. My Koran here"—he
tapped the lower side of his djellaba—"will keep me company
while you shooters are bursting your eardrums." Then he
showed me a box of earplugs. "This will help protect my nerves,
too—and allow me to dedicate some thoughts to Allah."

I suspected he was more apt to dedicate his time to observing
from some well-located observation post. Still pursuing my efforts to talk to the King, and afraid Rachid would move off, I

took a different tack. "I wonder," I said as casually as I could, "about General Oufkir's history, his background. How did he reach the high post he holds now?"

Rachid's eyes narrowed. "Oufkir . . ." he said, and cigarette smoke escaped from his mouth as he pronounced the name. "Comtesse, I think you have friends who know the General more intimately than I do, and who could answer that question better—which I am sure you have realized. Therefore I must conclude that you are asking me for another reason." He glanced at me mischievously. "Am I correct?"

I had the grace to blush, because he had, of course, seen straight through my ruse. "Avoiding the noise of gunfire has sharpened your ears to more than just sounds, Rachid," I said, and he inclined his head at the oblique compliment and at my admission of subterfuge.

"If you ask others, they will tell you foolish stories about Oufkir's ancestors and mine. I don't doubt you have already heard their babble about a feud that was supposed to have existed centuries ago. The fantasy is romantic, but may entertain your young ears, so I will amuse you further with what they tell me. In our country, nomad tribes have always depended upon dates and other fruit and, of course, the water of the oases for survival. In ancient times an oasis was not often shared peaceably. All tribes vied for control of these desert islands. Hearsay has it that Oufkir is a descendant of a tribe which waged a notorious and bitter blood feud with my ancestors for centuries, and the romance is based, as often happens, on an incident which did occur."

He lit another cigarette. His hooded eyes dropped to cover the dark pupils; as he inhaled deeply, the tip glowed red. Suddenly he seemed miles away: I sensed his mind drifting back in time. Was it my imagination or was I glimpsing how the pull of generations of blood relationships could forge and maintain a powerful and irreversible hatred? Here this man was reminiscing about times far past instead of concerning himself with the fact that his monarch was in jeopardy and could perhaps even be dead in the next few hours. His words had almost pulled me back into the past, too, but not the Ambassador and the Minister, who were still studying the map at our feet, oblivious to Rachid's remarks.

The silence between Rachid and myself lengthened. He was lost in his dreams, but I was still curious. "Please tell me," I urged. His story, I felt, would provide a clue for me, a piece to the puzzle of their culture, so different from that of Spain.

"This is the story as I know it, but doubtless Oufkir would tell a very different version." He shot me a wink of venomous amusement. "My ancestor, also named Rachid, was the Caliph of the tribe from which I have descended. About two hundred years ago, after a particularly bad dry spell, my ancestor's tribe, eighty people in all, finally arrived at an oasis on their usual grazing route. They had been forced to sacrifice many precious and meaningful possessions in order to spare the camels the weight. Many children and older people were sick and dying of disease, and water for them was more precious than gold. The wind had blown steadily for weeks and even the oasis was almost barren." Rachid looked up as the smoke disintegrated in the air. "I know well the feeling of the wind that blows in dry spells on the desert. It feels like powdered bone."

His next puff was long and slow, and for a while I thought he had nothing more to say, but he did go on. "It had been the hardest season in that century, and the tribe remained for weeks, exhausted from the grueling trek, weakened and ill. They needed at least two months on the oasis to regain their strength." He put his cigarette stub into a bowl of white sand at his side. "Then another tribe, supposedly Oufkir's ancestors, renowned for its great warriors, swooped down one day. They approached my ancestor and demanded water, food, and shelter for their animals. They were told that there was not enough to spare, that to share would mean death for half the camp. Nevertheless, my ancestor gave the newcomers enough water and dates to enable them to reach another oasis nearby. They pretended to leave, but that same night they returned to devastate the encampment and slit the throats even of small children. Miraculously, six men, three women, and a handful of children escaped, including the Sheik. His mourning, pitiful band struggled across the desert, accompanied by a few hastily loaded camels he had managed to rescue. He vowed that from that day on he and his descendants would wreak vengeance on that cruel tribe." Rachid looked at me quizzically, awaiting my reaction. The Ambassador and the Minister were still discussing something related to the posts on the map and had not heard my friend's romantic story.

"That's a fascinating story, Rachid," I said, hoping that he would go on. But he said nothing more, and I continued: "It's a pity that's not the true explanation of your misunderstanding with the General."

A sly smirk was my friend's only response. After what Fatima had said about power and favor, I did not believe that this legend, real or fictitious, was the answer to the hatred between Rachid and Oufkir.

He seemed to read my mind. "Of course I deny such frivolous explanations. General Oufkir and I have sufficient other causes for the argument you so unfortunately witnessed—" But before Rachid was able to say more, a bustle of running feet and the sound of automobiles told us that the King was arriving.

We jumped up and rushed out, and I never had the chance to ask this shrewd old man permission to warn the King, and never would. Perhaps his tale of ancient desert feuds was a skillful ploy to delay my question until it was too late. Already the cars of the advance guard were pulling up. Not until the King jumped from one was it apparent in which car he had been traveling—there were at least six, and all were identical. Prince Moulay Abdullah stepped forward, and the two brothers embraced, the King patting the Prince affectionately on the back. Although we were at a slight distance, and they both spoke in Arabic, the King's gestures and smiles made it clear he was kidding his brother about his fancy outfit. Hassan was wearing regular army boots, regular-issue army camouflage fatigues, a simple canvas army cap, sunglasses, and, hanging from his shoulder, were his field glasses. Nothing regal or ornate about his attire. The King had a nice caramel skin, extremely white teeth, a strong face—large black eyes, full lips revealing partially black blood, and a wonderful smile. He was not excessively tall, but had the powerful build of a bulldog, obviously a man of great physical and moral strength. Prince Moulay Abdullah was perhaps more handsome, but the King was stronger and more authoritative.

Carmen Franco, who knew Morocco well, had told me that the Moroccan royal family encouraged members of the aristocracy to take at least one black wife. This, she had said, was a smart political strategy to avoid ethnic clashes, and had completely removed any trace of racism in the country. The mixture of blood had sometimes resulted in beautiful people—blacks in certain parts of Morocco had pale blue eyes, fine features, and a lovely skin color.

One by one we were introduced. Carmen had met King Hassan during his visits to Spain, but I had never seen him before and was anxious to talk to this man who was reputed to be the most intelligent and powerful leader of the Arab world. As I looked at him, I wondered if he had donned his simple military uniform for the purpose of protection, since his attire was identical to that of the officers surrounding him, or if that was his usual shooting outfit. The King's cortege of officers and guards stood back while we were introduced. Meanwhile preparations for the shoot continued. Loaders transported equipment; cars were being hidden. The monarch moved easily and graciously through the guests, with a smile and a brief comment for each one. Suddenly I found myself alone with him, standing in the middle of all the bustle.

"Shooting in Spain is one of my favorite pastimes," King Hassan said amiably, "although I don't have as much time for it as I would like."

"For me, also, Your Majesty," I answered. "That's why it's such a treat to be invited to shoot in this beautiful country."

"And I understand that you are an excellent shot," he went on. "The trophies on that lovely hat attest to your skills." He smiled at me with warmth, and I was engulfed with a feeling of affection for this powerful man who had such grace and charm. I knew this was my chance to talk to him about the fact that today could be the fatal date, but Rachid, who had moved up quietly beside me, interrupted.

"Your Majesty will have a good shoot today. I'm told that over a thousand beaters have been rounding up the game for two days. They have more wild boar than usual."

Once again Rachid had stopped me. While we continued to converse, an endless line of men in rags and turbans was forming next to the King. Seeing them, he stretched out his hand, and while we continued to chat, one by one the men kissed it—first the palm and then the back of the hand. Hassan went through the ceremony of twisting his hand over, back and forth, back and forth, without even looking at those kissing it or acknowledging their presence.

"Our guests from Spain may be disappointed at the size of our wild boar," the King went on. He looked at me with those formidable black eyes and smiled that special smile. "But we make up for that in quantity. What's the saying? 'Quality over quantity'? Well, here we do it the other way around."

I marveled at his ability to carry on a normal conversation while turning his hand up and down and having so many people touch it. For me, the proximity of the silent file made it an effort merely to continue conversing normally. I would have preferred, like the King, not to look at them, but since I feared a traitor might be in the group, I found myself examining each one carefully. Their awed expressions made me realize that for them the King was not only their monarch but also their religious leader. The ragged men were so close that it would have been easy for any one of them to take a concealed knife from the folds of his djellaba and plunge the weapon into the King's heart, but the ceremony proceeded without mishap.

As I watched the armament being taken to each post, I wondered how any assassin could miss. The number of people present increased each second. If even a few were involved in that conspiracy, there would not be much chance that the King or anyone assisting him would escape alive. Luis passed by, his rifle on his shoulder, and squeezed my hand. I knew he was thinking the same. By the time General Oufkir suggested the King and his guests move on to the stands farther up the hill, I was perspiring with nervous tension.

As I walked up the mountain, General Oufkir accompanied me and chatted on about King Hassan being of the Alouite dynasty and a thirty-fifth-generation descendant of Mohammed, the Prophet, which explained the look of religious fervor on the faces of the men kissing His Majesty's hand. He also told me that his King was the seventeenth in that family to reign uninterruptedly since 1666. When Oufkir saw that I was interested, he went on to explain that Hassan had been educated in a French university and had participated in his father's governmental affairs since 1957. "During those difficult times of the Spanish and French protectorates," he continued, "although only seventeen years old, his intelligence and integrity already commanded respect. And he became King when Mohammed the Fifth died unexpectedly. That was back in '61. He—" General Oufkir's words were cut off. An officer appeared, requesting attention, and after making a hasty excuse, Oufkir rushed off.

Another officer approached me, saying he would take me to my post. We walked side by side along a grassy trail for a few minutes and then took a few steps up, in front of a huge green roofless room of three walls, where he left me. Branches of retama bushes had been intertwined with live oak to make the thick green walls. When I went inside, I was impressed. The floor of the roomlike enclosure was covered with beautiful red-and-orange carpets. Masses of colorful plush pillows were strewn about—a luxury unheard of in shooting posts in Spain or France or England. For a few moments the unreality of it all made me forget the danger; I stretched out on the thick carpet and leaned back Cleopatra-style on the sumptuous pillows, incredulous over the decor of my shooting post.

I looked up when I saw two officers with automatic weapons that looked like French MAT 49s appear in the back of my fancy blind, the only open side. They quietly stationed themselves there. Quickly, I stood up, wondering what would happen next and why they had come. Was this special protection provided by Rachid, or would they riddle me with bullets later on? Peering over the green cover of my stand, I looked down the line of guns—what I could see of it, since it wound around the hill, thick with underbrush. In the other posts I could barely recognize anyone; all were hiding behind the front wall, peering cautiously above it. In that crouching position, they would be invisible to the game when it was driven toward them. Each enclosure resembled mine, and I presumed that they also had

the same ornate interiors. Hoping to involve the officers in conversation, I approached one and asked why the stands were so
high off the ground.

"That's so the wild boar will not be able to get up into the
stand. When wounded, they're dangerous and are apt to attack."

Before I could ask why he and the other officers were on guard
with automatic weapons, Luis appeared, with a loader carrying
his shooting gear.

"They're changing almost everybody's post, even the King's.
So now we're sharing one," he informed me.

I was delighted, since the thought of being separated if some
outburst did occur added to my worries. I would prefer to die
fighting beside my husband if we were to be murdered. I surmised that Rachid or Oufkir was having the King's post changed
to foil any plans that might have been made by a conspirator.

"Wonderful," I whispered. "There's plenty of room for us
both here, and frankly I don't like being alone . . . just today."
I darted my eyes from one officer to the other so Luis would
know what I meant. Luis shrugged, indicating he didn't understand their presence either.

He peered over the wall of branches, as I had done before,
while speaking to me in English. "Frankly, I'm more worried
about a sniper out there than about these fellows or those
Moroccan *jabalís* they seem to think are so dangerous."

Men and officers continued to move about. There seemed to
be nothing we could do but wait. Our loaders appeared and took
their places on little stools, one next to Luis and one next to me,
and we spent a few moments practicing passing the guns back
and forth. Then three rifle shots rang out and we jumped to
attention. The shoot had begun.

Luis and I each leaned out over the leafy green wall, ready to
shoot the first animal that appeared or defend ourselves from an
assassin. We were accustomed to scanning the underbrush for
wild boar, which were always hard to see; their short legs kept
them close to the ground, not like deer, whose horns were easily
visible. But we needn't have made the effort. Hundreds of men
were suddenly racing down the mountain—screeching and
wailing. In front of them, masses of wild boar came rushing
toward us, running, bumping into each other in their haste to

get out of the thicket and away from the shouting beaters. There was such a mingling of men and wild boar that I was afraid to shoot—fearful of hitting a beater instead of an animal—and stood there with my gun poised. "Shoot, shoot!" cried one of the officers, who was now standing just beside me, with his automatic weapon aimed at the animal riot in front of us.

"But I might hit one of those beaters," I complained.

"*No importa.*" The man's voice was tense with excitement. "Señora Condesa, *tire, tire,* shoot. Shoot."

There was no way I could keep an eye on the other guns or try to see the King's blind. By now the first onslaught of animals was close to our platform, and the noise of the gunshots, the beaters' screams, the screeching of the animals, was deafening. Hundreds of wild boar materialized all at once. To me they looked like an army of gigantic bloated rats gone berserk. Maybe it was because they were smaller than our Spanish boar; also, there were so many—all running so fast.

I glanced questioningly at the young officer. Again he nodded, repeating, "Shoot. Shoot," his voice reduced to a thin, uptight shout. The other armed officer was next to Luis, who was shooting as rapidly as his loader was able to reload and pass the next shotgun.

"Shoot, Madame la Comtesse, shoot," my officer said desperately for the third time. "Don't be afraid. I'm here to kill any animals you may wound, so you don't have to fear they will get up onto this platform."

So that was why the officers were guarding our stand! I had no idea which station the King was in or who was supposedly protecting him. There was no way that Luis or I could help the King now. I also wondered where Rachid was located in this wild melange of automatic weapons, rifles, and shotguns. Around me, the bursts of gunfire resounded like the front line of trench warfare. I breathed deeply, not certain what to do. Those men out there, if I missed! Rifle blasts exploded from all directions. Luis was carefully picking off a number of wild boar. Already several lay dead in front of our stand. Some had even managed to reach the very edge of our platform. Now I understood why the wall had been laced so carefully with crisscrossing branches. The wild boar kept pouring down the mountain, and I realized that if I didn't help Luis, one might get into our blind. The beaters' inhuman screams became louder and louder as they came closer. The boar—many wounded—squealed frantically—each moment closer.

The racket was incredible and exhilarating. I took careful aim, but as I pulled the trigger, I realized the beasts were going almost as fast as our Spanish partridge. I missed. The officer at my side let off a short burst from his automatic and stopped two boar from jumping into our blind. Hastily, I grabbed the gun my loader handed me and shot again without aiming, just swinging the barrel, like wing-shooting. I did a fast double, killing two fat little ones. Then my loader handed me the guns quickly, rotating them in almost constant movement. I began to kill wild boar at breakneck speed. It was a slaughter, but exciting. Luis was using a rifle, but I had a twelve gauge, using solid shot. My loader soon started to rotate three of my guns because the continuous shooting was burning my hand despite my pigskin glove on the barrel.

The drive stopped as suddenly as it had begun. For a moment a heavy silence hung in the air. Forty-five minutes, and not one letup in the amount of game that had kept rushing at us off that mountain. In Spain we would have been in our posts about four or five hours, and with luck would have shot from one to three wild boar. Today we had seen thousands of animals all at once. The ground below us, all around and as far as we could see, was littered with carcasses.

Luis, a top shot, had killed many more than I, but nevertheless the officer beside me was enthusiastic with his praise. "Congratulations, Madame la Comtesse," he said. "Once you started, you shot beautifully. You handled those guns with great skill. Never have I seen a woman shoot so well." But I hardly heard him. Was the King still alive? With all the firing and bedlam of the drive, it would have been such a simple matter to put a bullet through his brain. I glanced at Luis and perceived his thoughts matched mine, as he too looked anxiously down the line where the King's stand was located. Nothing unusual seemed to be happening. A few shots rang out as soldiers and officers killed the remaining wounded animals. Still, a fatal shot could be aimed at the King.

Carefully, the men with machine guns moved out to ascertain there were no more wounded animals alive. Soon a sign was given that we could come down from our stands. I looked at Luis. We were still too astounded to speak. Neither of us had any idea how many animals we had downed. It had been a unique experience—the noise, the amount of game—but I knew he was thinking, as I, that our shoots in Spain were more sportive.

In the distance we saw General Oufkir and Rachid rushing down the hill to where the cars had been concealed under large oak trees. It took a few moments for us to recognize the King running between them. Thank God! He was alive, but why the hurry? Was something happening now that was placing his life in jeopardy? We raced to catch up and barely made it to the King's car, where we saw him dive inside in obvious good health. There were no goodbyes. The wheels of his black vehicle spun as the driver slammed the powerful engine into gear and started to move down the mountain. Beaters, servants, chauffeurs, officers, and soldiers ran toward it and tried to accompany the vehicle—running on either side, waving and screaming. Some managed to touch the window where he was sitting. Those who could not reach that touched the King's car anyplace they could.

Luis and I watched the amazing spectacle, astonished at the evident adoration these men had for their King. They kept running wildly, hysterically, next to their monarch's car, and it was quite staggering to see how long they managed to keep up with his big Mercedes. Like Olympic runners they raced, struggling to keep their balance, many slipping and falling off the steep incline on either side of the road, as the car moved down the curving dirt path. I grabbed Luis's field glasses to follow the scene. When the car took on greater speed, little by little most of the men were outdistanced, but one lone runner continued for another two hundred meters, racing like the wind. Only when the car turned a corner and sped off at the bottom of the hill did the sprinter stop and stand there motionless, watching his monarch's vehicle disappear. Through the field glasses I recognized Captain Omar Khalil's profile.

A great silence and peace engulfed the mountain. After the

thunderous racket of the shoot, the men's screams, the wild boars' screeching, and the bustle of jeeps and cars, we were suddenly wrapped in stillness. Luis and I looked at each other. The tension of the past twelve hours had left us drained. The King was safe. Not even a small accident had occurred. Did this mean that, after all, the rumors of a coup were incorrect?

As I turned, a cloud blotted out the sun and the entire mountain became shrouded in shadow, like an omen of tragedy. Whether or not the King was still in danger, there was still a mystery I had to solve.

Chapter 13

Luis and I returned to the *parador,* had a quick meal served in our room and, although it was only eight in the evening, fell into bed exhausted until eight the following morning. The next day we awoke refreshed and buoyant, relieved that the feared tenth day had passed. It was a beautiful morning as we set off for Marrakech, passing through a completely different terrain, a valley of almond trees in full bloom, their flurry of petals as pale and soft as fur. The drive was lovely, and comfortable, on magnificent highways that General Medbouh, who again had taken Omar Khalil's place in the front seat, said had been constructed by the French when they had controlled Morocco several decades before. As we came closer to the famous city, the snow-capped mountains in the distance made the view more spectacular than anything we had yet seen. Suddenly we entered a forest of palm trees. They stretched out on either side of the road and towered over the car, their huge leaves deflecting the sun, making intricate shadow patterns. General Medbouh told us that only two such enormous palm forests existed in the world—the other was in Tunis. The tall, graceful date palms continued almost until we reached the pink walls of the city of Marrakech, where the rich light of late afternoon heightened the tone of the adobe walls to deep rose.

It was almost dusk when we left our cars and entered the lobby of the exotic Hotel Mamounia, a building surrounded by walled gardens filled with orange trees and songbirds. Beyond the grand arched entrance, the lobby had painted ceilings, with lacy polychromia and colorful mosaics on the walls. I took Luis's hand and pulled him through the huge open arched doors to the garden, where above the waving palms and orange trees we looked up at the dark, scalloped silhouette of mountains against a rust-colored sky. Both of us were still relieved that the King was alive. Perhaps, after all, the plot had been aborted. Was that the reason the King had rushed back to his car so quickly? Whatever, we had both been under tremendous strain, and this beautiful garden helped to restore our equilibrium.

The Minister of Industry came bustling toward us. Since the Minister also sat on the board of Riff Mines, he and Luis were old friends, and now he had an invitation. "His Majesty and I will be playing golf tomorrow morning at nine, Luis, and he has asked that you join him."

I saw Luis hesitate. Despite there having been no coup, he still remembered the two attempts on our lives. But an invitation by His Majesty could not be refused. "But my golf clubs are in Madrid," Luis responded lamely.

"No problem," replied the Minister, laughing. "Everyone knows how much His Majesty enjoys playing golf, so manufacturers from all over the world have sent him dozens of sets, also shoes. And," he continued, "I hear you play very well."

"Well!" I exclaimed. "Luis was amateur champion of Spain when I married him."

This brought a glance of resigned disapproval from my husband.

"Then it's settled," concluded the Minister. "I'll pick you up at eight, which will give you ample time to select your clubs and hit a few practice balls. The course here is considered one of the best in this part of the world." Then he looked at me. "Aline, would you mind being on your own for the day?"

"That would be fine," I said. "I had intended to spend the day sightseeing and shopping anyway."

"Aline does her best shopping when I leave town," Luis said wryly. "She feels a sudden sense of pocketbook freedom." The Minister left laughing.

Luis didn't know it, but this arrangement was perfect for me. While Luis was on the golf course, I could finally approach

Serge without fear of my husband's jealousy. I hadn't recruited anyone since the Duchess of Windsor, and this recruit would be different—Serge was from the enemy camp!

I knew Jupiter would be anxious to have Serge as an agent—the sooner the better, especially since we had proof that the Soviets knew about the plot. Time was still important. Moreover, I suspected Serge was also anxious—he'd been watching me closely over the last two days. Fortunately he knew better than to approach me when Luis was around.

The next morning I woke up early, breakfasted with my husband, and saw him off with the Minister. I went back to my room, intending to form a plan for contacting Serge. No sooner had I closed the door than the telephone rang. It was Bill Casey.

"Just received a cable from Washington. My SEC swearing-in ceremony's scheduled for the fourteenth. The King was kind enough to send a plane for Sophia and me. We'll be able to catch the flight this afternoon from Rabat to the States. First thing, I'll talk to our mutual friend. Sorry I only have a minute to chat. Don't forget, when you and Luis come to the States, Sophia and I expect to see you." Bill was cautious, aware that other ears could be listening. "And say goodbye to Luis for both of us," he added.

What a disappointment! I was depending on Bill's experience to assist me with Serge; now I'd have to go it alone. Once again the phone rang. It was Serge! I realized that he must have seen my husband's departure.

"Good morning," he said. "I wondered if you would like to do some sightseeing with me today—that is, if you have not already made plans. I would like to talk to you alone."

"I'd be delighted," I answered. "I'm most anxious to talk to you, too."

"When shall we meet?"

"Why not now? We can take a walk and see some of the sights before lunch."

We agreed to meet at the big square at the entrance to the souk.

I waited several minutes before leaving, to allow Serge to precede me. In the lobby, I paused to ask directions. Fortunately both Salima and Fatima had left early to do some shopping. I had pleaded a headache when they asked me to accompany them—meeting Serge was far more important.

When I arrived at the large square, even at this early hour it was crowded—snake charmers, fortune-tellers, and child acrobats doing flips across the pavement. In front of me, a "dentist" was proudly displaying a variety of pulled teeth, along with sets, new and used. From across the square came an eerie, seductive music, and I spotted several men beating drums with large curved sticks, others playing stringed instruments. The air was filled with the smell of meat and spices.

I was so entranced that I jumped when Serge touched my arm. He smiled and we fell into step, side by side, both fascinated by the scenes. At first we walked in silence, just looking around us in awe. Several of the child acrobats were leading small monkeys around on long chains. Bearded vendors in bright-colored, fat bloomers mingled in the crowd, hawking candy, chickens, trinkets.

"I've thought a great deal about what you told me the night we first talked," I began. "About your admiration for my country of birth."

"Yes," Serge murmured, and I sensed his excitement over what I would say next.

We passed the doctor's stall, where a dusty human skeleton hung flapping in the breeze—no doubt a case where the cure had been worse than the illness.

"I asked myself over and over again why you would tell me such a thing," I said, faltering a little. "I felt sure you had a reason. And you do have a reason, don't you?"

Serge colored slightly. It occurred to me that having his fair skin might be a liability in his particular line of work—such a clear barometer of his state of mind.

"I knew you would understand," he said. "I have such faith in you, Aline."

We had reached a small shaded area off to one side of the square and paused. My heart was pounding.

"What I want to tell you, Serge, is that I think the thing you are interested in is a real possibility."

"Do you?" Serge asked, his eyes brightening. He understood

immediately. There could be no doubt he was anxious to join the Agency and help us.

"Absolutely. In fact, I want to arrange this for you."

Serge's breathing had quickened. His whole face was red now, and the pale blue eyes searched mine. He took my hand. "Really, Aline, this is more than I—"

"It gives me great pleasure," I assured him. "I'm as anxious as you are."

"But what about your husband?" he said, whispering.

"Oh, he won't know anything about it. Naturally I keep something like this from him. He shouldn't know. It would only upset him. Of course you'll say nothing to him."

"Of course not!" Serge cried. "I'm not crazy."

We stood somewhat awkwardly. I wanted to be careful how I worded my offer. "Well," I said, after a moment, "am I right in thinking you might be interested in moving forward with this?"

"Interested? I've been thinking of nothing else since I first saw you! For me it was love at first sight."

For a moment I was speechless. Was this some sort of code Serge was using to conceal our purpose from possible listeners? I looked around, but no one was paying any attention to us.

"I'm not sure I understand," I said, glancing tentatively about again.

Now Serge looked confused. "What else have we been talking about?" he said. "I'm madly in love with you and I don't know what to do about it. And you've just told me that you share my feelings."

"*What?*" I stared at him.

My thoughts were in chaos. Was the man serious? Had I completely misunderstood him, to the extent of dragging Washington and Langley into this? The implications of my error were so grave that I felt almost dizzy thinking about them.

I was still overwhelmed when we were interrupted by H. R. H. Prince Moulay Abdullah, accompanied by several cohorts. They were all laughing riotously, and I soon saw the reason. He was waving what appeared to be a brassiere in the air.

"We've been shopping," the Prince crowed as his friends wiped tears of laughter from their eyes.

Serge and I stood uncomfortably. The introduction of a brassiere was the last thing we needed in our already awkward conversation.

"Sir, you're beginning to remind me of Captain Omar," I said, struggling to sound lighthearted. "I'm surprised he didn't think of this first."

"Oh, Captain Omar Khalil is occupied with his new young wife at the moment," the Prince replied, winking at us in case we should miss the point. I felt the blood rise to my cheeks. Serge used his toe to poke at a stone.

"But you two are in serious moods this morning," the Prince said, letting the brassiere dangle at his side. "Aren't you enjoying our beautiful Marrakech?"

"Immensely," I said, smiling sweetly. "I'm only sorry my husband isn't here to see this wonderful square with us."

I shot a righteous look at Serge, who still stared purposefully at the ground.

"Not to worry, Countess," the Prince reassured me. "We have a second day here, and there will be time for Luis to see everything."

"Well," I said, "I suppose I have to get some shopping done before I go back to the hotel. See you later."

I left Serge with the Prince and his group. For the brief moment during which my eyes met Serge's, I saw the mirror of my own confusion. What was going on? I wanted to put the conversation behind me, but it continued to replay in my mind. What did it all mean—could it really be as simple as the Russian having a crush on me? That was impossible, I thought. I'd never given him any encouragement. Whatever the explanation, one thing was clear: I had acted too quickly in contacting Washington, and it was going to be difficult to extricate myself gracefully. What would be my excuse—and how would I convince them that I had made my proposal without blowing my cover in the process? Or had I? Consumed by these worries, I wandered out of the square in the direction of the hotel, along the narrow, curving streets, the pink houses dazzling as sugar candy in the sunlight.

As I was heading down a narrow lane, I saw Salima lingering listlessly at the window of a jeweler's shop. I felt I had never been so glad to see anyone in my life.

"Salima!" I called. She was clearly depressed, and I suspected it had to do with Michel, who had also gone to the golf club, being absent. But when she saw me she made an effort to put on a cheerful face. I decided to say nothing about Michel unless she did.

"Captain Khalil says many of our group are going to a feast-day celebration in a small nearby town this afternoon."

"That sounds like fun."

"Yes," she agreed, though her flat voice betrayed a lack of enthusiasm.

"Why don't we go, too?" I suggested.

She was making an unsuccessful effort to conceal her unhappiness, which reminded me of those first years with Luis, when even an hour away from him was torture.

We ambled among the streets, past walled gardens and shimmering houses, and gradually made our way back to the hotel for lunch. Both of us were silent, each occupied with our own thoughts. I dreaded bumping into Serge—how could I face him after such a blunder on my part and his embarrassing declaration? I found myself wishing Luis were still here and thinking that only this morning I'd been counting the moments until his departure. A pang of guilt struck me—here was my reward for operating behind my husband's back.

Luckily, Serge seemed no more eager to spend time with me than I was to spend it with him. We sat at opposite sides of the room, and when the meal was over, he bolted through the door. I wandered through the hotel's spectacular garden, filled with tropical parrots and dense, leafy trees, and when it came time for the cars to leave for the neighboring town, Salima met me and we walked out together.

About an hour later the cars parked outside the little walled village and we got out to make our way to the main plaza on foot. As we neared the plaza, the din increased and the enthusiasm of the inhabitants became contagious. Even Salima's flagging spirits lifted, and she seemed as caught up as anyone in the whirl of excitement which was enveloping our group like a happy breeze.

The level of activity in the small plaza was intense. Like the
Marrakech souk, acrobats, jugglers, and musicians were everywhere—one had to walk carefully for fear of finding oneself face
to face with the gleaming head of a swaying cobra. At the center
of the excitement stood Captain Omar. He was pointing to a
figure covered in goat skins, dolled up to look like a faun. The
man was playing the role of part goat, part man, enchanting the
populace with his frolicking—jumping and leaping. Salima and
I couldn't help laughing at his frenzied gestures. We followed
as the faun led the townsfolk from one little adobe house to
another. At each, someone came out to give him dates, toys,
flowers, or coins. A group of young soldiers accompanied him,
carrying the things people gave him. Salima explained. "On
feast days, the faun has the right to enter all the houses in the
village and take whatever he wishes. That's why the people have
gifts ready for him."

"That sounds like our Halloween."

Salima looked at me. "You're right. It's sort of like that. I
remember when I was in America how that first Halloween
reminded me of these ceremonies." She smiled as she watched
the faun prance and bound from an adobe hut, clutching two
flowerpots while trying to keep his head mask in place. "This
fellow is much more amusing than most," she said. "Look how
the people are charmed by him. I've never seen anyone get so
many gifts, nor go through such antics."

I looked at those with us. There were two groups—those from
our own tour and those from the town. There was also a number
of young local barefoot boys, grinning from ear to ear and nudg-
ing each other in their excitement. The crowd continued to
grow, with even the plaza vendors leaving their stalls and coming to watch the faun. I noticed Serge in the midst of our group,
and was unnerved to find him staring at me with renewed intensity. He seemed to have shed his shyness, as if some new idea
or question concerning me were now dominating his thoughts.
I looked quickly away, hoping that Luis would return from his
golf before Serge had another chance to approach me.

Captain Omar was positively bursting with excitement. Scanning the crowd, I saw his new wife from the City of Roses,
looking shy but happy. I assumed that festivities such as these

must have been common in her village, too. Omar clapped his hands. "Look, look what he's doing now," he exclaimed.

The faun was pushing his way into a crowd of children and giving them the gifts he had collected, and indicating to the soldiers who had carried his presents to do the same. The children were ecstatic with the toys and food and trinkets. They tried to get close to him, curious to know the identity of this wondrous faun. They grabbed the skins to uncover the faun's identity, making it impossible for him to keep his disguise in place. He made a leap high into the air to avoid them, but the skins started to fall off anyway. I surmised from the shouts of the locals that this was part of the game. Finally, one of the young boys managed to wrest the last goat skin from the fellow's shoulders, and another grabbed the headdress.

I was amused to see that it was the officer who had fooled Fatima and me in Tinerhir with the masks.

"Why, I know him." Salima's voice showed that she also was astonished. "That's Ahmed."

Crowds of children surrounded the new hero—all trying to touch him. Ahmed was obviously enjoying their attentions, and chatted with them while exchanging playful blows with the younger ones. Even at this distance when for a moment he looked our way, his wolfish, pale-blue eyes were piercing. I glanced at Salima to see if she was impressed by his good looks, and found her staring at him.

"Look at those children," Salima cried, laughing along with the rest of the group. "They're enchanted with Ahmed."

Near the mass of clamoring children was one lone, tall tree, and to escape the clawing hands and jabs, Ahmed stepped a few paces back and then leaped for the tree. A collective sigh rose from the crowd at the sight of him springing high into the air, taut as the tree itself. He leaped with incredible agility, as if someone had thrown him. The children tried to follow up the tree trunk but slid back down, while Ahmed's hands continued to clasp the trunk securely. As limber as a monkey, he even managed to hoist his lithe form higher, to the screams of the children. It seemed humanly impossible, absurd, how high he climbed. Finally, Ahmed dropped to the ground laughing, accompanied by cheers and applause.

Salima had been watching. "He always was an amusing, clever fellow," she said, her eyes bright with merriment. "I knew him well as a child—he was always playing tricks. Once he hid in the leaves of a tree and poured water on my head as I was walking to school. What he didn't expect was that I would climb another tree farther down the path and drop sand on him the next day!" She laughed at the memory.

"I think it's been twelve years since I last saw him," she said, turning to me. "One disadvantage of being away from home for so many years is that one loses touch with all of one's childhood friends."

"You must introduce yourself again," I said. "He'll probably be as surprised as you are."

Ahmed managed to separate himself from the clamoring youngsters, who soon started to chase through the crowd, whipping one another with bundles of palm leaves. Salima took my arm and we threaded our way through the crowd toward the triumphant Ahmed. I was pleased to see that the fellow's handsome face lit up on seeing her. Within moments the two were happily recounting their mischievous childhoods.

"Remember the time my friends and I disguised ourselves as beggars and frightened a whole group of you girls in the souk?" Ahmed cried.

"I wasn't frightened," Salima insisted. "I knew it was you. I only went along with it so the other girls would still be afraid."

"Frightening people in marketplaces seems to be a specialty of yours, Ahmed," I said.

"It was Captain Omar's idea," he admitted, grinning.

As the three of us talked, I noticed that a number of local girls were lingering nearby, in hopes of speaking with the flamboyant officer. Ahmed, however, now seemed oblivious to the stir he had created.

"You say that we boys were naughty," he said, smiling at Salima, "but what about you? She was a terror, Countess—you can't imagine." He proceeded to tell a story of how Salima had sent one of their friends, an arrogant, conceited boy, a series of anonymous love notes. Finally she had instructed him to appear at a designated place, where he had waited smugly for the fair Salima. Then she had emerged from the bushes with a band of girls. Laughing hysterically, they'd pelted the shocked boy with rotten oranges.

"He wasn't the same for weeks, and it served him right," Salima chortled, reliving her triumph.

"Are you still such a heartbreaker?" Ahmed asked, looking at her mischievously. Salima blushed.

What a favor the King had done, inviting Luis to play golf, or this conversation would never have occurred. But I knew that when someone is in love, all members of the opposite sex cease to exist, and I had little hope that today's excursion would make Salima forget Michel.

Chapter 14

When I left them, Ahmed and Salima were still chatting enthusiastically. I threaded my way along the narrow streets back to the cars, with the intention of contacting Jerry in Madrid before Luis returned, and hoping to find a way of extricating myself from the debacle I had created with Langley. Thanks to the feast-day celebration, this morning's anxiety had left me for a short time, but now I was again musing over the absurdity of my misunderstanding.

Arriving at the hotel, I was surprised by Serge, who appeared from nowhere. He walked briskly toward me, and there was no way to avoid him. It was now dusk. As I ascended the stairs, he blocked my path.

"Aline, I must talk to you," he said.

My heart slammed against my ribs, and the calm I had felt only moments before evaporated quickly.

"Haven't we talked enough for one day?" I said, trying to sound lighthearted.

Serge smiled, and his kind, spontaneous grin relieved me somewhat.

"That's true," he said. "However, I still don't understand the meaning of our conversation."

"You're not alone there," I said.

"What I mean is this," Serge said, more seriously now. "You spoke to me with something definite in mind. Clearly you thought that we had some understanding, and you were surprised to learn this wasn't the case. What was it, Aline, that you were trying to suggest?"

"I don't know what you mean," I fumbled, genuinely flustered now.

"How can that be?" Serge said. "You had a good idea several hours ago."

"It was only that I thought you might have some interest in going to America," I said, "and I thought you might want me to put you in touch with the American Ambassador."

Serge looked genuinely taken aback. "Go to America?" he repeated, bewildered.

"Well, yes, after what you told me about your feelings for our country, I interpreted that as—"

"Say no more about that," Serge said, looking furtively around.

For the second time that day, my mind reeled with confusion. Was he taunting me with the fact that he knew I worked for the Company? Or were his curiosity and confusion genuine? I stared at the horizon, which was burned deep orange, with the dramatic silhouettes of the Atlas Mountains against it. Serge's obvious discomfort strengthened my confidence.

"That's what I meant to tell you this morning—nothing more," I said coldly, "and if you wish not to speak of it now, then we have nothing more to talk about."

"But what about—"

I was already walking. At the door to the hotel I recognized the car which had taken Luis and the Minister to the golf club this morning. Frustrated that I had not been able to reach Jerry, I ran to our room to welcome Luis.

He was full of stories about his golf game, and as we headed for the dining room he said, "What about you, darling? I trust you managed to stay out of mischief for one day?"

His words caused me a jab of guilt. If you only knew, I thought and prayed we would not be seated near Serge.

Within moments, however, my nightmare came true.

"Welcome back, Luis," Prince Moulay Abdullah cried upon seeing us. "Did you enjoy your golf game?"

"Very much," Luis replied, "and I'm glad to find that my wife was well cared for."

"Oh, very well cared for," the Prince answered. "We found Aline at the square in deep conversation with Serge Lebedev only moments after you left."

Ever cool, Luis did not even flinch at the news or look my way. "Well, I'm glad to hear it," he said, smiling blandly at the Prince. "Come, my dear, let's find our places." And with that he took my hand and pulled me ahead. But his neck was crimson with anger. After a few steps he turned his back on me and stalked across the room. Ironically, because Serge was equally anxious to avoid me, the two men ended up sitting practically next to each other. I felt like a leper and found that I had lost my appetite.

Michel was seated between two women. I easily recognized Fatima's well-coiffed black hair, but from the back, the other woman was not familiar. All I could see was a luxurious mass of shiny, fluffy black hair, and not until I had sat down facing the three did I realize who she was. From a distance the two women looked so much alike. Again I realized what a resemblance there was between the two sisters—the same height, the same kind of beautiful figure and features. The difference was in the color of their hair and eyes. Salima saw me staring and jumped up.

"How do I look with black hair?" she laughed as she laced her two hands through the wig.

"To tell you the truth," I said, "you look like Fatima. It's amazing."

"I know," said Salima, still laughing. "That's why I wore it. At the beauty salon late this afternoon, the coiffeur remarked about the similarity of my features and Fatima's, who had been in yesterday. When I disagreed, he disappeared for a minute and returned with this wig. When he put it on me, I had to agree with him. Our resemblance is quite remarkable. Since I was meeting Michel, I wore the wig as a joke." She giggled. "You should have seen the shocked expression on his face. If it weren't for the blue eyes—"

One of the ministers walked over to our table, looking distressed. "My dear Salima," he said. "I've known you since you were a child. Like so many others, I have always admired your beautiful blonde hair. I don't understand why a woman like you would want to change its color."

"What a fuss I've created," responded Salima. "It's only a wig." And she pulled the black hair off, allowing her own light-toned locks to fall over her shoulders.

I moved over to where Fatima and Michel were talking. General Oufkir had come in shortly before, and Fatima was telling Michel more war stories about him. "It seems that the French forces in Vietnam were camped at night inside a walled enclosure for protection," she said, "but despite guards and walls, somehow the enemy was able to enter the camp in the darkness and regularly cut the throats of several guards each night. Nobody could understand how they did it. Oufkir decided to find out. Without the permission of his commanding officer, he hid near the wall and waited. After remaining immobile for hours, at about three A.M. he saw four men emerge silently, as if by magic, from under the water of the pond inside the camp, near the wall. They had been submerged, using bamboo sticks to breathe through. They knew the guards on watch would be scanning the jungle, not suspecting an attack from inside the camp. Oufkir made his own surprise attack, killing all four in the same way they had killed the guards—a slashed throat. The following morning Oufkir appeared with the head of one of the Vietnamese traitors and placed it on the desk of the French commanding officer. 'The guilty are our own Viet Cong. They come from inside, not outside, sir,' he said. The story ran through the entire camp and made him even more famous." As Fatima told Oufkir's story, I wondered if he'd received the scar on his face that night he had sliced the head off the Vietnamese traitor.

While Fatima talked I noticed that Michel's attention had strayed to Salima. Abruptly, Michel gave an involuntary jump and looked our way. I had the distinct impression that Fatima had kicked him under the table. "I've managed to get sessions with the best fortune-teller in Morocco for tomorrow, Michel," she said, smiling invitingly. "How about going?"

"Nothing I'd like better. You have me intrigued with this famous Señora See-It-All's supernatural powers. What's that name you call her?"

"Lalla Mira. She really is a remarkable fakir, and you told me you were fascinated by such things. This is a real opportunity. Sometimes people wait for weeks for an appointment. I have friends who make the trip to Marrakech only to see her." Fatima turned to me. "And Aline—you must come too. You may never have another opportunity. The women of her family have been fortune-tellers for centuries."

"To tell you the truth," I said, "although everyone on this side of the Atlantic seems to live by fortune-tellers, I've never put any faith in them."

"You're wrong this time," Fatima replied. "I won't let you miss the opportunity. We'll meet in the lobby around ten." I noticed that she had pointedly not included Salima in the invitation. When I left, I had the feeling that the two sisters were going to have it out as soon as they were alone.

I went into the bar, where a musician was playing wonderful old jazz on the piano and some of our group were having coffee. Since Luis didn't appear, I eventually left, determined to make use of my outcast state to put a call through to Jerry in Madrid to forward a message to Jupiter in Washington. After about an hour of waiting for the long-distance call, and also for Luis, I went out onto the terrace. There was no moon, but the palm trees were silhouetted against a sky filled with stars. As I looked up, enjoying the dramatic view, my eyes were attracted to the unusual sight of a man climbing over the balcony of the terrace above. Standing in the darkness, I clearly heard Fatima's laugh and then her familiar voice. "Come in—come in."

For some moments I stood there, considering what I had just observed. My instincts told me, although I had not been able to see him, that the man in Fatima's room was Michel. If Salima was not there too, it meant only one thing. Michel and Fatima were having an affair. Digesting the shock, I finally went to my room. Fatima had told me that Salima had adeptly arranged to be on the same floor as Michel. She had also ordered Fatima's reservation to be on the floor above, to avoid running into her.

So Michel was climbing up to Fatima's room. I picked up the telephone and asked for Salima. She answered.

"If you would like to go to the *kri-kri* tomorrow," I said, inventing the first excuse I could think of, "I have plenty of other things I would like to do at that time, and I insist that you go in my place."

"I'm afraid that would upset my sister," she answered, making no effort to hide her sarcasm.

I continued. "Have you seen Michel lately?"

"Not since dinner," she replied. "He said he didn't feel well and wanted to be sure that he didn't miss the fortune-teller tomorrow."

After goodnights, I hung up. I was astounded. I had caught Michel fondling Salima's breasts. Now I saw him entering Fatima's bedroom. What kind of game was he playing? Having an affair with two sisters at the same time, at the same hotel, on the same trip! Dangerous, careless, and thoughtless. I wanted to discuss the shameless new development with Luis, but I hadn't seen him since he had angrily left me before dinner. The connecting door between our rooms was shut. I was miserable but had no intention of crawling back to him.

The next morning I met Fatima and Michel in the lobby, and a few minutes later we were rolling toward the fortune-teller's house in the old section of Marrakech. As we rode, Fatima related some of the woman's eccentricities. "Lalla Mira," she said, "will be dressed in a special color. It changes every day, according to the genie she believes dominates that date. Take notice. The color will indicate what her mood is. For the séance she uses small hot stones."

Michel was in front, next to the driver. He turned around abruptly. "That's interesting," he said. "I've never heard of that technique."

"Do you know much about fortune-telling?" I asked.

Resting his arm on the back of the seat, he favored me with a smile. "My mother was obsessed by the supernatural," he explained. "I guess I acquired my penchant for this sort of thing from her. In fact, to tell you the truth, I'm always a bit afraid when I go to one." He ran his hand through his bushy hair. "I don't like admitting such a weakness, but there is an explanation. You see, during the war, we lived in Alsace-Lorraine, near the German frontier, and the Gestapo were constantly coming into the farmhouses, dragging out innocent people whom they suspected of harboring Allied pilots. Sometimes they would find pilots hidden behind a fake wall or in a cellar." My mind flashed back to Bill Casey, who had helped organize the safe houses where these pilots had been concealed.

"I was only six years old," continued Michel. "And they caught the Granjeans, neighbors who lived two houses from us, who were protecting two American pilots. They marched the pilots and the Granjeans and their four children—their youngest boy, Jean-Louis, was my best friend—to a spot in front of their house. The Gestapo shot all eight and marched away. We buried them in their backyard." He paused a long moment. "My father was away most of the time, helping the *maquis,* and my mother was always frightened. She spent hours crying. Neighbors often came for tea to cheer her up. Well, they called it tea, but we rarely had either tea or coffee in the house. My mother would heat water and mix it with a bit of milk from the cow. One of the people my mother most looked forward to seeing, though she ate most of our bread, was the local fortune-teller, Madame Dieulot. I usually sat on my mother's lap as Madame Dieulot took my mother's hand and ran her fingers back and forth across my mother's palm, telling her things which always made my mother feel better. Another neighbor, who was a clairvoyant, also came now and then. She used fancy cards which she carried in a big black bag. They fascinated me—with their bright designs of knights in armor and large golden cups. Sometimes I was allowed to play with them. My mother always felt better after those women talked to her. She would stop crying and take me in her arms and hug me. *'Mon petit Michel,'* she would say, *'tout va bien. Ton père est bien.'* Then she would tell me that we had to have faith in the supernatural. According to her, those women brought God's messages. 'Never forget that, Michel,' she would say. 'When you are unhappy or lonely, ask someone to tell you the message from up there above.' " Michel shook his head. "It's a weakness, I know that. But I can't help it. Fortune-tellers attract me like a magnet. Somehow I believe they will warn me, take care of me, just like my mother said." He shook his head again as if to rid himself of what he had just said.

Both Fatima and I were moved by this strong man's confession. Neither of us said anything, and he began to speak again, almost as if we weren't there. "My mother always seemed to know that both she and my father would not live to see the end of the war. She was frantic those last few months, mostly because she couldn't find Madame Dieulot, and my father was always away. The other fortune-teller had disappeared, too. My mother believed that was a bad omen. I always wondered if one of her fortune-teller friends might have warned her not to be in the station the day she went to meet my father, and the bomb fell, killing them both."

Silence reigned in the car until the driver pulled up to a small, pink adobe two-story building. Wooden lattice shutters covered the windows; boughs of purple bougainvillea framed the arched entrance. We followed Fatima into a small patio where, next to a well, were two goats tied to a chain, and after winding our way in between a clutter of empty orange crates, we climbed a narrow dark stairway with wobbly tile steps. The room at the top was packed with women in dreary dark djellabas. Many were veiled; some stood, others sat cross-legged on a dirty sheepskin rug that partially covered a cement floor. On seeing us, one black-robed figure stood up and disappeared behind a curtain at the far side of the room. In a few seconds she reappeared with two worn leather pillows, which she handed to us. Fatima and I placed them in the only empty area left, near a window, and sat down. Michel remained standing. The place smelled like an old Catholic church, and a light-gray haze of incense hung in the air like a cloud of chiffon. No one spoke, which gave the impression that behind the dirty curtain something as serious as life and death was occurring. Already, Michel's face had taken on a different expression. He stood, slightly isolated from the women, near the door through which we had entered, and as absorbed in his thoughts as if he were on a small solitary island. Outside, below the small window, was another patio. Chickens scratched around amidst a rubble of tin cans and old papers. Lalla Mira's business didn't appear especially prosperous, which made me skeptical about Fatima's claims that she was so famous. If it were true that people came from all over the country just to consult her, why didn't she raise her prices? Soon a veiled woman wrapped in masses of wrinkled black cotton emerged from behind the curtain and approached us. She mumbled a few words in Arabic to Fatima.

"Doña Lalla is heating the stones for our session," Fatima explained, whispering. "We have to wait. She heats the first stones over a brazier. Remember, she claims to be only the medium. Supposedly her information is transmitted to her by a superior force." Fatima patted the worn, dark-blue leather cushion. "This color indicates hope. Lalla Mira says hope is the greatest gift the Almighty has given humanity." Fatima smiled in anticipation. "Let's see what color she's wearing today. According to Lalla Mira, red's the favorite color of the genie of love. The genie who handles jealousy prefers yellow. Beware of green. That's the color of fear. In Lalla's world every human emotion has a supernatural spirit—and a color."

I asked Fatima if she would translate the Arabic for me during my séance. "Not necessary," she said. "Lalla speaks French. Most people in our cities do, you know. When Morocco became a French protectorate around the beginning of the century, they built *lycées* to teach their language." Hostile black eyes over thick veils glanced our way as she continued to whisper. Fatima was undaunted. "It's better to be alone during your séance. That way you can ask whatever you want." Clearly, Fatima took fortune-telling very seriously. The same veiled woman beckoned to me from the curtain. Fatima had insisted that I go first.

When I lifted the curtain and entered Lalla Mira's little abode, the woman was seated, bending over a round, shiny copper brazier. Shutters and curtains kept out the morning sunlight. The reflection of the red coals created flickers of light that darted around the dark room like lively ghosts. With a wave of her arm, and without looking at me, she pointed to a small stool on the opposite side of the brazier. "*Venez, venez, asseyez-vous.*"

Her scratchy voice was barely audible. Ample folds of purple shiny satin engulfed her body. The twisted loops of a huge turban of the same color curving down over her forehead made it difficult for me to determine her age, shape, or features. I wondered what particular genie purple indicated. Fatima had said the best color for Lalla Mira was blue, which represented hope, especially when it was a light blue, pale as a winter sky. Purple might be in the same vein, I hoped, and perhaps would indicate that the soothsayer was in an optimistic frame of mind today.

When I took the seat she indicated, I saw that the glowing embers had made the woman's face beet red. Perspiration hung in fat drops from her nose and chin. The air was stifling and the room reeked of cloves and incense, and something else less agreeable—maybe it was sweat. Not a word passed between us as she continued to drop little round stones on the gleaming coals. Slowly, she began to move her hands in circular motions over them. Now and then she looked up to the low, arched ceiling, as if communicating with the heavens. A long hiccup rolled up from her throat, then another, and still another. Gradually the sound became an outcry of something near to anguish. I wondered if she was having an attack. Then her eyeballs fell back into her head, so that only the whites were visible. No doubt about it, I thought, this woman has been overcome by the heat.

But as she began to chant, I changed my mind. She was playing a role she'd done many times before. At first her declarations about my coming from a far-off land, a visitor to her country, did not surprise me. Fatima might have told her she was bringing some foreigners. But when she peered at me across the haze of heat waves, her voice more intent, or so it seemed at the moment, and when she whispered the words "conspiracy against the leader" and "mortal danger," an icy draft ran up my spine. I listened attentively and she responded as if on cue.

"Beware! Watch out for a man in long dark robes. Gold will shine from his mouth. His hand will hold a long shiny blade. This is the emissary of the devil, who means to harm you." Throughout the dramatic recital, she frequently shivered as if consumed by fear. Then, abruptly, she indicated the session was finished. I had the distinct impression she wanted to tell me more, but did not care to. Or was that part of her ruse?

I walked out of the room confused. Something out of the ordinary had occurred in my séance which had little to do with the supernatural. I knew that. Yet my common sense told me that such a humble woman in this remote little house would not likely know anything related to the coup. I calmed myself with the thought that her words had merely been a strange coincidence, more obvious to me because of my current worries.

As I left the room, Fatima passed me going in—the tilt of her head indicated amazement that I had been inside such a short time. As I returned to my seat on the leather cushion near the window, Michel was still on his little island of thought.

Fatima was not happy, either, when she emerged about ten minutes later, indicating to Michel that it was his turn to pass into the darkened room. "Doña Lalla is not having one of her best days," she confided as she sat down. Glumly, she dedicated herself to observing the chickens down below. Strangely enough, neither of us felt like exchanging comments, and we continued to sit there in silence. Michel's session was lasting much longer than ours. Obviously, I thought, he knows how to handle these people. Then the curtains moved and he stumbled out, visibly upset. I wondered if Lalla Mira had told him a story like mine.

Michel went toward the stairway and we followed; without speaking, he stood aside so Fatima and I could go down the stairs before him. Fatima was still unhappy and I was worried. Despite my skepticism, Lalla Mira's remarks about a conspiracy kept ringing in my mind. I calculated that our silence made Fatima feel guilty for having taken us there.

When we were again in the car, Fatima tried to rescue Michel from his depression. "Lalla Mira has good days and bad days," she consoled him. "You mustn't take her too seriously. That purple was an unfortunate color. When she's in a trance the color takes over and she doesn't even know what she's saying." But nothing Fatima said improved the Frenchman's spirits nor led him to confide his worries.

As we stepped from the car out into the blinding sunlight, in

front of the Hotel Mamounia, I asked Fatima what genie the
color purple indicated. She looked at me for a moment, her
beautiful forehead creased in a frown.

"One of the worst. According to Lalla Mira, purple is the
favorite color of the genie of"—she paused and a frown of repug-
nance passed over her face—"of betrayal."

Chapter 15

General Oufkir and other officers were playing tennis on the hotel courts, and as I walked past the pool to join them I saw Salima just coming out of the water. She stood for a moment at the edge of the pool while removing her cap. A mass of thick shiny golden hair came tumbling down over her shoulders. Seeing me, she waved and sauntered in my direction with her usual feline grace, seemingly unaware of the attention her beautiful athletic body was creating. The brief French bikini make her the recipient of hostile stares from the Moroccan women around the pool. I understood, as never before, the difficulty for Salima and other Moroccan girls educated abroad. Once accustomed to freedom, how could they shroud their agile modern bodies in those voluminous clumsy robes?

When she arrived at my side, Salima asked me if I would accompany her for some more shopping in the souk that afternoon, and we settled on an hour after lunch. Then I continued on to the tennis courts. While I sat watching the game, I thought about Lalla Mira's reference to a conspiracy against the leader. My instinct told me that the strange woman somehow knew about the real plot, and once again I missed being able to consult with Bill Casey. Her prophecy was too vague to warrant transmitting to Jupiter, and at the same time I felt at a loss as to how to evaluate it.

That afternoon, when I joined Salima and others from our

group, the woman's omen was still on my mind, and as we walked across the big square I continued to mull over why she had mentioned that warning, precisely, to me. As we pushed through the crowd, children, chickens, donkeys, carts and wagons made progress difficult, but the joyous cries and picturesque appearance of the people gradually dissipated my worries. Farmers and tradesmen in colorful satin bloomers and turbans stood gaping at the street entertainers, their veiled wives in shabby drab djellabas standing behind them. Salima explained that these were country people from all over Morocco who came to the souk to buy and sell their wares. There was little doubt that in the street, at least, the men looked better than the women.

I became engrossed watching a blacksmith sitting barefoot and bare-legged in knee-length bloomers as he sharpened knives behind an ancient wheel which he spun with his foot. I was about to purchase a beautifully engraved small dagger when I became aware that an Arab in black djellaba and turban was staring at me. As I glanced at the black eyes, a slow, sinister-looking grin spread over his face—and as it broadened, a wave of terror overtook me. There it was—the gold. Two enormous gold teeth! And in his hand, a long silver knife. The mental image of the man that Lalla Mira had warned me about had remained in my mind like a hazy negative, and now the image had come to life.

In a daze, I turned around, looking for a companion. No one I knew was in sight. Now thoroughly frightened, I turned and walked as fast as possible away from the shop. After a few steps I increased my pace, my eyes searching each small alley in hopes of finding one of our group. My only thought was to get far away from that sinister face. No longer did I doubt that Lalla Mira knew more than she had told me. As I quickened my steps, I looked back and saw that the man was following me. The fortune-teller's prophecy seemed each moment more plausible—the black robe, gold in the mouth, the knife. The description could not have been more exact. Although I increased my pace, taking small paths, twisting and turning, I could not lose him. Even when I dashed in and out among those blocking my way, he was able to keep up. Now there was no doubt in my mind that he was after me. Throwing appearances to the wind, I raced toward a wider alley which I hoped would lead to an exit, but instead of finding the route to safety, I soon realized I was even more deeply enmeshed in the bowels of the souk. Running into a tiny shop, I pleaded with the owner for protection, but he didn't understand anything except Arabic, and instead of offering assistance, merely stared at me.

The back wall of the shop was a canvas cloth, which I lifted, and slipped out into another street parallel to the one I was on. For a few moments I thought I had escaped my pursuer, but then I heard him running softly behind me. The shopkeeper must have told him where I had gone. I raced through the maze of narrow passageways—none led out of the souk. Finally I found myself emerging from the dark confines of the souk into an area of small huts crowded with ragged children and weary adults. They all appeared poor and hungry, and irritated to see a foreigner invading their living quarters. But when I looked around, the man with the sinister face was still there, smiling that evil grin, the long narrow blade in his hand. I could practically feel it plunging through my stomach, impaling me on the wall.

I raced on, my hair disheveled; I had lost a heel. Then, at the end of the narrow street, I spotted one of Rachid's officers. I ran to him and practically fell into his arms.

"Madame la Comtesse," he said in an anxious tone, "are you all right? His Highness was worried."

"A man has been pursuing me," I whispered. I felt that terrible chill again. I turned, and there he was, some three feet from us: those black eyes, the gold teeth, the long deadly sword.

"That's the man!" I screamed.

"Please, Madame," said the officer, putting his arm around my shaking shoulders. "This is Ali Ben-Houssain, one of our best— how do you say in English—ah, plainclothesman detectives."

By now my pursuer was conversing in Arabic with the officer. Both looked at me with worried expressions.

"Oh, this is a pity, Comtesse," the officer said. "Ali recognized you from your pictures in our newspapers and he asks me to tell you that he believes you to be one of the most elegant women

that has ever walked through this souk." My pursuer was now
grinning at me benevolently.

"Then why was he following me?" I asked, my voice still
shaken.

"Because, Madame, while at the shop you left your bag on the
table in front of you and he was trying to return it."

First, Ali Ben-Houssain bowed deeply, then he mumbled a
few words and reached into his dirty djellaba. Ceremoniously he
handed me my handbag. His evil grin seemed less sinister as
with another bow he backed away and disappeared into the
souk. I apologized for the trouble I had caused, and hoped the
officer would keep my foolish mistake to himself.

When I finally got back to the hotel, I took a long hot bath in
the enormous tub, trying to relax. I was depressed. Luis still had
not returned from his golf game, but I hoped, when he learned
about my fright in the souk, that he would no longer be furious.
I needed comforting, and longed for his arms around me. Finally I pulled myself from the warm comfort of the tub, and my
thoughts turned to the necessity of notifying Jupiter about my
misrepresentation of Serge's motives. What an ass I was going
to appear when my friends in Washington learned the truth!
Even if I avoided details, I was certain Jupiter would suspect
how my mistake had come about. So as not to miss Luis's call,
and to put a call through to Jerry in Madrid, I decided to eat in
my room.

The telephone lines in Morocco were even worse than those
in Spain, and long-distance calls usually meant a lengthy or-
deal. My dinner arrived, and though it was beautifully presented I barely touched it. When the phone rang I jumped for
it, hoping it would be Luis or maybe my Madrid call. But to
my disappointment it was the concierge informing me that my
husband had remained at the golf club for dinner and not to
expect him.

I called the operator again. "Yes, Countess, I'm working on
your call to Madrid. I shall ring you back." So I stretched out
on the bed, staring up at the white silky fabric which covered
the ceiling. Every room in the Mamounia had double glass doors
giving onto a terrace with a view of the Atlas Mountains, and

now the moonlight set off their bulky shapes. I had closed the doors but left one window open. For a moment I shut my eyes, thinking of the day's incredible happenings while the warm night breeze blew across my face.

I must have remained like that for several minutes, when out of the silence came a sudden loud thump against the window. It was not a crack, like that of a stone, yet the force of it made the window rattle. The blow was so strong that I was surprised the glass remained intact.

I leaped from my bed and stood against the wall alongside the window so that I would be invisible to anyone looking in. The curtains were thin and light as shadows, and they billowed out with the night wind. After a moment I realized I was being ridiculous, and I opened the door and stepped outside. The night was deadly silent except for the faint shouts and music from below. Against the darkness and stillness which opened toward the mountains, these sounds were haunting rather than comforting, like memories from a place which no longer existed. Nothing could be seen outside, and as my adrenaline calmed down, I glanced at the terrace of the next room, wondering if someone could have jumped over the railing and banged on my window. For what purpose? Probably to frighten me, I conjectured. The shutters of the terrace next door were closed, and there was no one in sight, although the shadows were dark enough to hide several assassins. Really, I thought, these jitters are making me lose my common sense. Maybe it was my worrying about Luis's reaction when he had learned I had been with Serge that was upsetting me even more than the preposterous chase in the souk. Whatever, I would have to control myself. I went inside and shut the doors and drew the curtains, although they were not thick enough to block out shadows from inside the room. If someone was trying to frighten me, that person was succeeding.

Like the shot of a gun, the phone rang. I lunged for the receiver.

"Hello?" I cried. "Hello."

There was no answer, nor was there a crackle of long-distance. I thought at first that someone had dialed the wrong room and hung up until I detected the faint but distinct sound of someone's murmur. It was too low to determine whether it was male or female, but someone was on the other end.

I slammed down the phone. Pacing the room, I tried to calm myself. I had to talk to Luis. Then the phone rang again; I stood in front of it and prayed that this time it was my call to Jerry. I picked it up—silence again. I said "Hello" only once, and then I sat in silence again, listening to a murmur which I interpreted to be someone who wanted me to know the call was not a mistake—that it had a purpose.

I could think of nothing but finding Luis. I realized I was beginning to crack under the pressure. When I looked in the mirror, I discovered that my face was white as plaster, my pupils dilated so that the irises appeared completely black. I smoothed my hair, patted some rouge on my cheeks, my fingers trembling, and, feeling slightly lightheaded, went out to the long hallway and took the elevator down to the lobby.

It was only ten o'clock—early for Morocco—and people were still emerging from the dining room. The lobby was awash in confusion. Apparently, from the bits of conversation I could pick up, a large group of German tourists had just arrived and there was some problem with their rooms. Everyone was speaking in loud voices and the chaotic atmosphere only tightened my jittery nerves. In vain I walked from one salon to the next, back to the dining room, and finally into a bar whose doors opened onto a garden where a fountain made frail splashing sounds. There I found Luis with General Oufkir and Prince Moulay Abdullah.

"Aline," cried the Prince, "do join us. We've only just this minute been singing your praises."

"Oh, really?" I said. "How kind of you."

When I dared to glance at Luis, he raised an eyebrow at me and smiled ironically, which left me in no doubt that "we" meant the Prince and the General only.

"Please have a seat," cried the General with a majestic sweep of his arm. The three men were now standing, and Oufkir reached for a chair, knocking it over in the process. Then he took a step, moving uncertainly, as if he were on a ship at high sea. Luis and the Prince began giggling like little boys. I realized that all three were drunk.

"Well, gentlemen," I said, picking up the bottle of whiskey on the table. It was almost empty. "You seem to have made fast work of this."

"It was the Count," continued the Prince, wearing a silly grin which was completely out of keeping with his magnetic, regal stature. "Normally the Count drinks very little," he continued, as if this were valuable information I might not be aware of. "But tonight he was determined to 'tie one on,' as you Americans say—is that the expression?"

"That's it," I said, forcing a smile. I found my patience was wearing thin. "Luis, can I talk with you for a minute?"

"Certainly, my dear," Luis said with exaggerated grandness. He walked toward me with uneasy steps. It was true that he seldom drank, and I was not accustomed to seeing him in this state—moving with an unusual stiff formality. At least his drunkenness appeared to have diminished his anger.

"Good evening, gentlemen," he said, raising an arm in farewell. "You see I have no power against her—she calls and I obey. Her wish is my command."

The Prince, who was in the process of pouring two more glasses, raised the bottle in salute. "This is the trouble with having only one wife," he said, laughing mischievously.

Luis was weaving so chaotically as we left the bar that I had to suppress the urge to take his arm and guide him through the doors.

"Was your Russian boyfriend busy this evening?" he asked sourly when we reached the lobby. "I assume he must be or you wouldn't have come looking for me."

To my relief the lobby was still crowded with the German tourists. Some sort of quarrel had begun between the leader of the group and the concierge, and there was no chance of anyone noticing Luis's surly attitude toward me. Taking advantage of the general furor, I turned to him and spoke harshly.

"We have no more time for quarrels right now," I said. "I am frightened and I need your protection." I explained what had happened in the souk, my fright when I heard the sound against my window, and my nervousness about the telephone calls. As

I spoke, Luis snapped to attention and sobered considerably. Standing straight, his feet planted firmly on the floor, his eyes cleared, as if some cloudy liquid had been drained from them.

"You see, I've always told you a woman cannot withstand this kind of pressure. You're going to destroy your health," he said. "Look, if there is someone trying to get into your room, he's not going to find you. I've just thought of a plan." He giggled as he took my arm, and I wondered if he was reverting to his drunken state. He led me to the stairway instead of to the elevator and down the hall to our adjoining rooms on the second floor. When we reached my door, he made exaggerated gestures of looking to the left and to the right, then slowly opened the door. Silently, we entered. The room was as I had left it—with the lights on. He grabbed a chair and placed it against the door and solemnly sat down. "Now," he said, "I'm invisible to anyone who might be observing the room from outside. Go through the normal procedure of getting ready to go to bed," he ordered. I thought he was being ridiculous, but since the game he was playing seemed to have a sobering effect on him, I proceeded to undress. I put on my nightie and walked back and forth across the curtains a few times to the dressing table so that my silhouette would be visible through the window curtains. Luis sat calmly in the chair, watching me. He waved his hand when I looked at him. "Keep on," he said, "lie down on the bed with the lamp shining on you and pretend to read a book." I did as I was told. Luis must still be quite drunk, I mused.

"Now how do you feel?" Luis said in a stage whisper.

"Bored to death," I answered. "Really, Luis—"

"Just keep it up. I want you to be sure nobody is out there."

I continued to humor him, already thinking more about the idiosyncrasies of love than my premonitions of the past hour.

When five minutes had passed, I switched off the lamp and in total darkness slunk from the bed, feeling my way along the wall to where Luis was almost asleep in the chair. "What's up?" he said when I reached him. "Are you sure you didn't dream all this?"

"I'm sleepy," I whispered and started to creep back to my bed.

But Luis's hand grabbed me and plunked me down on his lap. "We're really acting like fools, don't you think?"

The pressure and anxiety of the past forty-eight hours seemed to disappear as by magic and suddenly I felt as if I too had been drinking, something I rarely did. A fit of laughter overtook me—the absurdity of it! Me in my nightgown, and Luis still reeking of whiskey—sitting together on a chair in the entrance of our bedroom and whispering to each other. My hilarity started Luis laughing, too, and the two of us scrambled along the carpeted floor like children, giggling all the way into his bedroom. We sneaked into bed, still laughing, without putting on the light. There I cuddled into his strong arms. How secure I felt; I began to relax and quickly fell asleep.

Chapter 16

The next morning was a beautiful, glittering day; the bright sun made everything gleam, and the palm trees in the garden sparkled as if it had just rained. When I went to join Luis for breakfast on the terrace, he was buttering a croissant while reading the newspaper and, amazingly, had no hangover. He looked up and smiled as I sat down. "I've a small surprise," he said. His white dressing gown made his face appear more tanned, and his eyes, catching the sunlight, sparkled like the surface of a sea. His good looks made me catch my breath for the millionth time since we'd met. Behind him in the distance were the mountains, their peaks frosted with snow; below, the garden was lush with camellias and orange blossoms. Tiny birds jumped on and off our railing, pecking at the stack of biscuits on the edge of the table; they were obviously accustomed to breakfasting with the guests.

"Look what I found," Luis said as he reached across the table and handed me a small, dark object. It was a tiny dead bird, just like those flitting around us.

"That's what you heard last night against your window. The bird must have hit the glass at top speed. I found it on the floor when I came out here this morning." I turned the soft feathery little creature over in my hand. "And those telephone calls," he went on, "could have been due to the service, which is always getting rooms mixed up. I hope that your fears of yesterday, my dear, will now be forgotten."

When I looked up at him, I didn't tell him that he'd long since eliminated those worries and that for this moment, at least, I couldn't even remember them.

After breakfast, when I went back inside the room, I saw an envelope under the hall door. "Must talk to you urgently," the handwritten note said. "Will be waiting in the garden after breakfast around ten-thirty. Salima."

When I was dressed and ready to meet Salima, Luis was still in his dressing gown, sitting in the sun reading the papers. "Say hello to Salima for me," he called as I left.

Downstairs, I was surprised to see Michel. He took my arm as we descended the steps leading to the lush, fragrant patio garden. "I'm part of this discussion too," he said with such a winning and joyful smile that it was impossible not to return it. Still, I felt a shadow of concern. What were the two of them up to?

He guided me along the path, past the swimming pool, and out into a smaller garden, where we found Salima. She was sitting on a small bench near a row of blooming orange trees, and leaped to her feet when she saw us. "Aline, I'm so glad you could meet us," she cried, grinning from ear to ear and taking Michel's arm.

There was a silence—none of us seemed sure of what to say next. Michel and Salima smiled helplessly at one another.

"Come on, you two," I said. "I can see that something is going on. Don't try to tell me it's a new factory you've decided to install in Marrakech."

Salima blushed and began to laugh. "You're right, Aline," she said. "It's something much better than that. Michel and I are going to be married."

I stared at her. My expression couldn't have been a happy one, but she was so ecstatic that she didn't notice.

"It's true," Michel said, putting his arm around Salima. "We're in love."

"Well . . ." I fumbled, astounded by the man's devious actions. "I don't know what to say. On the one hand I'm happy for you both; on the other, I can't help but worry. Have you told your parents, Salima?"

"Oh no," she said. "And I trust you'll not tell them either."

Then she added in a slightly incensed tone: "In fact I'm not even telling Fatima."

She glanced at Michel with such adoration in her eyes that I was sure she knew nothing of his duplicity with her older sister.

"Well, you put me in a strange position if you tell me and don't tell Fatima," I said with a note of sternness.

"Of course we'll tell her eventually," Michel broke in smoothly. "Fatima is also a close friend of mine and I confide many things to her." He took Salima's hand in his. "It's just," Michel went on, "that we don't want to tell her until I've finished my conversion to the Muslim faith."

"Your *what?*"

"Michel is more devout than I've ever been!" Salima cried. "You should see him poring over the Koran."

"It's a fascinating text. You could get lost in it. And the religion is inspiring."

I looked helplessly from one to the other. "So you'll have a Muslim wedding?"

"Yes, in secret," Salima said. I could see that the secrecy alone caused her pleasure.

"But then what?" I asked impatiently. "Surely you'll have to tell your family sooner or later. I don't know if you realize it, Michel," I said, turning to him, "but this girl's father is one of the most powerful men in Morocco. He could have you out of your job and back in Paris so quickly you'd be dizzy."

"I know," Michel said, somewhat sobered. "I'm aware of what an important family I'd be marrying into. But Salima thinks, and I agree, that once they've learned we're married and that I'm Muslim, they'll stand behind us."

"I wonder about that," I said.

"Oh, but I think they will," Salima said. "My father is harsh, but I've always been his favorite. If he knows I'll move to France and never see him again unless he accepts Michel, he'll soften."

There was little I could say. Clearly, love, youth, and hopefulness had completely blinded Salima to the realities of their situation. And Michel seemed to be as happy as she. Was his relationship with Fatima as intimate as I had imagined? My mind revolted at the idea of a man being ready to marry one girl while having an affair with another—and her sister at that!

"Funny," I couldn't resist saying. "When I first met you, Michel, you were talking nostalgically about your favorite bistros in Paris."

"That's true," he admitted. "Before I met Salima I would have preferred to live in France. But now I feel I could stay here forever. I've come to feel completely at home in this beautiful country. We can always go to Paris to visit, but this is where I'd like to live. I no longer have any family or roots in France; marrying into a family like Salima's, I would really belong somewhere again."

He spoke with such sincerity, I could almost believe him. My helplessness turned to frustration. I felt in my bones that no good would come of this, yet what could I do? I drove my heels into the soft earth and stared for a moment at a blue-and-yellow parrot perched overhead.

"Why did you decide to tell me this?" I asked.

"We need your help." Salima looked worried. "You see, Michel is going to finish his conversion in Madrid. Here in Morocco, his interest in our religion might make friends put two and two together, and that would uncover our plans too soon. We thought perhaps you could invite me to stay at your house in Madrid. That's the only way I could get permission from my father to leave, and he has my passport. Then we wouldn't be separated during this important time. We're going to arrange the marriage in Madrid, too." Both Michel and Salima were actually hanging on my reaction. I disliked intensely being put in such an uncomfortable situation and wondered which one of them had formulated this impossible plan.

"Look, Salima—under any other circumstances I would be delighted to have you visit me and stay as long as you like. But I cannot be made accessory to something which I know your family would not approve of. They may or may not accept Michel if he becomes Sunni, as you are, but I know your family will not agree to an elopement and I can take no part in it." They looked at each other crestfallen. "I'm sorry," I said to Salima as kindly as I could, then turned and walked back to the hotel.

As I left the bright, sun-drenched garden and entered the lobby, I immediately sensed a heaviness in the air that hadn't been there when I had walked out a short time before. In a room across the hall, several people from our group were huddled in a circle, talking gravely in low voices. As soon as the Prince saw me, he waved me over. I crossed the hallway with dread welling in my chest. What now?

"Terribly bad news," began the Prince, his handsome face pale and drawn. "Rachid has just been killed."

"Rachid," I repeated numbly. "How?"

"It was an accident. He was run over by a motorcycle just outside the souk." He rubbed his forehead. "He's dead, just like that! I can't believe it. I was just talking to him an hour ago, here in this very spot." Moulay Abdullah's worst fears had come true. The visit he had so carefully organized for General Franco's daughter had been plagued with trouble, and this was the worst yet. I knew that Carmen would not take a negative impression back to her father, and even if she did, Franco made his own political decisions with influence from no one, but it would be difficult to convince the Prince of this.

As I looked around the circle of faces, I wondered whether I was the only one who suspected that so many accidents in such a short time must have an explanation. General Oufkir appeared especially shaken. I felt an odd flash of sympathy for him: in its way, losing an enemy can be as much of a shock as losing a friend. There could be a sense of guilt connected to it.

"The King will be inconsolable," Prince Moulay Abdullah added softly. "This trip is touched by a bad omen. Accidents like these never occur all at one time. The idea that a man like Rachid should come to such an end—felled by a motorbike of all things—"

My stunned sadness was pierced by a pang of dismay. I had lost my cutout for the King.

"I will have to excuse myself," the Prince said with a deep sigh. "I must notify His Majesty, and Rachid's relatives, too."

I climbed the stairs with leaden feet. Luis was in the shower. I went into the bathroom, and over the sound of the water I told him the news. He came out, rubbing his head with a towel. "Did I hear right? Was it Rachid?" I nodded. Before he could say more, there was a knock on the door in the other room.

When I opened the door, Fatima crossed the threshold with urgent haste. "Isn't it terrible. Rachid, of all people," she said, pacing the floor. "One of the most important men in this country. And do you know, Lalla Mira was aware something like this was about to happen. She told me in my séance that someone near me would be killed. Can you imagine! I told you she is a great medium. She knows everything. It's so scary."

Luis came in at that moment in a white terrycloth robe. "I heard what you said, Fatima. But I think your imagination is getting the better of you. No one would consider Rachid a person close to you. I never noticed you speaking to him much on the trip. Those fortune-tellers just hit on something now and then that comes near to reality. There's nothing supernatural about it."

Fatima, not calmed in the least by this rational male reaction, went on. "Well, you might like to know that Lalla Mira intimated that a person would be murdered—and I can tell you that when someone needs to be removed in this country, a motorcycle accident or a car accident is often the way it's done. Rachid Salloum's death for me is just another proof that Lalla Mira is the best *kri-kri* in Morocco. And," she finished, looking at Luis, "you may think I give too much importance to fortune-tellers, but you should know that Lalla Mira also said that after the fatal accident something still worse was going to happen."

After Fatima had gone, silence hung in the air like a black ghost. I realized then that Luis had given Fatima's words as much importance as I had.

The next day before breakfast I received a call from Jerry, his voice disguised to give the impression that he was our home secretary. Although he maintained that formal manner, an inflection in his voice made me aware that he had important news to transmit. "Señora Condesa," he began, "a telegram from your mother in America has arrived." As usual, I asked him to read it. He enunciated each syllable slowly, as a non-English-speaking Spaniard would, of what I knew to be a coded message from Jupiter. That was how I learned that I had been right: new messages between Libya and Morocco had revealed that the coup had been postponed for the time being—why, they did not say. My heart leaped. Maybe I had been some help after all. It also said that Jupiter was anxious to see me in Washington as soon as I could arrange a trip to the United States. I presumed that the hollowed stone was still a source of valuable information.

Our visit was almost over. We were a somber group the next day as we left the hotel. Everyone was thinking of Rachid. Since Moroccans were buried quickly and in the intimacy of the family, there was little any of us could do. Cars were lined up as usual; suitcases, shooting equipment, boxes were shoved into the vans. People gave hasty farewells as they rushed to their cars; many were on their way to other places and would not be with us in Rabat.

Our normally happy Omar stood by himself near the car, staring unseeingly into the sky, unaware of the bustle around him. His attitude was in such marked contrast to his usual sunny efficiency that I felt compelled to say something.

"Captain Omar, I didn't know you were so fond of Monsieur Rachid Salloum. His death is indeed sad—he must have been a very good man to have so many friends mourning him."

He jumped and turned to me with a look of profound distress. His was a face incapable of guile; its childlike softness, its lack of crags and ridges, left it as open as a valley plain. "Yes, I'm sad for Monsieur Salloum, Madame la Comtesse, but today all I can think about is my new bride, the City of Roses girl."

"What's the matter? Is she homesick? Perhaps she is too young."

He grimaced. "Young? That little child has caused me a lot of trouble and hardship in only a few days. She's young—but not in the way you mean."

"What has she done?"

He glowered. "I am not an unkind man, Comtesse, but there are some things I will not allow." He started suddenly, as if he had just seen something painful. I followed the line of his gaze. Omar's new bride, Ayesha, stood near the fountain, her hand trailing in the water. She looked more mature; only a few days before she had been a lovely child, apparently barely able to understand what it meant to be taken away from her home by a stranger and added to his harem. Now she seemed to have blossomed into a graceful, willowy young woman. Her gaze was more direct; she had lost the fear of showing her face, which I'd last seen peering sadly from the back of the carpet truck. She was not only pretty but was quick and lively. The person she was gazing at seemed to inspire this transformation, and I understood immediately the cause of Captain Khalil's chagrined unhappiness.

I didn't pretend not to see the obvious. "How does she know Ahmed?" I asked. I watched as Ayesha laughed enthusiastically at something Ahmed said; his mischievous face lit up with appreciation at her laughter. However, he seemed to laugh with her more like a brother than a lover, and there appeared to be nothing secretive or clandestine in their mutual interest. It probably was perfectly innocent.

"They became friends because they both play the guitar, and one night he taught her some new chords. This is unseemly for a newly married woman. She has modern ideas, and she is not afraid of me, of being sent home again with her dowry. I think she wouldn't mind at all."

Omar's jealousy made me suspect that he had fallen in love with his new wife. "Naturally, she likes Ahmed," I said. "Who wouldn't? He's a lot of fun. But that doesn't necessarily mean she's flirting."

Captain Omar, nettled, said haughtily, "No, no. Her behavior is unacceptable. And Ahmed should not lead her on." He seemed to consider our conversation at an end now that I had expressed something other than complete accord with his misery. His face closed like a clamshell and I could tell that he regretted confiding in me. Then he thought of something else. "Anyway, this is all a matter of another few days, when my two older wives can teach her proper behavior." This thought cheered him up. He gave the little tableau by the fountain another quick glance, then, without another word, he dove into the sea of preparations for our departure.

"Aline," called Salima from across the courtyard. Her expression was somber as she came toward me. "Come sit with me while they finish loading the cars," she said. "On this bench over here."

When we had settled ourselves in the meager shade of a palm tree, she said, "I've been thinking about poor Rachid's death."

"So have I," I said. "He was a very kind man, and apparently everyone loved him."

"Not everyone." We exchanged a look and I wondered what she meant. "Fatima says Lalla Mira forecast that accident and that she also said something much worse would happen to one of us." She looked at me. "Doesn't that frighten you?"

"As I said before," I answered, "I don't believe in fortune-tellers, and I think it was just a coincidence. You shouldn't give that woman's words such importance. Let's talk about something more optimistic—"

Already my companion's attention was diverted to where Ahmed and Ayesha stood talking and laughing merrily. "That's Captain Khalil's new wife, isn't it?" she said. "What's Ahmed saying to her to make her laugh so hard?"

"Apparently they've become friends and Omar's upset about it. He was glaring at them a few minutes ago and telling me that his two older wives would have to teach her how to behave."

"What can Ahmed have to say to that country child?" Salima's large eyes smoldered and her face became sphinxlike, an expression I'd seen before when Fatima and Michel were talking together and ignoring her. "Ahmed is much too worldly and knowledgeable to care what an infant like that says." She gave a sniff. Her disdain amused me as much as Omar's jealousy. "You probably think it's strange for me to care what Ahmed does, when I'm marrying Michel, but Ahmed and I were close as children and I would like him to have the best of everything. I'd like to see him with a girl who's more—"

"More like you," I finished for her.

Salima, never afraid to admit the truth once it was pointed out to her, nodded. "Yes. Ayesha is pretty, and I understand she plays the guitar well, but she's ignorant and Ahmed is a cultured, highly educated man." She continued to observe them.

"It appears to me that Ahmed is merely being friendly to a lonely girl," I suggested.

"That would be just like him," said Salima. "He's always been nice to everyone." For the first time I caught a glimmer of her feelings for Ahmed. Perhaps if she had remained in Morocco instead of studying abroad, she might have married him and been happier.

Ahmed and Ayesha parted, going in different directions, and Salima turned her attention to me. "Why did your friends the

Caseys leave?" Her abrupt change of topic surprised me. "Is it true that Bill Casey had a run-in with Moustapha?"

For the second time now she was questioning me about the Caseys. "Salima," I told her, "I'm surprised at your interest. You hardly said three words to them the entire time they were here."

"Well, they're your friends, and they left so suddenly." Her blue eyes were as opaque as painted glass. "And I had heard about the chauffeur, and a fight in the garden at Tinerhir."

"Bill Casey has an important job in Washington and it's quite normal for him to be needed urgently," I answered.

The cars were ready for the trip back to Rabat, and Salima and I had to run, each to different ends of the caravan. I jumped in next to Luis. Omar Khalil, in his usual place next to the driver, appeared to be a bit more his old self than a short time before. As we started to roll, he pointed out details in the landscape, keeping up a relentless stream of interesting information. But even as he spoke, I heard instead Fatima's words about Lalla Mira's warning. No matter how much I told myself that it was ridiculous to give any importance to such things, the ominous prophecy made me uneasy. Perhaps one of her clients had inadvertently divulged some inside information about the coup in hopes of learning whether it would be successful. After all, according to Fatima, Lalla Mira was famous and people came from all over the country to consult her. But whether she had divined the warning or gleaned it from a more earthly source, I feared very much that something worse for Morocco's future than Rachid's accident was indeed about to occur.

Chapter 17

B y the time the car arrived in Rabat, it was late afternoon.
We barely had time to bathe and dress for the formal
dinner which had been arranged for those guests who
still had not left. In spite of Lalla Mira's prophecy, I felt more
relaxed now that the dangers of a coup were no longer threatening, and turned my thoughts to what I'd wear for the occasion.
When Luis saw me searching through my bag for an appropriate dress, he said slyly, "Stop looking. I've got something that'll
be just right for tonight."

I turned around and saw him pulling yards and yards of
glistening orange-and-gold silk from his large black suitcase. As
he stood up and handed it to me, I realized that he had somehow
found the time during our trip to sneak out to buy me a present.
That was typical of Luis, who was always giving me glamorous
gifts. He must have bought it in Marrakech, and I regretted that
I had not been so thoughtful about him.

"Put it on," he said.

Happily, I tore off my dressing gown and pulled the voluminous robe over my head. The shimmering kaftan fell around my
body in thick, graceful folds; the neckline and long, wide sleeves
were bordered with fine hand-crocheted green, gold, and orange
threads; the skirt of the gown had a small train.

"Here," said Luis, handing me a magnificent gilt metal belt
studded with semiprecious stones, another unexpected gift.
Thrilled, I wrapped the belt around my waist and hips as I had

seen Fatima and Salima do, and looked in the mirror. The effect was startling; I'd become completely Moroccan. "Wear your emeralds," suggested Luis. "The wives of the ministers will be there and they'll surely wear their jewels."

That night, as I entered the palace and joined the beautifully dressed Moroccan women, my luminous green emeralds sparkling on the orange silk kaftan made me feel that I blended into the exotic atmosphere. We joined a group near the entrance, and Prince Moulay Abdullah's aide approached, confiding in a low tone that there was a possibility the King might appear later on. He and Luis began to chat, and Salima came over to talk to me. She pulled me aside. "Aline . . ." she said. I was surprised to note that she was agitated and on the verge of tears. "I have something confidential to tell you. Michel and I have had to change our plans. The president of the company is arriving in Rabat this week to study the possibility of investing in another factory, and they're promoting Michel to vice-president. That's wonderful, of course, but with these developments, he cannot leave Morocco. Michel's also worried about my father's reaction—I think your arguments had an effect on him. He thinks we'd better wait to marry until he finds a way to win my father over. In a way I'm pleased that Michel is cautious. That shows that he'll make a good husband—but not getting married is a letdown." People were approaching. She hastened to add, "Please, please, Aline, I count on you to keep our secret." I asked her if Fatima knew about this. She said she had not spoken to her sister about any of their plans. As I watched her walk away, I couldn't quell a suspicion that the good-looking Frenchman had changed his mind about marrying her. Her dejected air seemed to indicate that she suspected this as well. Was Michel going to be the second man to make beautiful Salima miserable?

Serge Lebedev was also at the dinner and joined us. Even though I had convinced Luis that I had never flirted with the Russian, I was worried when I saw him approaching. But surprisingly enough Luis and Serge greeted each other quite pleasantly. Soon they began to talk about racehorses, and Serge managed to hide his infatuation well, if he still harbored one. I began to wonder. As we stood there, Serge introduced us to several diplomats and then went off to get Luis a drink. As soon as he left, Luis joked, "Your *conquista* is trying to make up to me. When he returns I'll get out of the way for a while, but make it clear this time that we Spaniards are dangerous."

Luis left me talking with a group of friends when Serge returned, and at first we spoke of nothing special—the beauty of Morocco, the hospitality of the people—but as soon as no one was within earshot, the Russian lowered his voice. "Frankly, Aline," he began, "ever since our last conversation I've wanted to talk to you about something, and this seems to be the only opportunity I may have."

I waited, determined to be careful.

"My intention has been to ask you a favor, but it is a matter of life and death for me. I . . ." He paused as the French Ambassador stopped by to say a few words. Others interrupted too, and although we were seated on a sofa, it was not possible to speak confidentially. Serge filled in, asking about my life in the United States and how I happened to go to Spain and marry. I said what I could, of course, avoiding any mention of my training in espionage and assignment to Spain during World War II. But when I described life in America, his eyes brightened. He took advantage of a moment when our neighbors were in a heated conversation to whisper, "I cannot talk freely to you now, but the time may come when I will turn to you for help. Please keep this in confidence until I contact you again."

Again, I had the very definite impression that this man was thinking of defecting, or something similar, but I wasn't able to ask him, because General Oufkir pulled a large pouf close to me and sat down. Just as our private conversation was ending, Serge leaned toward me. "We must remain friends," he said as he turned to talk to Oufkir. I observed the two men. They were both impressive, but Oufkir, although distinguished and honorable, did not inspire the confidence that Serge did. Everything about Serge confirmed my instinct that he was reliable. But I had been fooled once. This time I did not want to make another mistake in judgment.

Nevertheless, when General Oufkir began to speak, I think we felt more relaxed with each other than before. We both felt a bond of friendship. I believed that Serge was no longer flirting with me, and this made me much more comfortable. As the men spoke of general things, I realized that although Serge was Russian, his reactions to many of life's problems were not very different from mine. Eventually Oufkir and Lebedev got up and joined some officers, and I was taken up by one of the Moroccan wives whom I had met that first night in Rabat, before the trip began. Serge and I didn't have another opportunity to talk that evening.

People continued to arrive. About eleven a short man in a black djellaba raced into the marble patio, zigzagging between the groups of guests like a black bat. As he zeroed in on Serge Lebedev, I recognized Moustapha Benayad. When the two men separated from the others to talk, I again felt a pang of suspicion. Intuition told me Moustapha had something to do with the plot, and seeing him in close confidence again with Serge reawakened my worries about the Russian. A pity, I thought, that Bill Casey is not here to put that journalist in his place. The oily gray face, the snaky eyes with reptile lids, made my skin creep.

As time went by and the King did not appear, conversation lagged. It was known that he always came late, but this evening hope diminished when he had still not appeared by eleven-thirty. Finally General Oufkir announced that regrettably His Majesty would not be present this evening. We had expected that the King would say a few words in memory of Rachid. Instead, the French Ambassador spoke of his old friend, then introduced General Oufkir. Standing in his typical military pose, hands clasped behind his back, he surveyed us with those remarkable eyes. We presumed that he would give a brief speech, as if he were addressing his command on the loss of an officer. However, it was not that at all. In a quiet voice he told us that despite their personal differences he had respected Rachid tremendously. Rachid had been a wonderful link, Oufkir said, between ancient and modern Morocco. His death was a personal loss to the King as well as to himself and to the country. His words were thoughtful, and he had difficulty controlling his emotions. The military steel had turned soft and gentle—a side of this powerful man that I would never have suspected.

The next day we were driven to the golf course on the outskirts of the city, where Luis and I played nine holes and then went to a large tea at the home of one of Fatima's relatives. After admiring the house and strolling through the gardens, I came upon Omar Khalil, who stood looking out at the sunwashed landscape, the deep green shrubs of the garden bleached in the white light to pale gray, the brilliant flowers washed-out pastels. I squinted, following his gaze, and saw only the empty garden.

"Omar," I said, "this is the second time I've seen you so gloomy. It isn't like you. What has happened today?" A breeze moved in through the arched window. On the white stone wall of the garden, deep shadows danced and flickered.

Omar didn't even turn to look at me. "I don't know what is wrong with me, Señora Condesa," he said. "I am afraid that I'm ill, maybe even dying, but the doctor swears he can't find anything wrong, and he's the best in Morocco. Maybe I should go to a specialist in Europe."

Alarmed, I said, "What are your symptoms?"

"Oh," he sighed, "I can't eat or sleep. Sometimes I feel feverish. At first I thought it was just a bug I had caught. But I continue to feel weak. I'm not my former self at all."

"You may have eaten something poisonous," I suggested.

"She must be poisoning me," he said disconsolately. "I knew it. Nothing has been right since I married her. She has taken my strength and character away from me."

A light dawned in my head. "You can't eat or sleep? You feel weak and unhappy? Oh, Omar"—I couldn't help laughing—"you're in love."

He drew himself up with an injured stare. "Señora Condesa," he said, "this has never happened to me. This little girl is a witch of some sort."

"She's not a witch at all," I told him. I remembered the sleepless nights and untouched plates of food I'd suffered during my separations from Luis before he asked me to marry him. "Omar, haven't you ever been in love before?"

"I love all my wives, of course," he said. "The Koran commands it. But this Ayesha, now, she doesn't obey me or listen when I tell her something. She is out of my sight all day and won't go where I tell her, and at night"—he hesitated, remembering that he was talking to a woman—"well, she has her own ideas about what a wife is and isn't expected to do."

"She'll change. You have to be patient with women, not force them to feel something they don't yet feel."

"Force her to feel something?" He laughed bitterly. "My other wives I can force to feel or think whatever I want. Ayesha? She just laughs at me, Señora Condesa." Omar was so humbled that he hardly realized how much of his vulnerable state he was revealing. "A man is supposed to tell his wife what to think. This one thinks whatever she wants. I tell you—she is a terror!"

"You could send her home again," I said slyly, "if she makes you so miserable."

"No, no!" he cried. "I am already afraid that she'll take it into her head to leave. She's so independent for a country girl. And what will my other wives think? To them I am king of the household. When they see that I can't control my third wife, they may lose respect for me. Oh, this is terrible! Women should be obedient, useful, strong, quiet. Now and then you get a bad one. Why should this happen to me?"

"Whether you realize it or not, you're probably in love with Ayesha," I told him. "You cannot force her into anything. She'll become a good wife in her own time, and that's all you can hope for."

He looked aghast. "No Moroccan man should have to wait for his wife to love him," he said, shaking his head. But I could see that he had taken my words to heart and that something of what I had said had reached him.

When I told Carmen, she laughed. "Moroccan men," she said, "consider women necessary conveniences for life. They tend never to let a woman matter too much. Omar Khalil will be heckled if his friends hear of his infatuation with this little girl."

"They won't hear a word from me," I said. "I like that young man, and I hope Ayesha will fall in love with him."

"He has some nerve acting like a traditional Moroccan man, you know," said Carmen with a twinkle in her eye. "He was brought up in Granada and his mother is Spanish—he knows perfectly well that women aren't goods to be bartered and commandeered. He's just taking advantage of his adopted culture, so he doesn't have to do the hard work of a real marriage—so it serves him right that he's been upset by a child like her. But, actually, all men are a little like Omar," she added thoughtfully.

"They would like to believe that the man is the ruler and that the wife must obey. We're lucky in Spain—those customs went out long ago."

"Well," I laughed, "not so long ago. Until ten years ago I had to get written permission for an exit permit from my husband every time I wanted to leave the country. As an American woman, that really infuriated me, even though Luis always consented. And remember those laws that defended the husband's rights even when he was a drunkard, an adulterer, or a wife-beater. If she left the home for any one of those reasons, she would lose the children and all financial assistance. In Spain men still get away with a lot, but not in America. Few would dare even to keep secrets from their wives." As I pronounced those last words it occurred to me how many secrets I kept from my own husband. I hoped I would not one day live to regret it.

The next morning we left for Madrid.

Chapter 18

The day after we arrived in Madrid I called Jerry's wife and invited the two of them for lunch. It was safer to maintain our meetings under the guise of a normal social relationship, and by now our spouses were accustomed to it. While Luis and Jerry's wife walked in the garden, Jerry told me that Jupiter was anxious to know how soon I would be able to go to Washington. I told him that Luis and I were leaving in ten days, but not for Washington. We would first visit the Whitneys in Lexington for the weekend of the Kentucky Derby, and then go to Las Vegas, where we had been invited together with the daughter of the former King of Italy and other European friends. I told him to inform Jupiter that I dared not go to Washington. Luis simply would not have it. Perhaps Jupiter could come to Lexington, Kentucky? I gave him my itinerary.

"I don't know, Aline. I'll see. In the meantime be alert. Something tells me this Moroccan story isn't over yet."

Going to the United States was especially exciting for me. The trips were preceded by weeks of fittings—evening dresses with coats to match, suits, each with its hat, custom-made shoes—good ready-to-wear wasn't available in Spain—and proper clothes took weeks. Because of our trip to Morocco, my fittings were behind schedule and we had to postpone our visit several days, obliging us to go straight to Kentucky instead of having a few days in New York.

Luis complained as always about my many boxes and suit-cases, and he bristled when the customs official, turning over one embroidered dress after another, asked if his wife was a movie star.

"I hate this sort of thing," he groaned as the customs official plowed through my things. "But at least we'll be far away from the problems in Morocco." His remark hit me like a wave of icy water. If he only knew that Jupiter was waiting to talk to me!

A private plane was standing by in New York—which impressed us Spaniards—and we were whisked off to Lexington. In no time we were entering the gates of the C. V. Whitney Farm and going up the long drive to the old white colonial house. Accustomed to the sunbaked granite of ancient Spanish palaces, and pasture walls of crumbling stone, everything looked dazzlingly fresh and new to me: the white picket fences, like rows of bright teeth, the "bluegrass" lawns meticulously kept and very green. The trees stood in orderly rows in the slanting rays of the late sun, their shadows falling across the lawn in neat dark stripes.

Marylou and Sonny came out to greet us. "Right on time," she said. "We're so glad you're here. Let me show you your rooms in the guest house, which was the old slave quarters. You can rest before dinner. After that trip from Spain, you must be exhausted." After a brief chat, she left us, saying we had one hour before dinner. Gratefully, I stretched out on the bed, look-ing out the window at the rolling green fields, trying to imagine what it had been like in this building only a century ago when these rooms had still been inhabited by slaves. After a while I stood up and crossed into the next room. From my husband's window I could see the glass-walled building where the ball would take place tomorrow after the Derby. A dozen or so workmen were putting up the decorations; the swimming pool shimmered turquoise and blue, and the glass walls caught the light of the fading sun, reflecting it like a cut jewel. The air rang with the blows of the men's hammers and the scrape of a ladder being dragged across the tile floor.

Just when I was taking my shower, Luis knocked on the glass door. "Someone for you on the phone," he said. "Shall I tell her to call back?"

"No," I said as I came out dripping and grabbed a robe. "It's easier to take it now. Do you know who it is?"

"Some woman," he answered. "I didn't ask."

I went past him, an innocent look of expectation on my face. "Hello?" I said into the receiver, my heart in my throat, hoping Luis wouldn't catch on and begin our visit in a bad humor. As usual Jupiter was right on schedule. First it was his secretary asking for me, and then his cautious voice. "Can you talk?"

"Very well, thank you."

"Better I do the talking," Jupiter said. "Something's come up. You can help. I can't explain it on the phone. Las Vegas will be our meeting place. Can't manage Kentucky. Have you changed your hotel or the dates you'll be there?"

"No."

"Fine. Don't worry about anything. I'll find you. And I'll make our encounter appear coincidental so you'll have no trouble with your husband." Jupiter's voice was slow and cautious. "I know we can't talk now. Tell your husband it was a magazine interviewer trying to track you down."

Firmly, I said, "I don't have time to do any interviews."

"Good. I'm on my way out west and I can stop over in Las Vegas Tuesday night."

"What magazine is this for?" I asked. "An article on Americans married to foreign aristocrats? It sounds interesting, but I'm afraid I couldn't on this trip."

"See you then," he said and rang off.

"Thank you so much for asking, though," I said into the silent receiver and hung up.

Even from the air, Las Vegas was surreal. It lay on the desert floor like a toy oasis, dotted with perfect-green golf courses, turquoise swimming pools, and neon as bright as desert flowers, even in the daytime. Driving through the Strip to our hotel gave me the sensation of having been plunked down on a movie set. The gaudy façades, the unending line of billboards advertising weddings and divorces, the wild loops and swirls on the strident neon signs were like a set for an absurd cartoon Western. Fountains, not at all like those in Morocco, sent streams of water surging skywards from ornately designed bases.

Our hotel had an exaggerated ancient Roman decor, and the entrance to our suite was a series of glittering golden arches leading to a suite of elaborate rooms. From our windows the late-afternoon sun gilded a large expanse of open desert, and in the distance we could see the tips of a mountain range. We looked at each other, enchanted. This was going to be fun. Then I remembered, with a pang of sorrow, my meeting with Jupiter. I would have to make certain Luis did not find out, so that, at least, his enjoyment of this place would not be spoiled.

Friends of ours had arranged for us to meet Sammy Davis Jr., who was not performing but was in Las Vegas. Sure enough, within the hour Mr. Davis telephoned and invited us to join him for drinks at two A.M. at Caesar's, the Cleopatra Barge! That late hour was almost like being back in Madrid.

"Jane and Burt told me you'd be in town today," he said. "We also have other mutual friends. One of them will be there too, so be sure to come. It's a surprise," Sammy chuckled. "Don't get sidetracked—our mutual friend wants to see you."

"Of course we won't," I said and hung up. Luis was anxious to go downstairs, and I too wanted to see the gaming rooms, to give John Derby every possible chance to contact me. I wanted to get that over with as soon as possible so I could enjoy the incredible atmosphere. Hurriedly, we changed and went down.

The casino floor was a fantasy land, punctuated by the curious sound of the ringing and jangling of hundreds of slot machines. Men and women wearing anything from jeans and bright-colored shirts to skimpy satin skirts and full cowboy regalia were, despite their sartorial differences, united by their furrowed brows and intense stares as they concentrated on their respective one-armed bandits. They formed endless lines on either side of every aisle. The jangle of the slots, a roar from a crap table, the huge dissimilar crowd jammed together for one purpose—to have a good time—was intoxicating, so vastly different from the calm, centuries-old beauty of Morocco. The world of the casino was hermetically sealed, like a time capsule floating in the universe: no clocks, no windows, was it day or night outside? Like Oz, this could be anywhere at any time; evidently the casino never closed.

Luis bought a stack of chips and slipped them into his pocket.

I held his arm and directed our path toward the roped-off area where I saw the large gaming tables. "Ah, baccarat," he said, indicating an especially quiet area supervised by attendants in black tie. "My grandfather was a superb player and taught me when I was eight years old. One night he almost broke the bank at Monte Carlo." He gave me that wonderful smile. "Perhaps I can be as lucky."

"Luis," I said, pulling on a strand of loose hair, "my chignon is coming apart. Stay here. I'm going to the ladies' room to fix it. Just five minutes and I'll be back." I blew him a kiss as I rushed off. I knew that once he commenced playing he would forget about time.

I headed for the far end of the casino, looking for Jupiter. After covering the entire floor, I ducked into a side corridor and followed it out to the pool area, which was closed. I checked the restaurants and bars. Jupiter was not here. Glancing at my watch, I realized that I had been gone for three-quarters of an hour and rushed back to the baccarat table, where Luis was playing beside a stout Chinese gentleman. Seeing me, he rose, retrieved his by now much larger pile of chips, and smiled down at his Oriental friend. "I hope your luck improves."

Not looking at Luis, the man said quietly, "If I had your luck and what I'm betting, by now I'd own this place."

"What did that mean, Luis?" I asked.

"Well, that fellow arrived two days ago with a credit line of three million dollars, which he has exhausted. He's trying to extend it for another two million." He shook his head. "He takes too many risks, he plays with emotion, not his head—surprising for a Chinese."

"How much did you win?" I asked.

"Come, come," he responded with a grin. "You're not supposed to ask those questions. Anyhow, I shouldn't be too happy. As the old Spanish saying goes, 'Lucky at cards and unlucky in love.'" As he steered me to the main entrance, he said, "We're going to the Sands to see Danny Thomas. I enjoy American comedians and he's supposed to be very funny."

"Count," said the doorman, "here is your car." We stepped into a huge limousine and were whisked to the Sands. There, we were waved by a long line of people and seated immediately by the maître d' near the stage. "Really, Luis," I whispered, "you must have done extremely well at the baccarat table to get all this attention."

He grinned waggishly. "An excellent choice of words."

When we left after the show—which really was very good—Luis said, "We have some time left, so why don't we go to Binion's Horseshoe Club for half an hour? The World Series of Poker is going on and I'm curious."

The entry fee was ten thousand dollars, I found out—winner take all. They had some thirty-five or forty players, which also added up to a lot of money. They played a type of poker called Texas Hold 'Em. With all the excitement of the poker game, we were a bit late to meet Sammy Davis, whom we found sitting in a booth at Cleopatra's Barge with another man whose back was to us.

Sammy saw us approaching and waved us over. "This old friend of mine says he's also an old friend of yours," he told us, gesturing to his guest. "This is my little surprise."

"Why, John," I said, striving to keep my voice pleasantly surprised but not too surprised. "John Derby. To see you of all people in Las Vegas."

He quirked an eyebrow at me. "Ah well, you just don't know me well enough. I'm really quite a gambler at heart." I acknowledged this with a small smile: this was certainly not news to me! He turned to Luis and shook his hand in greeting. I wondered what Luis thought of this chance encounter. "Fortunately for me," John told him, "I ran into Sammy in the lobby and he told me you were here. I couldn't very well leave Las Vegas without saying hello, now, could I?"

We chatted for a while. John explained that he was on his way to Los Angeles and would be leaving early in the morning. He and Luis talked about horses while I talked to Sammy. Before long Jupiter got up to leave. "I'd love to stay and talk all night," he said, "but I've found other old friends crossing my path on this trip and I must check up on them. Perhaps we'll see each other in the casino later."

As he said goodbye to me, I ran over his words—old friends—

crossing paths—check up on them—everything Jupiter said in moments like these could hold a double meaning. Could it be that he was being trailed by the KGB?

My thoughts were interrupted by Sammy. "Maybe it's meeting you and Luis and running into John Derby. What a lucky night for me! And when I feel lucky, it's time to shoot craps." With a flourish he indicated to me the direction of the game room.

We left the bar and entered the crowded casino, where all the crap tables were jammed. A pit boss immediately recognized the problem and opened another table. The word spread quickly that Sammy Davis was about to shoot craps, and everyone, naturally, wanted to watch. After the initial clamor had subsided, Sammy picked up the dice and turned to me.

"Aline, you're my good-luck charm tonight," he smiled, handing me the dice.

Taken aback, I looked at Luis. Neither of us had ever played craps and didn't understand the game. Also, I had hoped to steal away in the excitement and talk to Jupiter, and now I was being put squarely into the spotlight. Luis just smiled, amused at Sammy's insistence.

"Give the lady some room here, fellas. She's about to make us all rich," Sammy cried.

I shook the dice, then dangled my arm into the well of the table and gave them a solid toss across the green felt top. The croupier read off their numbers, then returned them to me. I pretended to be delighted; I liked Sammy and I didn't want to disappoint him. But as I took the dice, I was wondering why on earth I had let him talk me into this. How could I talk to Jupiter when I was in the middle of a throng at a crap table?

"All you have to do is just roll 'em again, nice and easy," Sammy said, while people elbowed closer to watch.

I let the dice fly back down the table. The applause and chorus of approval told me that I had made my "point." Any efforts to back away now would have been greeted with great disapproval from the ever-increasing crowd. I was effectively trapped.

"Fire away, Aline," Sammy called out over the roar.

Again the dice left my hand and again the crowd ohhed and ahhed. A natural. The force of the crowd's admiration took hold, and I began to relax and enjoy myself: Jupiter could wait a few minutes, I thought. I rolled another seven and the crowd went wild. This was starting to be fun.

Just then I happened to look out at the far end of the room. Although he was too far away to see clearly, the shape of the face, the suit and graying baldish pate were unmistakable. Jupiter was waiting. He was always on the move, so I knew he was anxious to talk to me immediately. How could I get out of this predicament?

Sammy was pulling on my arm, telling me to throw again. My eyes strained to get another glimpse of my boss. To my absolute horror, I saw two men in dark navy suits come up behind him, one from each side. I ignored Sammy and continued to watch. Although the two men and Jupiter were far away and people milling about kept obstructing my vision, I saw them grab him, pin back his arms in a painful hold, and start propelling him forcibly from the casino. There was another glimpse of Jupiter struggling and resisting to no avail. I waited for someone to intervene, but no one seemed to notice. They were too busy gambling. Besides, the two men holding Jupiter were very professional. They were smiling and laughing, as if they were taking a drunken friend to his room. I knew Jupiter was in great shape, and an expert at extricating himself from predicaments like this. It would be a mistake for me to draw attention to him and perhaps alert someone to the reasons for the assault. I lost sight of the three again. Meanwhile the crowd at the table, led by Sammy, was urging me to throw the dice. A huge man bellowed, "One more time, lady. You're on a roll!" My mind was in a complete panic: I numbly took the dice from the croupier, since I had no choice and, mechanically, I threw again. Another natural! The sound of chips and the whirring of the roulette wheels, the calls of the croupiers, and the swelling applause reached me from a great distance, like the sound of waves in a conch shell. Already I was imagining John's body slumped motionless in a parking lot, shot from behind.

Full of dread and horror I choked out to Sammy and Luis, "I'll be right back—the ladies' room—" and raced across the room in the direction in which the men had disappeared with Jupiter. Now I had no doubt that they were KGB surveillance agents; they had tried to eliminate Jupiter before, but he had always been too wily and quick. Would he be now? Or would my intrepid, daring chief finally come to the end of his dangerous career? I had always thought of John Derby as immortal and indestructible, ever dapper and in control. Now I had seen with my own eyes that I might have been wrong.

I had no weapon. What could I do to help? Clutching my bag, I ran to where I had last seen them, but of course they had disappeared. For a few seconds I stood, panic-stricken, aware that every second I wasted could mean the difference between his escape or his death. What could I possibly do? Telephone Washington? Advise the Las Vegas police that a friend had been kidnapped?

The fact was, there was absolutely nothing I could do to help my friend. As the realization came to me with full force, I staggered a little and leaned against a column. Since he had not reappeared, I feared the worst. They could have hustled him into a waiting car; they could have taken him upstairs to a hotel room to torture him. I had always known very well from experience that espionage was a risky business, but somehow John Derby's gentlemanly, suave confidence in his wits and his knowledge had convinced me that he was immune to the lethal side of the business. Some people are hard to imagine dead, and he was one of them.

As I stood, frozen and staring into space, someone from behind tapped my shoulder. I started and turned around, afraid the same men had come back for me. "Don't fear, Aline, I'm all right."

There he was in front of me, alive and well. "But you're—but they just—" I stuttered, numb with relief.

I looked at John again. For all the world, he was the man I had just seen. I saw the identical tan silk gabardine suit, the gray, balding head. In each other's eyes we recognized the implications. They had grabbed the wrong man.

"It's all right, Tiger. I'm not quite sure who they grabbed, but needless to say I probably owe the poor devil my life. Or maybe it was this suit. Conservative clothes in Vegas make one stick out in the crowd. I should have worn blue jeans and a red-and-yellow shirt." I admired his cool control.

His eyes searched the room, flicked over people jostling around us. "I'm not sure exactly which job these fellows want to remove me from. It could be the Morocco problem, but it could just as well be something that took me to Singapore recently. There was a suspicious-looking fellow on the plane from Singapore to Washington, but I remained in Washington ten days and noticed no one trailing me during that time. But when I boarded to come here yesterday, it did seem to me that another questionable guy got on behind me. I smelled something wrong. I should have realized they were tailing me. The trouble is they hand the job over to another agent when one steps off the plane, and even when you're looking for them, it's hard to tell. I hope they discover they made a mistake with that poor fellow and let him go. Fortunately these KGB surveillance teams, like our own, are not always efficient. Thank God for that today. I remember what happened to your friend Magic in Paris a few years ago."

How could I forget? She had been my oldest colleague in espionage, and had trained with me in Washington at The Farm. A KGB surveillance team had not only murdered her, but she had died in agony, impaled on the spikes outside a subway entrance. Her gruesome death had disturbed my sleep for a long time. "I'm always afraid of torture," I said.

"You're right. Torture is the great concern. Do you know I still carry an L pill with me just in case."

His mention of the L pill reminded me again of the war, when I had also carried one. We had been taught in case of torture to place it between the back molars and bite hard, that death would come instantaneously. I shuddered. "Thank heavens, John, you didn't need it today."

"Try to compose yourself and listen carefully. We haven't much time. I don't know how long it will take those KGB guys to realize they made a mistake, but I want to get out of here before they return. If you're seen talking to me, you won't be safe either."

I was still too shaken to answer.

"Messages recently uncovered in that same dead drop in Morocco indicate that the coup has been postponed but is still planned for some future date," he told me. "We also now know that your friend Serge Lebedev holds a very important post in the Soviet Embassy there. It is most urgent that we encourage him to defect."

His mention of Serge reminded me of how uncertain I still was about Serge's intentions. Jupiter continued. "Rachid probably was murdered because he discovered who the leader was; the same could apply to your friend Abdul Nabil. They were going to attempt the assassination the day of the boar hunt, for obvious reasons—perfect cover for a murder. But that, you can be sure, was foiled by Rachid, who by that time, and certainly assisted by the information you gave him, had become aware of their intentions. Rachid's precautions that day frustrated the coup, but only temporarily. Temporarily," repeated Jupiter. "And as long as no one discovers who the leader is, the conspiracy will continue."

Jupiter paused and observed me. I was attentive to his every word, but had no idea what I could do to help. He continued. "Therefore the King's life is still in danger, which is of enormous concern to us. We could lose our most loyal ally in northern Africa. Our people in Morocco have found the guy who ran over Rachid in the souk. He was an ignorant mercenary, paid miserably for the job. He had no idea who was behind it."

John Derby took my arm and we walked to a more secluded corner of the huge game area. "I've talked confidentially to Bill Casey," he went on. "He told me about that journalist and the run-in with him. Since Bill came into the case so late and had to leave before the trip ended, he does not feel competent to give an opinion. But he has the interesting opinion, different from my own, that Rachid could have been involved with the conspirators. He might have been eliminated because of a power struggle within the group. I protested, and reminded him that Rachid was the Chief Intelligence Officer." Jupiter was smiling. "And do you know what he answered?"

I shook my head.

"Bill said, 'A great position from which to launch a coup.'" John nodded. "One has to admit Bill has a point there. But all this is really unimportant right now. Rachid is dead but the ringleader is not. And I believe the coup is still on."

"Why is it so important to tell me, John?" I asked.

"We need you to convince Lebedev to defect. We have other reasons to believe the guy may be ready. With the attention he paid you, your help at this moment is indispensable. I'm convinced he knows more than he let on to you. To make it brief, Tiger, I want you to make another visit to Morocco."

"I don't think there's any excuse Luis would accept right now for returning to Morocco. He'd be against it, you can be sure. He doesn't want me to get involved in that coup again."

"Tell your husband you'd be perfectly safe. We'll have you protected every minute. This would only take a day of your time. You could easily ask your friend Fatima to invite the Soviet to her house for a drink and talk to him there. We can make an offer he'd find difficult to refuse."

"First of all, Luis will never agree," I repeated. "And furthermore I may have misinterpreted Serge Lebedev's intentions. At first I thought he was interested, but later on I saw that he wanted to have an affair with me. And then the last time I saw him, he seemed to be thinking again about defecting, but he never said so exactly. I'm ashamed of having handled this so badly, but I'm still uncertain about that man. At any rate I can't go back there now."

"Think about it, Aline." John suddenly looked tired. "No matter what, at least you know the fellow. You can talk to him. We don't have anyone else who can get to him. Lebedev could very well know who the leader is, and right now he's our only hope."

I looked out across the crowded, noisy room and shook my head. "John, I have three children and a wonderful husband. I can't do it. I'm sorry." I touched his arm. "Why don't you get on that plane and take a vacation, for once? You're not going to live long if you don't relax now and then."

John shook his head without saying a word, but, giving my hand an affectionate squeeze, he turned and left. I walked back to the game room, feeling let-down, disgusted with myself, and worried. At least Luis would be pleased with what I had just told John. But I wasn't. Ahead, I saw Luis waving to me. He was still at the crap table with Sammy. As I walked toward him, I calculated that if he had seen me with John, I could tell him why I had left so abruptly. At least I could look at my husband with a clean conscience. I was not going to get involved in that Moroccan disaster again. And my return to throwing dice was a disaster too. I could not make a point. I crapped out. "Aline," said Sammy, "when you're hot, keep it going, never leave the table."

We quickly broke up and I fell into bed exhausted. We spent another full day and night enjoying the wonderful, wild world of Las Vegas, and the following morning were at the airport, on our way to Dallas. Our plane had a slight delay leaving, and Luis browsed through the bookstore while I picked up the Las Vegas newspaper. Scanning the headlines, I read: GOVERNMENT BANKS ACROSS WESTERN EUROPE SUSPEND TRADING IN U.S. DOLLARS IN AN EFFORT TO CHECK SPECULATORS SWAPPING U.S. CURRENCY FOR WEST GERMAN MARKS IN EXPECTATION OF AN UPWARD REVALUATION . . . THE SAIGON MILITARY POLICE DECLARES THAT SAIGON IS A SAFE CITY, THAT VIET CONG TERRORISM HAS ALMOST VANISHED, WITH ONLY ONE REPORTED BOMBING IN FIVE MONTHS . . . FRENCH PRESIDENT GEORGES POMPIDOU FLIES AT TWICE THE SPEED OF SOUND IN THE FRENCH-BRITISH CONCORDE IN A BID TO PROMOTE SALES OF THE WEST'S FIRST SUPERSONIC PASSENGER JETLINER.

Then, glancing at local news stories on an inside page, I recoiled in horror. The Las Vegas police had discovered the body of a mutilated man. There was no identification on him. No fingerprints were available, since each finger had been chopped off. The jaw had been so badly smashed that verification through dental records would be impossible. The article ended with a brief physical description—height, weight, coloring. It fitted John Derby perfectly. I said nothing to Luis.

Chapter 19

In the plane on our return trip to Madrid, I told Luis about John Derby asking me to go to Morocco. I had no choice, since he began the conversation by telling me he'd seen through my lame excuses. "Don't think you pulled the wool over my eyes, my dear," he said. "Not the telephone call in the Whitneys' house, nor in Las Vegas. I didn't mention it at the time because I didn't want to spoil your trip, but now I think you'd better tell me if you're involved again."

Luis's ability to keep his thoughts to himself and remain cool, when convenient, always astounded me. I, on the other hand, usually blurted out anything that might be bothering me. But once I'd told him the facts and proudly assured him I'd refused to help Jupiter, neither of us mentioned the Morocco case again. That is, not for several weeks, not until we received an invitation for dinner in early July at the Moroccan Embassy in Madrid in honor of General Oufkir. We accepted immediately. We felt indebted to the Moroccans for their kindness and looked forward to seeing the colorful, charming General again.

It was about nine forty-five the night of the dinner for Oufkir. Luis was driving our car toward the Moroccan Embassy in Puerta de Hierro, a residential area about fifteen minutes from the center of Madrid, when he broached our experiences at the casino in Las Vegas.

"I've been thinking about the men who thought they were grabbing John Derby in Las Vegas," he said. I still had not told him about the mutilated body. "Don't let this dinner tonight get you interested again in helping your old pals."

"Don't worry about that," I answered. "And anyhow we don't know that the men in Las Vegas had anything to do with the Moroccan affair. They could have been after John for another espionage case."

"Well, nobody can make me believe that they weren't connected to that plot. And tonight someone could be at the Embassy who is involved in the conspiracy. Remember what my friend Abdul said about the ringleader being a close associate of his and of the King, too. One never knows. So beware. John's a good friend, but he always means trouble. I wouldn't have agreed to his being godfather of a child of mine if I didn't like him, but usually our friendship with that man gets us both in over our heads." Luis slowed down for a red light and turned to look at me. "Don't say anything at the dinner that could lead anyone to suspect you know anything about a coup. We don't want to spend the rest of our lives being followed by assassins or maniacs."

The evening was full of surprises. Not only was Salima there, but Michel de Bonville as well. I took it for granted that Michel was in Madrid to pursue his conversion to the Sunni religion. But when I asked Salima, she told me she hadn't seen Michel in almost two months; he'd been in Paris all that time and had come to Madrid to meet her.

General Oufkir appeared at my side as I was taking a drink from a passing tray. "The lovely Countess," he beamed. "It seems only yesterday that we were touring through Morocco, doesn't it?"

I agreed, and asked what brought him to Spain.

"The main reason is for the horse racing tomorrow. There's a full card of racing. For centuries, fine horses have been highly valued in my country. It's in our blood. I love the races."

After a few minutes of talk about the race, I said, "You know, General Oufkir, I recently remembered a conversation I had during our visit with Rachid Salloum, and I think you might find it of interest." I told him what Rachid had said about the ancient feud between their two families. "Of course he said it was a romance, without a grain of truth in it."

Oufkir laughed heartily. "Our disagreements were very much in the present," he said. "With all due respects to my departed colleague, I think that Rachid might have benefited from spending less time strumming a guitar and singing in the desert sun. He liked to spin tales, Countess. That he told you this one at all indicates that he gave some credence to it, no matter how much he tried to mitigate it with disclaimers. Rachid was an intelligent, capable man, but he also had a head full of dreams."

"But," I persisted, "it fascinates me to learn that battles over an oasis did occur and were matters of life and death. You said your ancestors came from the desert, as did Rachid's. How can you be so certain at this date that your ancestors were not enemies?"

The General smiled. "You're right, Comtesse, about life and death. The oasis was life. Without it, the desert was death." Then his mood changed and he looked at me directly in his attractive masculine manner and added, "And if it makes you happier, Comtesse, I'm perfectly willing to say our ancestors were enemies."

After the dinner in the large Moroccan salon, while mint tea and coffee were being served, conversation turned to the importance of Mecca for Mohammedans. The Ambassador happened to remark that the name *"el hadj"* was bestowed upon those who had made their pilgrimage to Mecca, and that forever after those persons could use *el hadj* as part of their name. Since we Spaniards looked confused, he clarified that the word in Spanish meant *peregrino*, in English, pilgrim.

What he said hit me like a bomb. I remembered that the intercepted message had been signed *"El Hadj,"* which Jerry had considered the coup ringleader's code name. And I also remembered that our driver had referred constantly to Omar Khalil as *"el peregrino"* in Spanish, although they spoke together in Arabic. I had interpreted that as an affectionate nickname for Omar, since he was part Spanish, and had given it no importance. Now it occurred to me that being aware of the meaning of *"el hadj"* could shed light on many things related to the coup. I recalled both Casey's driver, Abdel, and Moustapha Benayad mentioning *"el hadj"* several times during their fight in the garden in Tinerhir. I remembered Casey's driver hovering near our car

during that luncheon in Msemrir. He had had plenty of opportunities to sabotage our brakes. And even Omar Khalil . . .

I called Jerry the next morning. His voice was enthusiastic.
"Strange that you called," he said. "I was just about to call you.
How about inviting me over for a cup of coffee?"

Jerry appeared at eleven, and as soon as no one was in hearing
distance he confided, "We've received news that your friend
Serge Lebedev boarded General Oufkir's plane yesterday in
Rabat, so if it didn't stop someplace before landing here, he
could be in Madrid right now. I don't suppose you've had any
word from him?"

I shook my head. His news about Serge had set bells ringing.
I did not confess to Jerry that I could have misinterpreted
Serge's intentions. Jupiter knew that now, and had most likely
told him. Despite my doubts, they both seemed determined to
believe there was a possibility of Serge defecting. I said nothing
and waited for him to continue.

"There's something else you should know," he went on,
calmly pouring himself another cup of coffee. "We've just found
out that Lebedev's the Soviet Resident in Morocco. He covers
all of northern Africa, too."

Nothing could have shocked me more. Serge, the Soviet Chief
of Station! A top KGB agent! And I had been so naive as to
consider him my friend despite his nationality. The man who
had pretended to be an admirer! Now I believed less than ever
that he had been interested in defecting; undoubtedly he'd been
playing up to me only in hopes of gleaning useful information
for his own intelligence service.

I tried to conceal my confusion by proceeding to tell Jerry the
meaning of *"el hadj"* and the connection with General Oufkir,
Omar Khalil, Moustapha, and Casey's chauffeur.

Jerry was annoyed. "Our translators should have told us that.
We'll look into all those close to the King with the nickname of
el hadj or *peregrino.*"

Before leaving, he insisted that I advise him immediately either at the office or at his home if Lebedev called. The knowledge that Serge might be in Madrid left me with mixed
emotions. That he might contact me, I doubted. It would be
different here in my own country. He would understand that I

could not have a friendship with anyone who had illegally entered Spain, especially not with a Communist who held a high post in Soviet intelligence. Yet I was excited. What a prize—to bring in Serge as a defector—if it were only possible.

The next day was the fourth of July, Sunday, race day in Madrid, one of the biggest racing days of the year. If it had been a less important day I might have begged off; I would have preferred to be riding my own horse in the Casa del Campo, ten minutes away. And I had never been able to get very excited about the races, not even when one of our own horses, bred in our stud in Pascualete, was running. Nevertheless, I wanted to help Luis, who was president of Spain's Thoroughbred Racing Association and had worked hard to improve the quality of the short racing in the country. Horse-racing had been started by his grandfather, Torre Arias, and was a family tradition. Today, General Franco and his wife would be there, and it was imperative that I assist with these prestigious guests. General Oufkir, I remembered, would be there as well.

The day was comfortably warm and dry. The bluish Guadarrama Mountains were etched clearly against the even bluer sky. I was standing in Luis's corner of the owners' paddock, talking with our trainer and jockey, when I felt a gentle nudge. I turned my head. Serge Lebedev was standing there grinning at me. His casual, well-cut sport jacket, beige slacks, pale blue shirt and red tie would not attract uncomfortable scrutiny. He looked like someone who went every Sunday to the paddocks in the Madrid Hippodrome of Lasarte. Despite Jerry's warning, I was astonished that he dared to come to the track today, of all days, when because of Franco's attendance the entire area was crawling with army personnel and police. It was not a small offense to be caught in a country like Spain, where Communists were prohibited and where his own country had no diplomatic representation. Franco was expected at any moment. Unconsciously I glanced around. No one seemed to find Serge's presence unusual, yet I wondered how Serge could imagine that I wouldn't denounce him.

As if reading my thoughts, he said, "Aline, please, I beg of you not to draw attention to my presence here." Serge's eyes followed my glance. "Not until I have a chance to talk to you. It is a matter of utmost importance." His expression seemed sincere, but I didn't trust him, and he was aware of that.

I remained silent. He continued to speak.

"I can prove my friendly intentions." His voice was so low that I wondered if I had misunderstood.

I was hopeful; this might be the manner in which he had planned his defection. I dismissed the trainer, who was waiting for me to continue our conversation. I looked to see where Luis was; I felt certain that he would denounce Serge as soon as he saw him. But Luis was not nearby. He was probably telling the jockey how he wanted his horse handled for the next race.

Serge's next words brought my attention back to him alone. "I'm here to protect you," he said. "You're in danger."

I frowned. So he wasn't here to defect. And how could he possibly think I would believe him? Me, in danger, here in my own country, surrounded by friends, guards, police, and military officers! No, I did not intend to be fooled by Serge again.

"You must believe me." He pulled me farther away from those nearby. We were now a bit isolated. No one could hear us. "Do not be alone for one minute today. I will be watching. And try to be near your telephone this evening. I will call you about another matter, but I have to take care of some unfinished business first."

I suppose my expression of disbelief had not changed. In desperation he pulled on my arm again. "Please, please have faith in me. I am your friend and I want to help you. I'll prove that in a few hours."

My head was reeling, trying to interpret the meaning of his words. Although I had no intention of being taken in, I sensed that he was sincere. Quickly I told him that I could not help him in Spain unless it would be to defect. I told him that over one million people had died in the Spanish Civil War against Communism, and that many of those surrounding us at this moment had been tragically affected by that massacre, that I felt compelled to denounce him.

"Not yet. It is critical that you do not mention my presence to anyone. Give me a few hours at least. I should not have approached you in this place, but I had to warn you. When I see you, I lose my head." His words were pronounced with a mean-

ing I preferred not to notice, and I wanted to turn away. Yet I
lingered. He had not taken up my reference to defecting, but the
fact that he dared to appear in a place where General Franco and
most of his staff of military officers were present gave some
weight to his declarations. At the same time, since Jerry had told
me that Serge was the Soviet Resident in Morocco, he could be
clever enough to deceive me—but also, as KGB chief in Algeria
and Libya, he certainly knew more about the coup than we did.
What a quandary. It might be worthwhile if I could discover
who was behind the plot and warn General Oufkir, who would
be here today. If . . . if . . .

While these thoughts were whirling through my head, Serge's
face suddenly broke into a smile. He bowed slightly and calmly
kissed my hand, then turned and walked away, leaving me still
more perplexed, until I saw Luis approaching with his trainer
and jockey. He had not seen Serge, of that I was certain. I looked
in the direction in which Serge had gone, but he had disappeared into the crowd. At that moment I made up my mind not
to tell Luis—not yet, although I harbored many doubts. But how
could I face him? I was so nervous that he would realize something was up as soon as he saw me. Fortunately he stopped to
talk to another owner and several officers. Soon I was swamped
by the officers' wives, and I had no opportunity to talk to General Oufkir, or to Luis either. The crowd waiting for the
Generalissimo's arrival grew by the moment.

Every year on the day of the Chief of State's cup, our *palco* and
the small room attached to it were filled with generals resplendent in dress uniform, with row upon row of medals from the
Civil War. Some decorations denoted that they had served in the
Blue Division, which had fought against Russia in the first years
of World War II. As usual I was busy introducing people and
offering drinks, until Luis and I had to make our way to the
main entrance to greet the Chief of State.

We arrived just in time. The three cars which usually preceded Franco were already entering the driveway outside the
recinto. With very little fanfare, the Generalissimo and his wife
descended from their black Mercedes. When Luis and I greeted
them, I saw that Franco seemed to have recovered from his
illness of a few months before. He looked well and was in good

spirits. Doña Carmen was elegant in a large-brimmed beige hat, a matching Pedro Rodriguez beige silk suit, and her beautiful pearls, necklace and earrings, which had become famous. Franco's entrance across the proprietors' paddock was received with enthusiastic ovations and cries. "Fraaan . . . co, Fraan . . . co, Fraaan . . . co" rang out everywhere in the stadium, as with one voice the crowd acclaimed him. And when General and Señora Franco appeared in the President's box, all those in the stands stood up, and again the same familiar fervent salutation rang out: "Fraaan . . . co, Fraaan . . . co, Fraaan . . . co," over and over, until the Chief of State silenced them with a wave of his hand and sat down.

General Franco had no special fondness for horse races or for bullfights, but he came to each one that was celebrated in his honor. Fishing was his favorite sport, and shooting partridge came second.

Once the excitement had died down, he turned to me and asked what I'd been doing lately. I reminded him that his daughter and I had been shooting in Morocco. I knew that he was especially interested in that country because of his thirteen years in Spanish-controlled Morocco before the Civil War. General Franco was an unusual person; his cabinet ministers had enormous respect for him, but were at the same time impressed by his austerity. He was a man not given to luxury of any kind, and gave much attention to saving money. He incurred no unnecessary expenses, neither official nor private, and it was a standing joke among cabinet members that when Friday cabinet meetings at the Pardo continued through lunch, they had to fill up with something more substantial when they went home. However, I knew that he could be different, and that his commanding reserved manner was due in part to his military background, and also to an unsuspected innate shyness. Carmen had told me that she often placed me next to her father at dinner on shoots because he found me easy to talk to. I enjoyed sitting next to him, and although at the beginning of the dinner he was a bit stiff, he gradually became warm and entertaining, and usually had several amusing stories to tell. When I mentioned Morocco, he told me that he could fill a book with anecdotes related to that country.

"You know for years we had a *capitán general* in Tangier called Jordana, an admirable man." The Generalissimo chuckled in remembrance. "Well, he had a charming and intelligent wife, but she was far from beautiful. One day Jordana invited the Sheik of Tetuan to the *Capitanía General*. Jordana's wife happened to be in the patio of the building as the Sheik entered. Naturally, Jordana introduced her to the Sheik before passing on into his office. When the Moroccan Sheik was about to leave about an hour later, he paused in the doorway. '*Mi General*,' he said, 'was that woman you introduced me to when I came in one of your wives?' Jordana nodded. 'She is my wife and my only wife.' The Sheik asked again, 'Your only wife?' Jordana smiled and said 'Yes. You know my religion permits only one.' The Sheik looked at Jordana for a moment and then patted him on the back. Looking puzzled and impressed, the Sheik said, 'General Jordana, you are really a good man. A very good man.' "

General Franco laughed heartily. Those nearby looked at us astounded. None of them were aware that the Generalissimo had a keen sense of humor.

With all the excitement of the Chief of State's visit to the Hippodrome, I had almost forgotten Serge Lebedev. After the feature race and the presentation of his trophy, the Caudillo and his wife left, and Salima, who had been sitting in a nearby box, came to look for me.

"Aline, did you see Michel?" she asked, her voice obviously distraught.

I told her I didn't even know he was at the races.

"Well, he is," she whispered. "And he was quarreling with Serge Lebedev, who's also here. Michel has not called me since the Embassy dinner yesterday." She shook her head. "He's changed so. I don't know what's come over him."

We walked together down the steps and across the green enclosure. Already, the horses for the last race were parading around the paddock. We stood in the middle of the enclosure, studying the horses, although I'm sure Salima's thoughts, like mine, were on other things. In the distance, on the path that was used to bring the horses into the paddock, I saw Serge in heated conversation with Michel. At that moment General Oufkir joined us, and Salima and I were obliged to turn our attention to him. But the afternoon had been long and exhausting, and when Oufkir and Salima started to walk toward the stands to watch the last race, I sneaked away toward the parking lot. If I hurried, I calculated, I could avoid the rush by leaving the Hippodrome now. Luis had come earlier than I, as he always did, in his own car, and I had arrived later in my small Seat, precisely so I'd be able to leave when I wanted.

The parking lot was still filled with cars. Climbing into mine, I started the engine and drove out toward the main road. Just as I was about to merge into the traffic on the main highway, I heard a voice behind me. Immediately I realized a man must have been hiding behind the backseat. Naturally it had never occurred to me to look.

"Change your direction." The voice was harsh, and to make certain I followed his orders, he jabbed my ribs with the barrel of a revolver. I recognized the voice immediately, though the timbre was totally different. "Follow this road out of Madrid." I did as he said. "Now make another turn." Again the barrel shoved painfully into my side.

There were few cars going in our direction; most of the traffic was returning to Madrid at this hour. I did not initiate the turn, and he leaned over my shoulder and grabbed the wheel, swerving in the direction he wanted. I didn't have to see his face. It was Michel de Bonville. Why was he being so violent with me? My car merged with the other cars headed toward El Escorial. At first I was not too frightened. I imagined that he had had a quarrel with Salima and wanted me to help. She's lucky to be rid of him, I thought as I continued along the highway, his gun still shoved in my ribs. The man's mad, I said to myself. With a gun, he's dangerous.

"Don't stop until we get to that fork, where the sign says 'Las Rosas.' Turn in there," he ordered. I was amazed that he knew this area so well, and with each moment that passed, I became increasingly apprehensive. I drove on and on for what seemed a lifetime. Now it was dark. Since Luis always remained at the track to discuss his horses with his trainer, he would not be home for hours. When he missed me and became alarmed, where would he look? And I had nothing—no weapon I could use to defend myself.

Making a great effort, I spoke to Michel calmly, asking what it was he wanted from me. Why was he behaving in such a manner with a friend? His answer stunned me, like a dash of ice water.

"Ha, ha. Some friend. A tool of the CIA." As he pronounced "CIA," he gave another painful jab into my ribs. I heard the click as he removed the safety and decided not to excite him further. His mention of the CIA made me realize he might not be crazy. Could he be connected with the Moroccan plot?

At Las Rosas I turned in as he had commanded, but in my rearview mirror I saw another auto turn off the road behind us, lower its lights, then put them out altogether. I knew we were being followed, but Michel de Bonville did not, unless the person behind was an accomplice. But he never looked back, so I surmised that he did not expect anyone to be there. He was concentrating on the road, his head close to mine, looking for something, perhaps a turnoff to a smaller road. What was he planning? To rape me, torture me, or just to murder me? And why? If he intended to kill me, I hoped he would have the decency to do it quickly. I'd seen people die in agony from a bullet in the abdomen. I kept wondering who was in the car behind. My heart raced, my hands were damp on the steering wheel. Whatever action I took to save myself had to be immediate—now!

Though close, the trailing vehicle in my rearview mirror was barely discernible, because it still maneuvered without lights. Whoever it was, was going to be my only chance. Bracing my weight against the backseat, I pounded down on the brake pedal. As we ground to a frantic stop, the car behind tore into the rear of my little Seat. Both violent, unexpected shocks—the car braking and the blow from behind—coming almost simultaneously hurled Michel de Bonville over the front seat, and his head smashed into the windshield. I jumped out and ran for the shadowy bushes on the side of the road into the safety of darkness.

As I brushed aside the retama bushes, ripping my dress, slipping and falling on pine needles, I was oblivious to whatever was happening behind me. I concentrated only on reaching the highway as fast as possible. For a moment I stopped to catch my breath, but strangely enough there were no sounds of pursuit. Only the dull hum of vehicles on the main road, where the headlights of cars going toward Madrid glowed in a steady stream and the taillights of those going toward El Escorial looked like an endless red snake. Not a branch moved. Again, I raced through the underbrush.

It must have been a full half-hour later before I reached the highway. Even then, my trials were not over. Cars and trucks sped by. No one stopped, despite my frantic waving. Finally an elderly couple in a battered Seat took pity and stopped. They were caretakers from the *finca* of the Señores de Arburua, and had come from their daughter's house in Madrid where they'd spent Sunday afternoon with their grandchildren. When they heard my story about a crazy foreigner who had tried to kidnap me, even though they were headed in the opposite direction, they turned around and drove me to the entrance of the city, where I took a taxi home.

I rang my doorbell—I had left my keys and handbag in the abandoned car—and our butler, Andres, was aghast when he saw me. "Señora Condesa," he said, appraising my torn dress, scratched face, and disheveled hair, "was there an accident? The Señor Conde has been calling all over Madrid."

Luis raced down the steps to the front door and turned pale when he saw me. "My God, Aline," he cried. "Are you all right? What happened, darling?"

I nodded, close to tears. "Pay the cab and I'll tell you." Luis dispatched Andres to take care of the driver, and with a firm arm around my waist, assisted me upstairs, where he forced me to lie down on a couch. He quickly came back with a glass of water. Down on his knees, he gently raised my head. "Here—take a sip and relax." By this time my maid had appeared with some hot milk and was running hysterically around the room, closing windows and shades. I must have been on the couch for some time, with Luis holding my hand and gently stroking my hair.

Gradually I told him what had happened. He was shaken before I began, but livid when I gave him the details. Michel's reason for attacking me was an enigma. "He probably blames you for some problem he's run into with those two sisters," Luis mused at first. Then I remembered Serge, and told Luis about seeing him in conversation with Michel. Luis didn't scold me for my espionage activities at once, probably because, seeing my frightful state, he felt sorry for me. We tried to determine how much we dared tell the authorities. Neither of us wanted to risk giving a clue to my activities on behalf of the CIA. After hashing over everything, we decided that Michel de Bonville had to be involved in the plot against King Hassan. At the same time, however, we also knew that if he were picked up by the Spanish police and questioned, he would have no qualms about telling them I worked for the Agency. We tried to figure out who had been in the second car. Intentionally or unintentionally, that car had saved my life.

Finally we decided to do nothing until we could talk to Jerry or contact Jupiter. Jerry's home number didn't answer.

Chapter 20

It must have been about an hour after I arrived home that the doorbell rang. The servants had gone to bed, and Luis and I were still talking in the upstairs sitting room. I stood up to go to the door, but Luis stopped me.

"Slow down. Don't always be so imprudent. Haven't you been in enough danger for one night? Let me see who it is." He went quickly to his room for his revolver.

Nevertheless I followed him down the steps and across the garden, and looked over his shoulder from between the poplar trees to the door on the street below.

"Who's there?" Luis called.

"It's me—Serge," the voice answered. "Please let me in."

"What are you doing here at this hour?" Luis's voice was not friendly.

"For God's sake, please let me in. I'm here to ask asylum. There's no one I trust at this moment except your wife. Can't you see I am alone? And, here, I have a pistol. I'll drop it."

Now I leaned over Luis's shoulder. There was no one in the street at this hour, and I could barely distinguish Serge in the shadows. "I know you're the KGB Resident, Serge," I butted in. "How can I trust you?"

"Because I was the one who followed you when Michel hid in your car. I knew that he intended to kill you, and I wanted to stop him. Fortunately I've taken care of him for the time being. I gave him an extra knock on the head, but he may have come to his senses by now and he'll be after us both. I want to defect. There's no way I can go to the American Embassy at this hour. That's the first place they would go to look. I'm counting on you to help me."

Luis was still against opening the door, but I insisted. Serge climbed the steps painfully. I saw that his head had been bleeding, and he limped severely. When he came in the house, he collapsed onto the floor.

While my husband tried to help him, I went to the phone and dialed Jerry's home number. Still no answer. When I returned, Serge was able to sit up and began to explain what had happened.

In faltering words—he was still obviously exhausted from the efforts of the past hours—he told me that Michel de Bonville was a Soviet "illegal," in other words, a Soviet intelligence officer, a Russian citizen posing as a Frenchman while doing his job for the KGB. In this particular case, his job was coordinating the efforts of the Libyans and the leftist groups in Morocco, which, together with high Moroccan officials, were plotting the assassination of King Hassan. Serge said that Michel had been using Salima and her family, who were completely unaware of his purposes, as an entrée into Morocco's most powerful inner circle: a brilliant cover-up.

When I mentioned that I was aware Michel had been flirting with both sisters, Serge interrupted to say that Michel's male ego and his success with women had led to a serious reprimand from Moscow. He said the KGB felt that this double affair could be discovered and would seriously jeopardize his position and the assassination plot. "Michel always plays this kind of a chancy game with the opposite sex. One day," said Serge, "this will be his downfall."

Serge went on to explain that he had been with Michel every minute that afternoon at the races. "I was afraid to leave him alone," he said.

"I saw you with Michel. What were you two arguing about?" I asked.

Serge's response shocked me. "Whether to kill you or not. Michel suspected all along that you were aware of the planned coup. We intercepted your messages, and he saw them, no matter how I tried to avoid that." For the first time a slight smile crossed Serge's face. "Aline, you are too beautiful and too smart. That almost got you killed."

Seeing that I was puzzled, Serge continued: "Michel is a tough, shrewd operator. Though you might not have realized it, he kept you under close surveillance. Your room was bugged. He used Salima, who was innocent of his actual role, to obtain bits of information from you about people on the trip."

I remembered Salima's questions about Bill Casey and doubted she'd been able to report anything worthwhile; I remember having been distrustful of her questions and cautious in my responses.

"He began to realize that somehow you were suspicious of a conspiracy to kill the King," Serge went on. "He counted on your being unaware of his involvement but feared you were getting close." Serge was hardly able to speak. "When we heard through the hidden mike in your room that you and Luis were talking about the tenth day, and being on the alert, and arming yourselves, he convinced everyone to call off the plot. With all the noise of the hunt, the shooting and the confusion, it would have been a simple matter to put a bullet through the King. But you would have informed the CIA that it was no accident. It was important to the instigators that the killing be above suspicion. I never was able to find out who the Moroccan leader of this coup was. Of course he wanted to keep his identity secret and obviously had the ability to do so." Serge paused again, then struggled on. "That meant somebody would have to kill you and Luis, too, before proceeding with the plot. Three deaths could not be accidental. So, because of you, Aline, Michel's carefully laid plans, which had taken months to set up, were blown apart."

Serge rubbed his injured leg. "Of course Michel was wild with anger. He knew that you would continue to be a menace. That automobile crash in the mountains was no accident, and neither was the tent pole. At the races today, Michel said he was going to damn well take care of you himself. I argued against it, but he told me that it was his operation and he was going to do it his way." Serge raised his arms in a gesture of futility. "What could I do? I had no time to warn you. My only recourse was to keep my eyes on Michel and follow you when I saw you get into your car. The KGB will know what I have done—attacked a colleague. Since there is no Soviet Embassy in Spain, it will take them longer to catch me, but by now they know I have not checked in with the KGB illegal who was putting me up in Madrid. I'm sure that right now he's rounded up five or six illegals in Madrid and they're looking for me. If Michel has recovered, he'll have a good idea where to send them. Though they don't want to risk having their illegals picked up by the Spanish police, they will come to this house to take me. My defection is too important."

As he said the words, the terror in his face grew. He hastened to say, "For years I've wanted to make this break, but not until I met you, Aline, did I dare try. I checked up on you. I listened to you. I believed in you and realized that you were the only reliable person I knew whom I could turn to for help. That's why I managed to get to Spain on an illegal visa, using General Oufkir's plane. He is unaware of what's going on. Just when I wanted to tell you of my intentions to defect, I discovered that Michel was planning to kill you, and naturally I had to protect you first."

Serge spoke more quickly as he went on. He was tense and frightened. There was little I could do without Jerry. Again, I went to the phone, praying as I dialed. After some ten rings, which seemed like an eternity, Jerry finally answered. Knowing me so well, and also the timbre of my voice, I knew he would be aware that this was an emergency. Deducing now that there might be a tap on my phone, I invited him as gaily as possible to come to my house, though it was late, to meet a famous American movie star who had just dropped in. I suggested he bring his sons, too. Jerry had no sons.

By the time I returned and let Luis and Serge know that Jerry was on his way, Serge was almost beside himself with fear.

"Time is running out. I have only minutes before our under-cover agents in Madrid come for me." His face was white, the lips blue, the gashes on his head more livid than before. He was suffering from shock. He looked at me—imploringly. "You have to believe me or I'm dead now. Three months ago, during your Morocco trip, just when I was about to tell you how I felt, I discovered that Michel had also checked up on you and knew your connections to the CIA. So I had to stay in my post at the Soviet Embassy to monitor his intentions with respect to you."

Luis spoke up. "You could be lying." He was still belligerent. "You could have been helping Michel kill my wife, too." Training his pistol on the Russian, Luis went on coolly, "After killing Aline, you both could have made your escape in your car."

"No, no!" Serge shouted desperately. Frantically he turned to me. "If my people pick me up, they'll assassinate me. They might try to break into this house to get me. We have illegals in Madrid trained for this sort of thing. People who know this city well."

Both men turned to me. I realized the enormity of the moment. To throw Serge out to the KGB would mean instant death if he were telling the truth. To give him sanctuary meant enlisting an invaluable new agent for the U.S.—but if he were lying, everything was at stake, even our lives and my wonderful marriage, my three boys.

Years ago, when I first joined the OSS, our Director, General Bill Donovan, had stressed the importance of one's own instinctive judgment. "Part of your training is to hone that judgment," he had said. "On many occasions it will mean life or death . . . maybe yours."

I looked from Luis to Serge. "Serge is telling the truth."

Luis stared at me—for an unforgettable moment. All his love and trust were reflected in that look. Then, swiftly, he turned back to Serge. "Do you really think that the KGB will try to take you by force?"

Serge's head bobbed affirmatively.

"My God, you must be important," Luis muttered. Suddenly I heard a door open in another part of the house, and I jumped.

"They're in the house," groaned Serge. As I walked toward the door, Luis grabbed my arm. "Stay here with your Soviet friend," he said, and quietly left the room. There was not a sound except Serge's rapid breathing. Again I jumped and Serge gasped as the door opened. It was Luis. With a grin he said, "The noise you heard was Andres, the butler. Hearing our voices, he woke up, and like a good servant was coming to ask if we needed anything. I met him in the butler's pantry. When he saw my gun his eyes became huge circles. I suggested that he go back to bed. I've never seen him move so quickly."

"Don't you think we should have some weapons just in case those KGB agents do appear?" I said to Luis.

Giving me his pistol, he raced upstairs and returned with his pair of Purdy twelve-gauge shotguns, his hunting rifle, and another pistol tucked into his belt. "Here," he said, giving one Purdy, a pistol, and ammunition to Serge. "You'd better be prepared to defend yourself. We only have to watch the front of the house. There's no way they can attack from the back. This house is separated from the Calle Serrano by our own walled-in garden and two other houses behind." Handing me the other Purdy, Luis's mouth creased in a wry smile. "If we have to use these things tonight, our neighbors may think that my American wife is having a Fourth of July celebration." Taking the other pistol from me, he slipped out the door with his hunting rifle in hand. I followed him, with Serge limping slowly behind, into the garden. Each of us stood concealed behind a poplar tree and peered over the railing down into the street.

We did not wait long. A car turned into our street from the corner—headlights out—and stopped at the door. Three men quickly slipped out, and from the dull streetlamp below came the brief reflection of a gun barrel: KGB or U.S.A.?

The short ring of the doorbell and a voice called quietly, "Aline?" Thank God! It was Jerry with two men. I felt weak with relief.

Luis raced down our stairway to the street, unlocked the door, and led them upstairs. I explained the situation, and was just presenting Jerry to Serge when the sound of squealing tires made us all dart to the wall and look down again. First, the headlights of one car came around the corner, illuminating the road, and then the flashing lights of two more just behind. The five men in our garden now took positions—all armed—along the front wall, well hidden by the poplar trees. One car raced by our door and screeched to a halt twenty-five yards beyond, blocking the road from that end, while the second stopped opposite our door; the third blocked the other end of the street. The headlights were extinguished. There was not a sound. A few minutes later the click of a car door opening was matched by the sound of Jerry releasing the safety on his automatic rifle. A figure slowly emerged from the backseat of the car directly in front of our door, faced the house, and put two empty hands on the roof of the car. Standing there, shrouded in the darkness, he surveyed the scene. Nobody moved, nobody talked; just silence as the seconds slowly ticked by. Then the figure below walked deliberately to Jerry's car, and with the snap of a cigarette lighter bent over the license plate, running the tiny sliver of light along the numbers. With a wave of his hand toward the other cars he quickly returned to his own and carefully lowered himself back in. The door slammed, engines started, lights flashed, and the three autos disappeared around the corner.

Giving terse orders to his two assistants to stay on guard, Jerry beckoned Serge and me to enter the house. Luis joined us just as Jerry was saying, "We've got to get this man out of here fast." Turning to me, Jerry said, "Are you willing to go on record backing this man? You realize he could be double-crossing you."

Then a quiet voice said, "Aline has already made that decision." It was Luis, and I never loved him more.

While Jerry hastened to the phone, Serge limped to me and, taking my hand, bent over and kissed it. "It's because of Americans like you that I've been able to make this decision," he said. Striding over to Luis as best he could, the Russian said, "Thank you. You've been very kind."

Jerry was at his side. "We must hurry. We have to get you out of the country before your friends devise a plan to get you back."

Serge spun on his heel and was hustled downstairs with Jerry's help. As our street door clanged shut behind them and the car moved away, Luis said softly, "You know, that Russian's quite a decent fellow after all." Then he put his arm around me and we turned and walked up the stairs. "You've had quite a day, *guapa*. But at least your job's over. I doubt that Michel de Bonville will dare return to Morocco to create trouble when he learns that his colleague has defected. King Hassan is safe and there's not much chance that anything will happen now."

Chapter 21

O n Saturday, six days later, I boarded the Iberia plane
for New York and then took the shuttle to Washington, D.C. Jupiter had asked me to sit in on the debriefing of Serge Lebedev. Jerry had explained that Jupiter wanted
me to make certain they did not skip over any personalities in
Morocco or Spain whom Serge had known. This was also his
way of complimenting me for my role in the defection.

Serge had flown in an army transport plane to Washington on
the previous Tuesday from Torrejón, a U.S. air base just outside
Madrid, but I would not be seeing either him or Jupiter until
Monday. I had the Sunday to recover from the flight, and would
be rested for the meeting with Serge and Jupiter. During these
several days in Washington, I was to dine with Bill and Sophia
Casey. After the debriefing I intended to go to Pearl River to
visit my parents, then back to Spain and Marbella for a vacation
with Luis and the children. Now that there was no cause for
tension, I looked forward to a wonderful summer.

When the plane landed in Washington, it was late. The Iberia
flight from Spain had been delayed three hours in the Madrid
airport because of weather, so I'd missed my connection to our
capital. But despite being tired from so many hours en route, I
was in a buoyant mood. King Hassan was safe for the time
being, and his pro-American government had been untouched
by the events of the past months. As a reward for my efforts, we
had Serge as a defector, and I felt certain that his information

would help our side in many ways, especially in clearing up the still-unknown details of the attempted coup, perhaps even in uncovering the identities of the plotters. It was such a relief to know that the whole mission had ended with no serious repercussions, outside of Rachid Salloum's death, which still made me sad. I arrived at my hotel and was given the key to my room; the luggage would be sent up. It was almost midnight and I was finally feeling the strain of the transatlantic flight and the time difference; my eyelids were so heavy they felt like cement. When I stepped across the threshold, I received such a shock that I took another large step backwards, my hand on my mouth. In the middle of the darkened room was the face of King Hassan, fixing me with a fierce stare.

After an instant of stunned bewilderment, I rushed across the room to the television and turned up the sound. I sank to the floor in disbelief and horror as the announcer's cool, modulated voice described the terrible massacre which had taken place that day at the King's Summer Palace near Rabat. My hand covered my mouth; my heart raced. The coup had taken place. In despair I watched the clips of carnage and combat that flickered across the screen. Was the King dead or alive? Who was responsible? My face was so close to the screen that they were almost touching.

The spot ended abruptly and the announcer moved on to other stories. Frantically, I turned the knob, jumping from one channel to another, but I learned no more.

My mind was reeling. It had seemed that plans for the coup had halted. How was it Serge hadn't warned us? At this hour on a weekend I knew it would be impossible to contact Jupiter or anyone else. Finally, despite my agitation, I fell into bed from sheer exhaustion. My dreams were a jumble of bright, chaotic images, and I slept badly.

The next morning I called for the newspapers as soon as I awoke. It was still quite early, and it took fifteen rings before anyone downstairs picked up the phone. The sleepy voice I eventually reached said that the *Times* hadn't been delivered yet, but as soon as it was he would send up a copy. I paced for twenty minutes, too jittery to eat or shower, then at last the paper arrived and I had written evidence, with photographs.

The *New York Times,* Sunday, July 11, 1971, had front-page headlines: SOLDIERS ATTACK MOROCCAN SUMMER PALACE; KING HASSAN CAPTIVE. Below that, "Hassan, on radio, asserts 10 officers led 3-hour raid by 1,400 men. A captive for 2 hours, monarch says 3 generals were killed—he accuses Libya of inciting uprising." Then the story: "Palace sources said that King Hassan has authorized the Interior Minister, Gen. Mohammed Oufkir, to take over all civil and military power to regain control of the situation." On the second page was a picture of Prince Moulay Abdullah. The caption stated that he was reported wounded. Another picture of General Mohammed Oufkir in battle helmet was captioned "Gen. Mohammed Oufkir, Interior Chief, assumed civil and military powers."

There were few details about the coup itself, although much background material about King Hassan. I tried the radio for up-to-the-minute news, but I could learn little more. All the TV channels and radio stations transmitted "news bites" about the coup in Morocco, but there were few details. Who had been responsible? Who was dead? Was the King still in power? How badly was the Prince wounded?

Jupiter was not in Washington, nor in his apartment in New York. I called Bill Casey. He said that he had heard the sad news; General Medbouh had been killed during the skirmish. Another friend dead! I hoped against hope that there was some mistake. Casey knew little else, and was as anxious as I was to learn more.

All day Sunday I contacted friends from the Moroccan Embassy and little by little some facts became clearer, although there was a certain restraint in all of their reports; I could tell that it was a censored version of what had really taken place. Nobody seemed to know much. I gradually pieced together a story of sorts: The coup had been planned for the forty-second birthday of the King, a large celebration with eight hundred guests scheduled to take place at the King's Summer Palace in Skhirat, near Rabat.

Festivities had begun early in the morning, with golf, tennis, and swimming in the palace pools. Diplomats, government ministers, artists, writers and scientists, and friends from all over the world had been invited, but only men, as was customary in Morocco for official affairs. The ambassadors of the USSR, the

U.S.A., France, Belgium, Great Britain, and many Arab countries had been there.

A few minutes after two o'clock, while King Hassan was lunching under a large tent in front of the palace, sounds of firing were heard. At first the guests and the King thought the explosions were fireworks. But once the first moment of shock had passed, the King realized it was gunfire. He ran from the tent, accompanied by General Oufkir and ten others, and took refuge in the throne room, where he telephoned some motorized units that were loyal to him and ordered them to intervene. His call got through just before all telephone communications were cut.

A moment later armed soldiers and officers broke into the palace grounds, shooting and throwing hand grenades, and killing people left and right. The guests who started to run were mowed down. Others threw themselves on the ground.

The King's forces, greatly outnumbered, were caught in a severe crossfire. By three o'clock the situation was desperate. The King had no means of communication; he and his small group had no weapons. Since firing was still continuing outside the palace, they understood that they could be slaughtered. Realizing his only chance was to conceal himself, the King moved to a small, unimportant room in the palace.

One thousand four hundred cadets from the Military Academy of Ahermoumou, 130 miles from Rabat, had left their barracks at three-fifteen that morning in two motorized columns. They had been informed only that they would be performing a tactical assault with live ammunition somewhere between Rabat and Casablanca. By eleven o'clock the two groups had stopped at Sidi Bouknadel, sixteen kilometers from Rabat. There, Lieutenant Colonel Ababou, head of the Academy, had met with four battalion leaders and told them that the purpose of the maneuver was to neutralize subversive elements which were endangering the liberty and life of the King at the Skhirat Summer Palace. He ordered them to attack in strength, to hit quickly and hard.

From two o'clock until three, it was a massacre. One hundred dead, more than two hundred wounded, the King's motorized division quickly annihilated.

The insurgents looked in vain for the King on the golf course, in the palace, and among the hundreds of guests who were herded together. Some had been lined up against a wall, and others were forced to lie for hours facedown on the ground in the relentless heat of the July sun.

Medbouh, who knew the palace well, found the King. Reports of their conversation differed, and were often heavily spiced with speculation, but as far as I could tell, Medbouh told King Hassan that Lieutenant Colonel Ababou was the ringleader of the attack, and he recommended the King speak with Ababou.

The King refused to speak to Ababou, the man responsible for murdering so many innocent people. General Medbouh left to relay the King's answer, but was accidentally killed by a stray bullet moments later.

At ten after three the King and his group noticed that the sounds outside the palace had changed drastically. The firing had almost stopped, and through the small window of their enclosure, they could see that the young cadets who led the attack were confused. The soldiers were awaiting orders and none were forthcoming. Ababou, thinking that the King had been captured by Medbouh, not realizing that Medbouh was dead, had gone in triumph to Rabat, where he took over the radio and television stations and broadcast the news of the successful overthrow of the government.

Meanwhile, when Medbouh and Ababou failed to appear, the young cadets began to wonder what was happening and why they had been ordered to fire on the motorized troops. This situation reigned until five o'clock, when the King courageously took action. Despite the knowledge that he could easily be shot, he stepped out of the palace alone and walked among the fourteen hundred cadets who were scattered in ragged formations throughout the grounds. When the cadets recognized their monarch, they crowded around him. The King began to recite the Our Father of Islam, the Al-Fatiha . . .

> *"In the name of God,*
> *He who accords mercy*
> *The Merciful one*
> *Praise be to God,*

> *King of the Day of Judgment . . .*
> *Direct us on the straight and narrow path . . ."*

The six or seven cadets standing nearest to him came to attention, and one of them addressed the King, explaining that they had been told their monarch was in danger, and that was why they had surrounded the palace. A young cadet officer explained that they were then ordered to open fire, and begged the King to realize that they had been deceived, and affirmed that they were now awaiting their King's orders.

The coup was over.

This information took me all day and Sunday evening to obtain. I questioned everyone and telephoned Morocco repeatedly, but could reach no one. I slept badly again Sunday night, and Monday morning waited anxiously for the newspapers to arrive.

From the *New York Times* on Monday, July 12, 1971:

It began on the grounds of the Summer Palace with a golf match organized by General Medbouh, who was chief of the royal household and regarded as the most important officer in the army.

The United States Ambassador, Stuart W. Rockwell, said in an interview tonight that he chatted with the General (Medbouh), who was in sports clothes, at the 18th hole of the golf course at about noon. Then the Ambassador went to a courtyard, where a buffet lunch was served to some 500 guests. There were diplomats, ministers, officers, and politicians in a variety of costumes ranging from bathing suits to Arab galabias.

"All of a sudden popping sounds were heard," Ambassador Rockwell said, "and most of us thought they were firecrackers. But a man staggered through the open doors onto the patio, bleeding profusely from his legs."

Hundreds of cadet officers had arrived in trucks and charged the palace gate, killing those guards who resisted and hurling grenades.

Mr. Rockwell said that in the confusion, "a number of guests dashed out of the main entrance of the palace, where they were mowed down by a hail of fire. Others jumped through the windows facing the sea, and still others, among whom I found myself, found that the safest place was the throne room itself."

It was in the early shooting that most of the casualties occurred. Among those killed were the Belgian Ambassador, Marcel Duprat; Morocco's 24-year-old Minister of Tourism, Mohammed Lazrak; and the Minister of Justice, Mohammed Bahnini. Also killed in undetermined circumstances were a number of high military officers.

The King and his party came to the throne room for a time, but left for a hiding place without speaking to the other guests, Ambassador Rockwell said. Soon afterward, soldiers came and ordered the guests out with hands in the air.

"We were made to walk through the patio over the bodies and through pools of blood and over piles of broken glass and through the main entrance of the palace, which was clogged with bodies of the original guests who made the original dash for freedom," Mr. Rockwell said.

The guests, about 300 in number, were ordered to lie down in the flower beds at the edge of the road outside, first on their backs and with hands in the air, and then on their faces with hands behind them.

"We were kept this way in the hot Moroccan sun for two hours by very nervous young soldiers who were, to say the least, very trigger-happy," the Ambassador continued.

He said palace servants and guards were brought out and beaten with rifle butts and kicked.

Finally, he said, the prisoners were ordered to walk down the road, three by three, "to an unknown destination." A helicopter circled overhead, suggesting to them that loyal forces might be approaching. They had heard an order given to most of the rebels to mount the trucks, which drove off, leaving a small force in charge of the prisoners.

Half an hour later, Ambassador Rockwell recounted, "to our great surprise, the King and General Oufkir returned, and the same soldiers who had been carrying on all this bloodshed clapped hands and proclaimed their loyalty to the King."

It was now about 6 P.M., some four hours after the attack. At this time, some two hundred rebels occupied the broadcasting station and the interior ministry. The station broadcast announcements that the monarchy had been overthrown and that a new era had begun.

King Hassan said three rebel generals at the army headquarters beside the interior ministry had called on units in the field to join the rebellion, but they had not only spurned them but began a siege of the area held by the rebels.

Armored troops captured the radio building during the night. This morning, residents saw several hundred dazed young soldiers in fatigues being marched away with their hands on their heads.

Throughout the area today, the royal troops under the command of General Oufkir, the Interior Minister, conducted a house-to-house search marked by occasional bursts of firing. Now and then, two or three prisoners, sometimes stripped of their uniforms, were led away. There were unconfirmed reports that they had been summarily executed.

The last firing was heard about 7 P.M., but King Hassan said his troops were still cleaning out a few pockets of resistance. The market quarter was blocked off.

The King, speaking in French, began his news conference with an expression of regret for the loss of foreign lives and of hope that the incident would lead to a "resurrection" of Morocco. Then, in reply to questions submitted in writing, he talked about the coup with occasional humor and relish.

He said the decisive moments were the accidental killing of General Medbouh, which left the remaining "pawns" in panic, and the remorse of the lieutenant who was guarding him.

I read this last paragraph twice and still could not make sense out of it. Why was Medbouh giving orders, and what was this "remorse" all about? I read on:

Earlier he said: "General Medbouh came to me with a dagger in a daze and said, 'Follow me, I'll save you.' I said there was no need.

"These people were drugged," the King said. He said that their gestures were jerky and their eyes staring and they sweated profusely. He added that a flask of an unknown liquid had been found on each of them.

"It's a *coup d'état à la libyenne,* with all that that implies in imperfections, shortcomings, and all that is infantile," he said. "They took the radio out, but not the post office, they took the interior ministry, but not the state security department, Rabat radio but not Tangier radio."

"It was," he repeated, "a Libyan-style coup typical of an undeveloped country." He jested that he himself had neglected to take out war-risk insurance on his person.

The King indicated that the special powers given General Oufkir were only "transitory" and a case, he added in English, of "the right man in the right place."

The *New York Times* continued on the same page with the following:

LIBYA AGAIN BACKS REBELS, Special to the New York Times. BEIRUT, LEBANON, July 11—Libya today continued to extend support to the rebels who yesterday tried to assassinate King Hassan.

The Tripoli radio, monitored here, said this evening that Libya "has dedicated itself to helping the revolutionary tide in the Arab world against reaction and feudalism."

Arab diplomatic sources here believe a serious crisis is building up between Libya and Morocco.

In another paper I read that Malcolm Forbes had been in the palace when the shooting broke out. Forbes said that at first he had also thought the noise was firecrackers, but that a Moroccan who accompanied him had realized it was gunfire and grabbed a chair, using it to break a window through which they had escaped to the golf course. In short time, however, they had been apprehended by soldiers and led back to the palace. As they were being led there, Mr. Forbes said that they saw many dead bodies in the patio, and he felt certain that they too were going to be executed.

I rubbed my eyes, distressed and incredulous. Hearing about the slaughter of the innocent guests made me nauseated: I was disgusted with myself for not having foreseen the imminence of the coup, for feeling smugly satisfied only hours before when I had landed in Washington, thinking my mission was accomplished and neatly laid to rest.

It was frustrating, too, that so many things still didn't add up. Casey had mentioned to me when we'd spoken on the phone Sunday afternoon that the reports we'd be getting from Morocco would be the "official" ones, and the real story wouldn't surface for a while, if ever. I wondered now which officers besides Colonel Ababou had been involved in orchestrating the coup.

As I was dressing to go to the debriefing, I listened to the radio, hoping for a further update. While I was rummaging through my suitcase for stockings, it came. It made everything leap into focus. I sat down on the edge of my bed with my stockings in my hand and stared at the instrument as if it were the person speaking.

"And this just in from Rabat: Our sources have revealed that the leader of the recent coup attempt in Morocco against King Hassan has been identified as General Mohammed Medbouh. The General apparently masterminded and directed the entire plan to assassinate the King. He was accidentally shot and killed by his own men as he left the King's hiding place, where he had gone to negotiate with Hassan. Lieutenant Colonel Ababou, heretofore believed the sole leader and instigator of the rebellion, had already left for Rabat, thinking that Medbouh had succeeded in capturing the King. With no further instructions from either of their leaders, the troops disbanded in confusion."

There was no time to call Morocco again: I would be late for the meeting if I didn't leave immediately. I arranged my chignon, hardly seeing my reflection in the mirror. Medbouh! That handsome, charming, interesting man! He had been the one, the whole time. How had he organized the coup, and with the help of whom? Was Moustapha involved? Had Medbouh ordered Rachid's death? What about our accidents, the tent pole, and the brakes of our car? And if Fatima had really had an affair with Medbouh, as Salima claimed, then did she have any suspicion about the coup? And what had really happened when Medbouh and King Hassan met that last time?

I left for the debriefing with my mind in hopeless confusion.

Chapter 22

Jupiter had decided that it would be more convenient for me to stay near the safe house while I was taking part in Serge's debriefing, and two of his men were in the lobby to take me to a motel in Tysons Corner, Virginia. We drove the forty-five minutes in silence and after checking in I went with them to the safe house, which was about ten minutes away from the motel.

We entered the narrow cobblestone path which wound through a thick forest of green trees and ended in front of a small, unimpressive brown stucco house with gray shingles. To one side, near the small garage, stood a shabby delivery van of ancient vintage, and parked in front was a blue Ford. Nothing about the house or the entrance would attract attention.

As I climbed the steps, Jupiter opened the door and grinned at me. "Well, Aline," he said as I reached the top step, "you made it. Good girl." He took my hand, patted my shoulder, and he pulled me into the room. A smiling Serge was walking toward me, his hand outstretched. For a few minutes the excitement of finding myself with the two men who had consumed my thoughts during the past months made me forget my preoccupations about the Moroccan coup.

Jupiter motioned for me to sit down on the sofa. One of the men called from the small kitchen, "You guys want some coffee?" An affirmative rang back and then we settled ourselves comfortably, Serge and Jupiter in two armchairs and I on the sofa. Two men who had been in a back room came in. Jupiter introduced me to Rob and Jim, and then they pulled up straight chairs and joined our little group.

Serge was the first to bring up the coup. "What do you think of that attempt to kill King Hassan?" His face had taken on a somber expression.

I almost shot my question at him: "Didn't you know this was going to happen so soon?"

Jupiter turned on the recorder that was on the table nearby. I reminded myself to curb my impetuosity in the future.

Serge looked more ill-at-ease than I had ever seen him, and I regretted having been so abrupt.

"No, I had no knowledge of the timing of the coup. In fact," he said, "we weren't in on all the secrets of the people behind it, not by any means. Our principal contacts worked through the Libyans, whom we supported in many covert actions, often without knowing the whole story."

"At least we know the King is safe and that he's placed General Oufkir in charge of things for the time being," interrupted Jupiter. "There'll be plenty of time to fit the pieces of the Moroccan *putsch* together. Right now we should talk about other subjects." He turned to Serge. "Do you know, Mr. Lebedev, anything on any topic that you think should be reported immediately to the policymakers of the United States government? I assume that someone has already asked you that question but I must be sure."

Serge paused to think and then said, "You mean for example that the Soviet Union will attack day after tomorrow, or that Henry Kissinger is selling secrets to Moscow?"

Jupiter nodded and grinned.

"Well," Serge went on, "in that kind of case, no. But I do know a lot about how Soviet policy is made, how information is used in the Soviet system, and of course, a lot about who supplies that information, at least from North Africa."

Again Jupiter interrupted. "The identity of KGB spies in the West, and those not connected with the plot and King Hassan's government, can wait."

I understood. No matter how much Jupiter might trust me, the code of the professional involves not revealing information on subjects like the identity of spies, either theirs or ours, to anyone who does not need to know. Serge understood, too. He stopped cold on that topic and waited for Jupiter to continue.

"Where do you think we can find Michel de Bonville?" he asked. "Any chance he'll return to Morocco to make more trouble?"

"No," Serge answered. "Once he saw that I was against him—and of course when he learned that I had defected—he would not dare return to Rabat. He knows that his game is up there. He'll be heading for Moscow. He'll assume that the DST [the French equivalent of the FBI] will be looking for him. Bonville is not dead. He'll show up again with a different name and history, maybe in some place like Quebec. If he's ever sent to Paris again, he'd have to change everything, even his appearance. Of course he'll use my defection as his excuse for his cover being blown. He's not apt to recount to his superiors his failure with you, at least not how it happened. He probably had to remain in Madrid for several days." He smiled. "After Aline jammed on the brakes and he smashed his head into her windshield, and I squashed her car from the rear, plus a few little things I added, Monsieur de Bonville was in no condition to travel."

The fellow called Rob came in and put a cup of coffee in front of each of us, but Serge left his untouched and continued speaking. "If you'd like to know more about Bonville, he was born Mikhail Almatov." Serge sat back in his chair, warming to the topic. "An only child," he went on, "in a poor section of Moscow. His father was a drunk and a wife-beater, too, who could not hold a job and survived by making illegal vodka in his apartment, but consumed most of the profits.

"In a drunken rage one night, his father strangled his wife. The neighbors called the police, who dragged him off to jail. Realizing he'd be sent to an orphanage, Mikhail, although only ten years old, escaped to the streets, where he survived by his wits, stealing, delivering drugs, selling black-market goods."

I think Serge was flattered by our undivided attention. He paused. "Do you really want me to go into such detail?" he asked. "You see, I was the one asked to prepare Mikhail's case history for the KGB files, so I know it well."

Jupiter nodded assent and Rob stacked a few tapes on the table next to the recorder. "On a street corner near the KGB head-quarters," Serge continued, "Mikhail made a black-market sale of a cake of Palmolive soap to an expert Soviet cryptologist called Vladimir Noginsky. Noginsky was attracted by the boy's alert good looks and seeming intelligence." Serge nodded. "I've had long talks with Noginsky about this. He told me the boy reminded him of his only son, who had been killed with his young wife in the defense of Stalingrad in World War Two. Vladimir asked young Mikhail to procure some Gillette razor blades, which the kid did, though the price was exorbitant. After that, Mikhail never failed to find what Vladimir wanted, but always for a high price. Repeatedly impressed by the child's intelligence, one day he asked the boy to put together a good picnic, which Vladimir would pay for, and to join him in Gorky Park to enjoy it the following Sunday. Caviar, smoked salmon, Norwegian dark bread, Danish Tuborg beer, and a Coke along with dessert comprised the picnic. As Vladimir was eating his Sacher Torte, he realized that the food was the most sumptuous he had consumed in a long time, and when presented the bill by Mikhail, the most expensive. Vladimir, expecting to spend a pleasant afternoon in the park, had brought several books along, which Mikhail regarded enviously. When asked if he cared to borrow one, Mikhail could hardly restrain his delight. The boy confessed that he loved to read anything that he could find or steal. Vladimir began to lend the boy all the books he wanted.

"After several months, Vladimir noticed that Mikhail appeared wan and thin. He confessed that he was spending so much time reading that he had little time for racketeering and that his eating had suffered. Vladimir made the decision that he had been mulling over in his mind for months. He suggested that Mikhail come live with him. He would put a small cot in his little library. For the privilege, Mikhail would clean the small apartment and buy and cook the food. Vladimir laughed when he told me this, because he said the boy did not really want to come to live with him, and only agreed to do so when Vladimir told him he would have access to his library.

"Vladimir went with the boy to retrieve his meager belongings. He was curious to see how the boy had survived. They entered the crumbling foundations of an abandoned building and climbed down a rickety staircase into total darkness. Groping about, Mikhail found a match and lit the stub of a candle. Followed by Vladimir, both on hands and knees, they squeezed through a small opening and came into a tiny room created by a fault in the foundation. There was no light, but by the glimmer of the candle, Vladimir could see a pile of filthy blankets. The room surprised him, because it was warm, and then he realized that he was standing on top of a steam pipe. Mikhail crawled across the small space, carefully removed a small concrete block, reached behind it, and retrieved three small silver spoons—his worldly possessions.

"The routine improved at the apartment. Vladimir awoke to the aroma of real coffee, ate a delicious breakfast, usually sliced bread and butter and jam. He never asked Mikhail how he procured such delicacies considering the meager allowance he gave him for supplies. He left for the KGB office with Mikhail reading, and when he returned that evening, it seemed that Mikhail had not moved, but dinner was ready. While the two ate, they discussed Mikhail's reading of the day. The boy was fascinated by stories of reincarnation, fables about the Goddess of Prophecy, Cassandra. He loved novels which involved fortune-tellers, and began to believe in transphysical science. Vladimir, being a cryptologist, belonged to the world of cold, hard facts, and he said that the two used to argue for hours, but he could never convince the boy that the world of metaphysics was nonsense. He felt that Mikhail had undergone such a brutal physical childhood that, psychologically, he sought refuge in mysticism."

My mind flashed to Michel's fabrication of his early life in Alsace-Lorraine during World War II, and the emphasis on the two fortune-tellers, also his distressed reaction after seeing the soothsayer in Marrakech. What had she told him?

Serge went on: "They watched the TV news and shared comments, both from the daily newspapers and the TV news. Vladimir himself was an outstanding scholar and linguist. His favorite language was French; he started to speak to Mikhail in French. The boy picked up the language with an astonishing facility.

"Vladimir decided to adopt the boy in order to enter him into

Moscow's best school, available only to children of members of the Communist Party elite, senior KGB officers, and their ilk. He urged Mikhail to concentrate on French, which he felt might provide the child with a good future. When the boy became proficient in the language, he gave him books from the library he had compiled while serving eight years as an expert on codes at the Soviet Residency in Paris. Mikhail started to read Voltaire, Rousseau, Proust, Balzac, and other French classics, becoming familiar with French customs and thought. The school soon became aware that Mikhail was an outstanding student, not only in languages, but in whatever he put his mind to.

"When he reached the proper age, he entered the Institute for Foreign Languages. Though Vladimir and Mikhail had been living together for some eight years now, there was no communal bond of affection between the two. But there was respect. Though Vladimir had adopted Mikhail, he had not replaced his lost son, as he had hoped. He found himself wishing for Mikhail to move on, and recommended him as a candidate for the KGB's program to prepare 'illegal' officers for service abroad.

"His wish came true when Mikhail was recruited by the KGB. The young man packed his few belongings; there was a formal handshake and farewell, and the two parted for life." Serge changed his tone. "Vladimir did not seem to be much affected by the young Mikhail's moving. I found that strange— since he had lived with the boy for so long. When I asked, he said that Mikhail was not a person anyone could get close to. Maybe it was the home life the child had had, or losing his mother in such a way. I always felt that coldness from Mikhail, as well. It amazed me that the women he seduced did not miss the warmth that usually goes with physical relationships. They certainly did not get that from Mikhail.

"Would you like to know more?" Serge asked.

"By all means," insisted Jupiter. "Aline wouldn't let you stop, anyway."

"Well," Serge went on, "Mikhail was intrigued by his new life. The wide diversity of his experience made him a unique candidate for the KGB First Chief Directorate. When it came to hand weapons, deception, falsification, subterfuge, knives, guns, his years surviving on the Moscow streets had given him a huge head start. He astonished the linguistic department by his French and his knowledge of French literature and culture. He took to the training of the illegals program with great interest—that involves a long assignment abroad, posing as somebody from a Western country. He was assessed as perhaps the best young KGB spy ever trained. Besides, he was lean and handsome, with a sense of humor which belied his killer training.

"His only weakness was his attraction for the opposite sex, which was keenly reciprocated. He had several affairs with KGB women, but later on he had assignments to pick up wives of specific Western officials who might have knowledge useful to the Soviet Union. He often helped the KGB obtain photographs for blackmailing, and as a result he quickly gained the reputation as the KGB Don Juan, which stimulated his ego. His success was spectacular, but he had a cynical opinion of women, especially Western women, regarding them as mere sexual playthings for his own physical desires. It amused him to play one woman against the other. There was no thought of love or respect, just the amusement of physical pleasure.

"His superiors saw that he was ideally suited for work as an illegal agent in France, and with great care, a credible case history was prepared for him, which he adopted to perfection. In some way, the improvised childhood during the war in Alsace-Lorraine was similar to his experiences near the front lines in Russia during World War Two.

"After two years of *stazhifouka* in France, establishing himself and his cover, learning how to be a perfect Frenchman, he was sent to Rabat.

"Mikhail did not take long to discover that the two most attractive women with the best connections in Morocco were Fatima and Salima, and he was soon on intimate terms with both—thanks, in part, to you, Aline." I sighed. "His preference was Fatima, who was the first woman he discovered who could match his sensual pleasure. Her sexuality was incredible; we saw that by the erotic dance she performed at her uncle's palace. She came to exert a surprising influence on him, but her jealousy over his attentions to her sister was a constant problem."

What Serge had just said about my friend Fatima shocked me.

Salima had intimated that her sister had been Medbouh's mistress, and I suspected her relationship with Michel—two traitors. Could Fatima have been involved in the coup, too?

Serge breathed deeply. "That's about it. The rest you know too well." No one said anything for a moment. Jupiter changed the tape in the recorder and asked Serge what he knew about Moustapha Benayad. Serge's answer startled me.

"He had nothing to do with the coup. His interest was only in getting paid by either side for any information he could pick up. In fact, I always suspected him of being loyal to Rachid and the Moroccan government. Otherwise how would he get his stuff in the censored press? It created a great cover to enable him to work for us—and to pick up useful information for the Moroccans at the same time. If he had known about the coup, Moustapha would probably have gone to Rachid with the information—if Rachid paid enough. I always felt that Moustapha was unbalanced, brilliant but crazy—he loved those two damn knives he always carried. He would gleefully relate how many times in fights he had dropped his knife and pleaded for mercy. When his opponent would bend over to retrieve the knife, he would draw the second one and cut his throat."

Jupiter finally asked Serge if he knew of General Medbouh's disloyalty to the King.

"I didn't know, nor did anyone, I believe, outside of the tight little circle of plotters. When I saw the television and heard the radio reports about Medbouh being the top man, I was as surprised as anyone else. It must have been a shock for the King to learn that the trusted head of his military guard had been plotting against him."

We spent several hours that first day with Serge. Later, about three o'clock, as Jupiter and I left the safe house, he told me that I might hear from a friend that evening. At the hotel I found a note from Bill Casey asking me to join him and Sophia for dinner. At dinner Bill wanted to hear all about the coup attempt—who was involved, who was caught, and who might have escaped detection. After I had carefully reviewed all I knew, he was silent for a moment. Then he said, "Something doesn't make sense to me. General Medbouh doesn't sound like the right man to be the mastermind of the plot. His post does not give him enough power or influence over enough men. I've also learned that when there is a seed of political unrest in the bowels of a government, there is usually a bigger shark than Medbouh involved." He puffed out his cheeks and turned his lips down in the pouting expression he often wore when thinking a problem through. Then he said, "It's not over, Aline. I'll bet that we still are going to see another act of this drama."

Meditatively, he drew on his cigar and blew a few smoke rings in the air. I interrupted his reveries. "How about telling me the story about Moustapha Benayad in World War Two in Algiers? Do you believe Serge's analysis of him, that he plays both sides and is too paranoid to be trusted?"

"Yes, I do. Fellows like that have a tendency to be mixed up in crooked deals. When you hear his story, you can decide for yourself."

Sophia got up to refresh our drinks. "You'd better have another one, Aline. Bill, too. When he gets started on war tales"—she gave me her wonderful warm smile—"sometimes they're longer than the war."

Bill swirled the ice in his glass. When he began to speak, his slow mumble was barely audible. "Remember those drops our agents made behind enemy lines in southern France?"

I nodded. One of the OSS Madrid jobs had been to prepare information about safe spots for these sabotage experts to land. They were dropped from planes flying out of Algiers on nights with a full moon. That light, although meager, was necessary for the small aircraft to spot the improvised landing areas. Then the parachutists, if they had landed safely, would set up radio contact with us in Madrid. Sometimes I went to the radio-transmitter room in our Madrid office to watch our radioman trying to receive a contact from an agent who had been dropped that very night. Most times there were shouts of joy as the Morse Code contact came clicking in. However, despite hours of frantic effort by our radio operator tuning and retuning his dials, sometimes no message was received, which meant that the fellow had been picked up by the enemy instead of friends, a trap sometimes deliberately set up by traitors.

Slowly, Bill shook the gray cigar ash into the ashtray. "To make a long story short," he said, "Ali, being an Algerian national, was able to move to and from France, and he set up some landing spots for us. We had a great guy called Jack Crackton who'd waited the longest time in Algiers before we had what we believed to be a reliable landing setup. But the poor guy had the bad luck of falling into a trap. He was caught and tortured. Suspicions fell upon Ali, but he was well prepared to defend himself. It was not until after the war ended that friends in the *maquis* let us know that he'd been the one responsible, not only for Jack Crackton, but for several others who were captured as well. While being paid by us, the bastard was on the German payroll. Yes, he's a betrayer by nature, and to make money, he would lie, cheat, kill, whatever. He certainly could be mixed up in this murky affair. How far, it's hard to tell. Serge may be right; I wouldn't trust the son of a bitch to bring me the evening paper."

That night from the motel, I telephoned Fatima for the first time; she had been out when I had called on Sunday. Jupiter was anxious to hear anything that she might say about the coup, and I had prepared a logical excuse for why I was in the United States to give her: a niece's wedding, which was in part true. Now aware of Fatima's intimate relationship with two traitors, I had to concentrate on keeping my voice warm and casual. We discussed the coup, but she had nothing new that we did not already know. But just before hanging up she said, "You may be interested to know that among those who were killed was that young officer who was assigned to you and Luis during your trip."

"Not Omar Khalil?" I asked. Suddenly his warm smile as he used to open the car door flashed before me.

"Yes, that was his name. You might say he committed suicide in his loyalty to the King. When the insurgents attacked, Omar drew his sidearm, advanced toward them, and started shooting. His body was practically destroyed in a hail of gunfire." She talked about other victims whom we had both known. I was so upset about Omar that I paid little heed to the names she mentioned. What would happen to his pretty new bride, and his other wives? She went on to say that everyone was pleased that the King had placed a man as reliable as General Oufkir in charge of the country. I wondered what Fatima's reaction would be if she knew Michel had tried to kill me. She did not mention Salima, and I refrained from bringing her name up. Nor did she mention Serge. I realized that the KGB would have covered up his disappearance, and fortunately no mention of his defection had appeared in the press.

For the next two days I remained in the motel and took part daily in the debriefing. I was particularly anxious to ask Serge if he knew why attempts had been made to kill me. Serge seemed to have been thinking about this, as well. "Michel wanted to eliminate you because he thought you had uncovered him. The day after the automobile accident I confronted Michel and he swore he had nothing to do with it. And later I discovered that certain cars had been changed that particular day."

"What do you mean?" I asked.

"Well, that last day in Marrakech, when we were getting ready to drive back to Rabat after Rachid had had that accident, I put my own bags in the trunk of my car instead of waiting for the driver as was the usual custom during our tour. When I arrived in Rabat, my bags were not in the trunk. I knew they had to be, because I had placed them there myself. After much telephoning and questioning, it turned out that my luggage was in another car. I had concentrated on the license numbers to distinguish mine from the others. Remember they were all alike? All black Mercedes?"

I nodded.

"Through that mixup I found out that some of those Mercedes had been changed during the trip, because now and then one broke down. And I suspect that the car you were riding in the day of the accident could have been a car destined for someone else."

"Why?"

"Because in searching for my bags, my driver discovered them in your car—which had previously been Rachid's car. I know, because I was driving with him." Serge lit a cigarette. "At any rate, when I found that out, I began to realize that whoever the coup leader was might very well have had Rachid or someone else in mind for elimination and not you."

"I'm beginning to feel like a fool," I said. "I was almost hysterical about someone trying to kill me during that trip." I took the cigarette Serge offered me. "What you say makes me remember that Rachid was the one who was supposed to occupy the seat next to me in the tent that day."

Jupiter broke in. "I've often told you, Aline, that we never know all the answers. You may be right, you may be wrong."

One morning, almost my last day of the debriefing, I arrived a bit late. When I sat down, Serge was sweating and looking unhappy. Jupiter was absent and a man who called himself Mr. Roberts was in charge. Roberts was going back over all the events in Serge's life, or so it seemed to me, implying that there were contradictions in some places and that Serge was withholding information. Serge looked at me frequently, in a mute appeal for support. Sometimes all he would say was that what happened, happened, whether it seemed probable or not to an American who had never lived in the Soviet Union. I felt a strong sense of sympathy for him, but tried to keep a cold, impersonal expression on my face. I knew that if Roberts came to suspect that I was moved by Serge's protests, he would discount my opinion of Serge's statements as the emotions of a flighty woman at seeing a man under pressure. By keeping calm and even joining in on some of the questioning, I knew I would be more able to influence Roberts to accept what Serge had said.

Roberts proceeded to ask details about the Moroccans Serge knew, and other Soviets serving in Rabat and Algiers. On most of the questions, Serge appeared ready to tell all he knew, even the seamy details of their personal lives. But there were times when he simply said no. Roberts became exasperated. One of the Soviets who piqued his curiosity was the secretary to the Ambassador to Morocco. Serge realized that Roberts was searching for information that might make people vulnerable to recruitment as spies. These ranged from indications of a concealed moral or ideological rejection of the Soviet system, to accounts of acts that might be used for blackmail, whether or not they opposed the Communist Party—drunkenness, extramarital sex, homosexuality, theft, embezzlement of government funds by padding expense accounts, or taking kickbacks. With this particular woman, however, Serge made the mistake of saying she was a very good, decent person.

"Ah ha," Roberts cried. "You think she really hates the system?"

"She's not a hating person," replied Serge. "She isn't the kind who hates people, no matter what they do or believe."

"But tell me," Roberts asked. "Does she have a boyfriend on the embassy staff? Does she know any Moroccans?"

I could see Serge become tense. "I don't know," he answered.

"What do you mean, you don't know? You must know. Hell, you knew everybody there, and this woman was a friend of your wife's, wasn't she?"

"I don't know," Serge said.

"Don't know or won't tell?" Roberts countered.

"Take your pick."

"I thought you were on our side, guy," said Roberts.

"I didn't change sides to exploit the innocent," Serge shot back. "I left because I'm fed up with the morals of the KGB— and I won't adopt them here. If you bastards want to play games with their bastards, I'll help you out. But keep your hands off those who aren't part of the game."

"You're calling me a bastard!" Roberts shouted, rising from his chair.

Serge got up, too. I had to do something to cut this off. I jumped up and asked, as coolly as possible, "Are you two starting World War Three?" They looked at each other and realized that they were behaving like little boys—both looked sheepish. "Let's call it a day, it's late," I said. We left Serge at the safe house; on the way to the motel Roberts admitted that he'd gone too far. Jupiter, who was waiting for us to report anything new, thanked me for saving the situation.

The next day, just before lunch, I was alone with Serge. He told me that the woman in question was his dead wife's best friend, a single woman who was the sole support for a child and her mother back in Moscow. He would do nothing, he said, to subject her to any risk or to encourage an attempt to recruit her, even if she were the most dedicated anti-Communist in the USSR. "Some people you don't touch. You know that, Aline. Sometimes you can be too professional, too cold and calculating. Do that and you don't defeat the enemy, you join him."

Chapter 23

S ometime during the first days of 1972, I received a letter that brought back the preceding spring all of a sudden— memories of Morocco, the picturesque scenes, the interesting people, the exotic seduction of Marrakech—and also the fear and the tension.

"Dear Aline," it began, "I am marrying Ahmed in April, and we would like you to attend our wedding!" It was from Salima. A formal invitation followed. The wedding was to last six days, but she said the most important ceremonies would be on the third, fourth, and fifth days, when there were parties at the houses of the bride and groom. I decided to go, though Luis could not accompany me. In addition to the wedding, I wanted to pick up a gold and emerald bracelet which Fatima had designed for me. She was frequently in Paris now, overseeing the opening of her boutique there, so she came less to Madrid than before and had not been able to deliver the piece.

I arrived in the midst of the wedding celebrations on the second day. The evening sky was cloudless and blue, just as it had been in Spain, but the Moroccan sky stretched out, embracing the sea. On the horizon, graceful lavender-and-rose clouds moved like gossamer in the breeze. As the car took me to Fatima's, we passed her father's house, where the party was to be held the following day. Bright images of the previous spring crowded my head: Rachid's wise, bearded face deep in the hood of his djellaba, Fatima's dance, Ahmed's goat mask in the souk.

I was pleased to be back, but also curious to see how the coup had affected my friends.

When I arrived, a manservant took my luggage and led me through a wide corridor to a guest room, where a smiling young maid in white bandanna and pale yellow, soft cotton djellaba was waiting to unpack my things. She welcomed me in French and made a small curtsy. Then, in a soft voice, she explained that Fatima was due home soon and that Salima had just arrived at the house to greet me. While she began to hang up my dresses, she told me that there had been a small wedding party that day, a henna party for the bride and her family and close friends, during which the bride's hands and feet had been painted a lovely reddish tone with henna powder. I knew that hands dyed with henna were considered more beautiful, and that the color lasted for weeks, until the dye washed off.

Through the open door to the garden a steaming pot of mint tea, and cookies, awaited on a table on the small terrace. I was sipping my tea and admiring the cascading fountain in the middle of the garden when I heard a door in the house open and close. A moment later quick, light footsteps sounded along the marble floor of the hallway. Then there was a crash. Someone had dropped something on the floor outside my room. Then a distraught Salima burst through the open door, holding up to me two pieces of green pottery. "Aline," she called, "I've just broken this little vase that came this morning. This is terrible! It means bad luck." She placed the broken parts carefully on the table and turned to embrace me. "Oh, it's so good to see you. I'm so glad you've come to my wedding. Let me show you what the artist did today at my henna party."

She held out her palms. They had been painstakingly designed in intricate patterns in red henna dye. "What a fascinating custom," I said.

But she was still thinking about the vase. She picked up one of the pieces and said, "Do you think it can be mended?"

I took both pieces in my hand and placed them together. "It looks to me as if they can be glued," I said.

"This is a lovely little Roman vase with the design of a fish carved around it," she said. "Many centuries old." Salima sighed. "I was bringing it with me to show you, and I tripped over that horrible rug in the hallway. The gift arrived this morning, without a card, but I'm sure Ahmed sent it as a surprise. He was in Rome this winter. He'll be so upset—what will I say to him?"

She had never looked lovelier, and to take her mind off the vase, I told her so. She smiled. "That's because I'm so happy, Aline." Her huge eyes gave off sparks. "Who would have thought a year ago that I'd marry Ahmed? Suddenly everything seems right—Fatima and I are friends, my father is pleased, and I am marrying the most wonderful man I could ever have hoped for. That whole nightmare of Michel seems like a lifetime ago."

"But he's gone now, out of your life," I said.

"That disgusting, vile man," she replied, with real venom. I was too startled to say anything. "To think that I ever let such a snake touch me—it makes me shudder. I hate him. I still can't bear to talk about him."

"Then let's not," I said. "Let's talk about your wedding."

"All right," she said, and tried to calm herself. On the first day of the wedding, as was the Moroccan custom, there had been a bridal party for women only. They had all undergone a purification ritual in the *hammon,* or pool, at her father's palace. A women's orchestra consisting of drums, castanets, and flutes played all the afternoon, while relatives and close friends had accompanied her into the sauna, where they had been massaged with traditional powders, and then they had gone with her to the large *hammon.* Meanwhile the rest of the party was enjoying the banquet and the music. "We had such fun talking and laughing," Salima went on. "And today, the henna party."

"It sounds fascinating," I said. "Western weddings are so simple in comparison. What will happen tomorrow?"

"Tomorrow night and the next day are the official ceremonies," she said. "There's a party at Ahmed's house, and at the same time one at mine, and then at midnight Ahmed comes with his musicians and friends to fetch me to his family's house. The party goes on while Ahmed and I are led to our wedding chamber and supposedly left alone. But the guests spend much of the time outside the door teasing us." She laughed and her long-lashed eyes were two slices of deep azure sky on a sunny day. "On the fourth day," she went on, "we hold the final ceremony.

There's a procession—you'll see, it's spectacular—and then the party goes on until dawn. Hundreds of guests attend, and I have so many beautiful new silk kaftans made especially for those two days." Another radiant smile. "The last two days are small parties for our two families only, with lots of good food and more music. This festivity signifies the union of our families, which have now become one."

I looked down involuntarily at the broken vase, which I still held, and her eyes followed mine. Her frown made me realize that she had been reminded of her worry about bad luck on her wedding day.

"Oh, Aline, I'm so glad you're here. I must talk to you. I am worried sick." Her eyes were filled with anxiety. "You see," she began, "I have seen Michel again."

Immediately my thoughts jumped to the day of the races, when Michel had tried to kill me. "When was that?" I asked, trying to sound matter-of-fact. Little could Salima imagine how her mention of Michel affected me.

"About four months ago," she answered, "when I was in Fatima's boutique in Paris looking over some silk brocades for my wedding kaftans. He appeared unexpectedly. What a shock! After almost seven months!"

"What did you say to him?" I asked, wondering how Michel would dare to see someone who knew him and who could tip off the French DST. Would his superiors in the KGB permit such an indiscretion?

"Fatima had gone out for a moment, so I was alone when he came in," she went on. "I said nothing to him then, and I have nothing to say to him now. I suspect that Fatima saw him, too, when she returned." Her voice was hard. "To think that he still lives and breathes—it's enough to make me want to break something."

I lifted the broken vase and we both laughed. Although her tension passed, I had seen that her hatred for Michel matched the intensity of her love a year before. "There's more to the story, but I can't tell you now," Salima said. "Ahmed will be here any minute."

"Then tell me how you and Ahmed became engaged."

"About six months ago, while I was working for Fatima in

Paris, he just came into the shop to say hello. He brought croissants, café-au-lait, and the *Paris-Match*, and we had a French breakfast together, reading the paper and talking. And by the time we'd finished our coffee and discussed the news, I was head over heels in love with him. He made me laugh so hard. He asked me to marry him a month later."

"You must be talking about me," joked Ahmed as he appeared in the doorway and then crossed the threshold into the room. He came to the low, pillowed couches where we sat, and smiled down at Salima. I sensed her panic as she hid the broken vase, which I had placed on the sofa, under a pillow. "I always knew my practical joking would pay off one day." He kissed Salima and sat down. We chatted until it was time for them to drive out to visit Ahmed's grandmother. "She wants to tell Salima all the old family secrets and warn her about my bad character," Ahmed jested as they said goodbye.

Shortly after they had gone, Fatima arrived. She poured herself a glass of tea and collapsed gracefully onto a cushion. "Aline," she said, "your bracelet is going to be sensational. I can't wait to show it to you."

"When will your new collection be ready?" I asked her.

"Soon. I'm going to Paris every month now, seeing to everything. Salima helped me for a while, then she became engaged to Ahmed and I hired a very bright girl to take her place. But I need to go as often as possible, to see that all goes smoothly." She looked a little tired; I noticed new lines around her mouth, and the skin under the black eyes looked smudged. Maybe it was from fatigue, but it looked more like traces of kohl after crying. Her eyes were as bright as ever, though, and she spoke with her characteristic energy. I remembered that Salima had speculated that her sister had seen Michel; I wondered if it were true, but I dared not ask her. I wondered what Jupiter, and Serge too, would say when they heard that Michel had reappeared in Paris. Jupiter would probably order a surveillance team to determine what Michel was doing. I had never talked to Fatima about her affair with Michel. Our friendship had begun with discussions of our husbands and children. I decided to leave it that way.

But I did ask, "Does your husband often go with you to Paris? It's such a romantic city—Luis and I love to go together."

She shook her head. "Raoul and I have different tastes." She sipped her tea and changed the subject. I could see that she didn't want to discuss her marriage or anything to do with romance. "I'm delighted about Salima and Ahmed," she said. "Do you remember when I said they would be perfect for each other, and you teased me about being a matchmaker? Well, I was right, and my little sister is finally going to be happy."

Deliberately I blurted, "Yes, and to think that only a year ago she was engaged to Michel. It all turned out for the best, didn't it?"

Her face darkened but she said only, "Ahmed is far more appropriate. Thanks to Allah, he doesn't know a thing about her past." She leaned back and ran her long red nails nervously along the fat belly of the cushion under her arm. I wondered what flashed through her mind behind that impassive, perfectly made-up face. I felt sorry for Fatima at that moment. In spite of her beauty and wealth, in spite of the rewards of the career she had fashioned for herself, she did not love her husband, which seemed to me a life of such emptiness I could hardly imagine.

Her hand continued to pluck restlessly at the pillow, then went underneath it. She gave a sudden gasp and sat straight up. "What's this?" she cried, pulling a piece of the broken vase from under the cushion. She lifted the pillow and found the other part.

"That's a wedding present Salima says is from Ahmed. Unfortunately she tripped and dropped it and now she doesn't know how to tell him it's broken."

Fatima was looking at the vase with an unreadable expression. "No, it's not from Ahmed," she said, her voice strangled with emotion, hardly aware of what she was saying. "Oh, that despicable, hateful—" She broke off and shrugged, recovering her poise. "Anyway," she continued coolly, "it doesn't matter if she broke it. I'll have it glued back together and she can display it with the other presents." She put the pieces into the pocket of her pale-blue silk kaftan, which she had worn to the wedding party that afternoon. However, I knew she did not wear the traditional Moroccan dress so frequently, now that *Vogue* had complimented her stunning European clothes and referred to her as one of the most chic businesswomen in Paris.

I wondered who could have sent the vase, and how Fatima knew the sender when her sister did not; I assumed that it was from Michel; who else would make Fatima react so violently? Yet for Michel to send such a valuable piece of ancient pottery to Salima at this time did not make sense. I wondered again what Michel would be doing in France. Maybe he intended to return to Morocco. I had to advise Jupiter as soon as possible.

Later that night, after we had all dined together, we went out to sit in the cool night air in the garden. It was a festive, merry group, mostly young people, friends of the bride and groom, and we sat on the low benches in the garden. Lanterns had been lit here and there; the warm yellow flames danced in the night breeze, and shadows spilled onto shrubs and walkways. The light fell on faces, making them bloom out of the darkness like flowers. Salima and Ahmed were inseparable during the entire evening, giving each other secret, happy smiles, talking and laughing in low, intimate tones.

As soon as Ahmed went inside the house, I walked over to Salima, where she sat on a bench slightly apart from the rest of the group. As I sat down, Salima glanced at me, her face suddenly solemn. "Aline," she murmured, "I went back to get the broken vase and it was gone! Did you take it to your room?"

"No," I said. "I'm surprised Fatima didn't tell you. She's having it glued together. Maybe she wanted to surprise you."

"I couldn't stop worrying about breaking it all evening," she said. "I hate to think that Ahmed's gift was destroyed the day I received it. That's a bad omen." She was truly distressed. "Aline, I wanted to tell you the whole story before, but I couldn't. Something terrible happened in Paris when Michel appeared that day in Fatima's shop, and I can't stop worrying that my wedding still can be spoiled."

I leaned forward so as not to miss a single word.

"At first I didn't even recognize Michel," she began. "He had a beard and long filthy hair, and he was dressed in blue jeans streaked with paint and a torn, dirty cotton shirt. And, can you imagine, he had wire-rimmed glasses." She shook her head. "He looked awful. Not at all the handsome elegant man I had met in Rabat."

Salima looked off into the dark night. For a moment I feared her story was going to stop there, but then her soft low voice began again. "He said he was living on the Left Bank and doing what he had always dreamed of. He said he was painting, and that he hoped to be a world-famous artist one day." Salima looked at me. "Do you know, I never had an inkling that he enjoyed paintings, much less that he could paint."

Salima looked around at those walking nearby and almost whispered. "He said that after seeing me that night in the Moroccan Embassy in Madrid, he decided marrying me would mean my ruin, that my family would disown me, and my father would ruin his business. So instead of playing the hero and explaining that he was going to leave me, he just disappeared, although it meant heartbreak for him."

Salima moved closer; she was trembling. "Then Michel turned dark and almost cruel. He told me that it almost killed him to give me up, and when he read in the Rabat newspaper that I was getting married to someone else, he decided he had to see me again. He grabbed my shoulders and tried to embrace me, there, right in the shop!" Salima shivered. "And when I tried to get away he tightened his grip until it hurt. Then he screamed at me. I can still remember his words. 'Don't try to avoid me, Salima,' he said. 'I can still ruin you. I can tell your Ahmed a thing or two about us. Things a proper old-fashioned Sunni would be devastated to learn about the pure girl he thinks he's marrying. And I will tell him, Salima, if you do not spend one night with me.' "

Salima's voice broke. "What could I do?" she sobbed. "I was trapped."

"Well, did you go with him?" I asked.

"No, I hated him so much, I could hardly bear to look at him." She rubbed her arms as if she were cold. "Why did I ever have anything to do with that man? I was too afraid of him that day to ignore his threat, so I agreed and took the telephone number. He told me to ask for Michel when I called, that all the other artists went by first names in his boardinghouse. But when I did call, to tell him never to contact me, the woman who answered said, 'Michel, Michel who?' I said 'Michel de Bonville,' and she said that there was no one by that name there. When I described him, she told me that was Michel Dupont, but that he was never at home. I didn't leave my name. I haven't heard from him since. It was all so strange, like a bad dream. The way he looked, the different name! But the worry that he could destroy my marriage keeps me awake at night. If I had gone with him, I would have betrayed Ahmed. I can't do that, not even to protect my reputation. But now I know Michel is angry and perhaps somewhat unbalanced. Every day that goes by, I'm more on edge. It's the one thing that's marring my perfect wedding. Even if he told Ahmed about our affair, Ahmed might not believe him. I know that Ahmed would tell me and would believe anything I said, but I don't want to begin our life together with a lie. I would have to tell him the truth." She raised her hands in a gesture of despair.

"Why on earth is Michel still hounding you?" I asked. "Do you believe that he's still so in love that he would carry out his threat?" I remembered the man who had killed himself when Fatima rejected him. Men apparently did strange things for love of these Karam sisters.

"He's evil!" She spat out the words so vehemently that her small nostrils flared and her eyes went dark. "He doesn't need a reason. I hate him, Aline." Although she said this in low tones, the intensity of her voice was almost a scream.

Footsteps were making crunching sounds on the gravel path. I looked into the lights and shadows of the garden. Fatima was approaching. "Salima," she called out. "Is that you?"

"Yes," her sister answered, hastily rubbing the skin under her eyes.

Fatima came close enough to see us both. She sat next to me on the bench so that I was between the two. She seemed to have been about to say something when she called out to her sister, but when she saw that Salima was not alone, she had changed her mind. "It's a lovely night," she said instead.

"Fatima," said Salima, "Aline told me you found my vase. I hid it so Ahmed wouldn't see it. Can it be fixed?"

Fatima coughed, then in a flat voice said, "Yes. I gave it to a pottery expert. He said that the cracks will not even show."

"Thank you!" Salima cried, her relief evident. "It's lovely, isn't it?"

Fatima nodded and the three of us sat in silence. I decided to let the sisters talk in peace, and excused myself and went to my room. It had been a long day and I was tired.

The next morning, before anyone else had stirred, Fatima and I drove to her jewelry studio, a high-ceilinged atelier several kilometers from her house. She seemed preoccupied and drove with both hands tightly on the wheel. We made desultory conversation, chatter about the wedding and Fatima's problems with her decorators for the boutique. She led me into the workshop and closed the door behind us. The little room was filled with boxes of cutting tools, machines for molding and others for pouring metals, sketches of necklaces and bracelets and earrings. She unlocked a drawer in one of the long workbenches and took out a small box. Opening it, she removed the bracelet she was making for me and slipped it onto my wrist.

I gasped aloud with delight. "Fatima," I said, "it's incredibly beautiful. I can hardly believe it!"

She had fashioned a gold vine with emerald grapes that wound and twisted around my wrist as if it were growing there. The brilliant green grapes flashed in the morning sunlight; the rich gold looked molten, encircling my wrist, an incredibly intricate, delicate triple vine with tiny sharp leaves. I gazed at it for a long moment in silence. "You're going to be a great success, Fatima," I said quietly. "I feel very fortunate to have something so beautiful. You're a true artist."

The distance I had felt between us in the car melted away, and I realized that her constraint had been caused by her nervousness. Like any artist she worried before the unveiling of her creations. "I'm so happy that you like it, Aline," she said. "Your praise means a great deal to me. Few people know more about jewels than you."

By the time we returned, the household was awake and preparing for the big day. Guests began arriving at Fatima's parents' palace in the late morning, and the musicians were already tuning their instruments when we walked in. Tables laden with food lined the halls. The atmosphere was festive and exciting. I imagined Ahmed's family, several kilometers away, doing exactly the same thing. Salima entered, dressed in a beautiful rose silk kaftan. I embraced and congratulated her, then complimented her on the stunning gold embroidery and lovely rose color of her dress. "I have three dresses for today," she said, as excited as a child. "This one, and a green one, and a white one. All with hand embroidery that took months to sew."

All day we ate, drank, and talked. People arrived and greeted each other; the musicians played ancient Moroccan music and servants kept long tables stocked with cous-cous, lamb, flaky honey pastries, vegetables, and chicken pastry. Salima changed her dresses throughout the day, and each time she reappeared, she looked lovelier than before. She did a special ceremonial entrance, almost like a dance, something which Fatima told me all brides did. I thought of Salima's reaction to the dance Fatima had done, and although her bridal appearance was chaste and virginal in comparison, it still struck me how much she had changed, to perform a traditional ceremony in public, especially one which represented her acceptance of Morocco and her role as the wife of a traditional Moroccan man.

The sun went down; night came. The party continued, unabated. Shortly after midnight Ahmed, handsome in a white djellaba, appeared with a parade of friends and musicians who swooped down on Salima's party. Then we all went with them to his house, where the party continued until three or four in the morning. Finally, Salima and Ahmed were led up the stairs to a grand suite, with much teasing and laughter. Then everyone drifted away to their own houses and beds, and we all slept until late morning.

The next day was another party at Ahmed's family's house. This was the official ceremony, the showing of the bride. Salima wore an enormous embroidered headdress and rode a float surrounded by attendants. Musicians played and the party went on until almost sunup, at which point we were all so exhausted we could hardly stand.

My plane back to Madrid was at ten the following morning, so I snatched what little sleep I could and awoke at eight. While the maid packed my things, I breakfasted on a small terrace overlooking the garden. Fatima came out to say goodbye, wearing a pale pink djellaba. Her hair was already bound up in a sleek chignon, but her eyes had dark circles under them. She looked exhausted and I realized the wedding had been a strain on her.

"I'm very tired," she said when I asked how she was. "This wedding seems to go on forever. I love the traditional Moroccan customs, but this one comes at a bad time for me. I should be in Paris every minute right now, overseeing my boutique, and this whole week I keep getting telephone calls from the decorators, my assistant, my gem supplier, several department stores interested in my jewelry. My assistant handles as much as she can, but there are so many decisions only I can make." There was something unconvincing in her tone, and I knew this was not what was really bothering her. I took a deep breath and plunged in.

"Fatima," I said firmly, "what was it about the vase that startled you so?" My heart was beating fast—I had never confronted Fatima before.

She looked keenly at me, her eyes cool and appraising. "So you noticed," she said. "I may as well tell you, Aline. I didn't want to bother you with this, but since you asked, I'm glad to have an objective listener." She poured some tea from the pitcher on my tray. "Michel sent it to Salima as a warning to me." The hand that held the tea glass began to tremble. "I don't want Salima to know this, because it would upset her, but he threatened me with exposure of their affair, which would ruin her marriage to Ahmed and bring disgrace on our family. He sent the green vase anonymously, as a warning to me that if I don't give him what he wants, he will send Ahmed a letter describing certain . . . encounters that he had with his new wife."

"What do you have to give him?" I asked, my mind in a whirl. Was he threatening Fatima with exposure to her own husband as well? How did she know the vase was from Michel? And did Fatima know that Michel had threatened Salima also and that she had refused to comply with his demands? Or had she?

"Money, of course," she replied coolly. "He's blackmailing

me. Aline, don't ever breathe a word of this to anyone in my family. They cannot know."

Several things began to make sense now. The trips to Paris, the lines of worry around her eyes, the panic when she saw the vase. "What does the vase mean?" I asked.

"I gave it to him," she answered wearily. "Instead of money, every now and then I buy expensive gifts for him, which he then sells. It looks more innocent."

To whom? I wondered. Fatima had bought her lover valuable trinkets, and he sent one of them to her sister for her wedding as a warning to Fatima that he meant business; this all seemed extremely convoluted. The game Michel was playing was beginning to look darker and darker. I wasn't sure which sister to believe, and which version of the happenings was real, or if any version was even near the truth. I remembered Serge's warning that women would be the downfall of Michel. Instead, at this moment it looked to me as if Michel was going to be the downfall of two women. I decided not to pursue the conversation any further and expressed sympathy to Fatima for this trying situation and for her efforts to protect her sister. Anyway, it was time to leave for the airport. Fatima walked with me to the front door and waved goodbye as my car pulled away.

On the airplane back to Spain, I thought about the beauty of the wedding and how starkly it contrasted with Fatima's secret dealings with Michel. I wondered whether she was protecting her sister or herself. And I worried about the venom with which Salima spoke about Michel; both sisters were still deeply involved with him, to what extent I would probably never know. I decided to give Jerry a message for John Derby as soon as I arrived. Jupiter would be fascinated to learn that Michel de Bonville had surfaced in Paris as Michel Dupont, this time a young painter. As the plane crossed the narrow channel separating Morocco from Spain, I felt a weight lifting from my mind. In a short time I would be home with Luis.

Chapter 24

Four months later, August sixteenth to be exact, after not having seen nor heard from Fatima or Salima since the wedding, I was in my house in Marbella, looking out at the great expanse of the blue Mediterranean. In the distance, the gigantic rock of Gibraltar loomed gray and majestic, and squeezed close to it, jutting up over the sea line, were the two hazy round bumps of Ceuta's mountains, the first view of Morocco's coastline on the northern tip of Africa.

My maid, Maria Luisa, interrupted my reveries. "Señora Condesa, the Marquesa de Villaverde is on the phone."

As I picked up the receiver, Carmen Franco's voice was unusually excited. "Aline, turn on Radio Nacional. There's another coup taking place in Morocco—right now. The commentator is broadcasting tapes of radio messages . . . hurry. It's fascinating."

When I found the station, the Spanish commentator was saying, "At two-thirty this afternoon, three Royal Moroccan Air Force fighters from the Royal Moroccan Air Force base in Kenitra attacked King Hassan's 727 over the Strait of Gibraltar on his return from a trip to Paris, after refueling in Barcelona. The planes were F-5's, supersonic, capable of 925 miles per hour, or Mach 1.4, with a climbing ability of 30,000 feet per minute, a deadly efficient fighting machine. They were fully armed with two 20-millimeter M-39 A-2 cannons capable of firing 280 rounds per minute. We are able to reproduce a tape of messages between the F-5's and the Moroccan air base as well as voices from the King's 727. These transcripts were picked up and taped by a Spanish radio ham in Tangier. Over the original voices in Arabic will be heard the translation in Spanish."

A second later another voice, barely distinguishable over the background of Arabic sounds and airplane engines, came through. "Kenitra tower, this is General Kouera. Freedom Wing Leader and flight are prepared for takeoff."

With a moment's delay, the answering voice could be heard. "Freedom Wing, switch to departure control, maintain runway heading. Cleared for takeoff."

The Spanish commentator interrupted. "The three F-5's started their roll down the runway and were quickly airborne. Meanwhile, King Hassan's 727 was nearing the Strait of Gibraltar, cleared the Spanish coast, and commenced descent to Kenitra, expecting to be on the ground in twelve minutes. At that moment three Moroccan F-5's appeared about 500 hundred feet above the King's plane. We now play the next tape from the rebel plane."

"Kenitra tower, this is Freedom Wing Leader. I have a visual on the target and I'm preparing to attack."

"Roger, Freedom Wing Leader. Good luck."

"Freedom Wing, this is Freedom Leader. Maintain your altitude until further orders."

"Roger, Freedom Leader."

The Spanish commentator interrupted. "At that moment, the lead F-5 peeled off and attacked the King's plane and opened fire, making numerous hits. King Hassan is known to be an experienced pilot, and it is believed that he took over the controls of the 727 personally. The first awareness Rabat Military had of the attack was a radio message from the King's plane that he was hit and landing there, instead of at Kenitra air base, and that the plane would make a low-level, high-speed approach. Our experts tell us that the King probably threw the 727 over on its back, a fighter maneuver called a split-S, a tactic which avoids unloading the surface of the wings, thus preventing a flame-out of the three engines, and placed the engines at maximum thrust while deploying his speed brakes. The three Pratt and Whitney

J-T 8D-7 engines, each capable of 14,000 pounds of thrust, quickly reached the speed of Mach 1 or 750 miles per hour, as the 727 headed straight down. When the King reached the critical point, he had to pull out of the dive to avoid a high-speed stall which would plunge him into the ocean. At that speed there would be no chance of survival. His only hope was to come in as low as possible, a slim chance against an F-5. The attacking F-5 made another pass at the King's plane. We are switching our listeners once more back to the F-5 tape of the rebel pilots' communication with each other."

The Moroccan voice was as taut as a guitar string. "Kenitra tower, this is Freedom Wing. Freedom Wing Leader has bailed out, over . . ."

Answer on tower from Kenitra tower: "Say again, Freedom Wing."

"This is Freedom Wing. Freedom Wing Leader has bailed out: his chute has deployed. He'll land in the water some ten miles off the coast of Rabat."

"Kenitra tower. Freedom Wing—why did Freedom Wing Leader bail out?"

"Freedom Wing to Kenitra tower. No idea. He was on afterburner some time; he might have run out of fuel or had a mechanical problem."

"Kenitra tower to Freedom Wing. Did Freedom Leader destroy the King's plane?"

"Freedom Wing to Kenitra tower. That's a negative. He made two passes. Must have hit it fifty times. The right engine is smoking."

"Kenitra tower to Freedom Wing. The position of the King's plane?"

"Freedom Wing to Kenitra tower. About 500 feet off the water, speed near Mach 1. Why the wings didn't collapse when he did that pullout I'll never know. . . . By Allah, he's heading for the Rabat airport! Over."

"Kenitra tower to Freedom Wing. Follow the King's plane at 10,000 feet and stand by for further orders."

A pause while another tape came on. The Spanish commentator gave the time as 15:00.

"Rabat tower, this is Captain Hashid. His Majesty is at the controls. You should have us in sight. His Majesty will make a high-speed landing on the east runway. We'll exit over the wings. Have all emergency equipment standing by."

The time was announced again, as 15:00:30. "Freedom Wing, Kenitra tower. The position and altitude of the King's plane."

"Kenitra tower, this is Freedom Wing. The King's plane must have come in at around 250 knots, dropped full flaps and wheels, and has touched down on the east runway . . . helluva bit of great flying."

Time announced: 15:01:50: "Kenitra tower to Freedom Wing. Attack the King's plane. He must not escape alive . . . repeat, he must not escape alive."

"Roger, Kenitra."

I was trembling when the report put together by the Spanish radio ended. The commentator announced that there would be a replay two hours later accompanied by further details.

Immediately, I tried to reach Fatima, but the lines to Morocco were busy. Then I telephoned to Moroccan friends vacationing in Marbella, but they hadn't even heard the radio report. When I called back to Carmen, she had no further information either. I was a nervous wreck, calling Jerry in Madrid, trying to reach Jupiter. No one had news. Early the next morning I called all the newspaper dealers. Spanish papers told me more or less what I had heard on the radio and added that the King was safe, but about the middle of the morning, the *New York Times* of Thursday, August 17, carried front-page headlines with more details:

MOROCCAN JETS FIRE ON KING'S AIRLINER

WARPLANES ALSO ATTACK PALACE AND AIRPORT

Moroccan Air Force jets fired on the Boeing 727 carrying King Hassan II as it returned from France today, and later pumped machine-gun and rocket fire into the royal palace and strafed the airport.

The Moroccan King, who survived an attack by an army faction just over a year ago, reportedly stepped unhurt from his plane at Rabat Civil Airport. Loyal troops in full battle gear were reported to have surrounded the military airfield Kenitra, 25 miles north of Rabat, where the apparently rebellious fighter pilots were based. Tonight loyal troops took the field without firing a shot. . . .

It was hard to believe that another coup had taken place. My only sense of relief was in knowing that the King was safe, but I knew there had to be some one person responsible for organizing the coup, and no name had been mentioned. It was also clear to me that it had to be the same person who had prepared the coup the year before, when so many people had been killed at the King's birthday party. General Medbouh and Lieutenant Colonel Ababou had been taking orders from someone. Who? The bitter feeling of having botched my job made me miserable. I knew Jupiter would be desperate that we had all failed so completely. At that moment Jerry called. "I'm planning to go to Malaga tomorrow and would like to see you." The reason for his trip, I presumed, was to discuss the latest happenings. Jupiter had probably told him that it was more urgent than ever to uncover the leader, and he wanted to convince me to return to Morocco.

Luis had learned the news only a few minutes after I had, and had read the papers with the same astonishment. Both of us had taken for granted that the most important news of the coup had already been divulged. Therefore I was incredulous when he burst into my room, shoving the *New York Times* before my eyes. On the first page of another edition of the same day, I read, KEY MOROCCO AIDE APPARENT SUICIDE, DEFENSE CHIEF FOUND DEAD AFTER 2ND ATTEMPT ON LIFE OF KING IN 13 MONTHS.

Since I knew that King Hassan had named General Oufkir Defense Minister a year ago, these words told me my friend Oufkir was dead! I could hardly believe it. The most courageous officer in the Moroccan Army and the most powerful! With a heavy heart I continued to read.

RABAT, MOROCCO, Aug. 17— King Hassan II, who yesterday escaped the second attempt on his life in 13 months, lost his principal military supporter early today with the death of Gen. Mohammed Oufkir, the Minister of Defense. Official and unofficial sources concurred that the General had committed suicide.

General Oufkir was found in an undisclosed place with a bullet through his head a few hours after Moroccan Air Force fighters had attempted to shoot down the airliner carrying the King home from a visit to France.

When the attack began, the General was reported to have been swimming at the beach south of here.

Informed sources expressed the view that the General had felt he had failed the King yesterday, as he had in July of last year, when he failed to head off an attack by an army faction in the King's Summer Palace. The General, who was then Interior Minister, was reported to have been on the verge of suicide after that attack.

I continued reading:

Strafing of the airport and terminal caused several injuries, according to the medical report, and cars in the airport were set ablaze. . . .

From an observer at Rabat Airport: "It was only when we saw this thing coming at us with puffs of smoke trailing behind and kicking up dirt in front that we realized something was abnormal."

Luis handed me the Spanish *ABC*, which had a front-page article about the coup. He pointed with his finger to a column: FREEDOM WING LEADER WAS GENERAL KOUERA, WHO WAS PLUCKED FROM THE OCEAN BY THE CREW OF A MOROCCAN NAVAL CRASH BOAT LOYAL TO THE KING.

We looked at each other, shaking our heads; neither of us had ever heard of or met General Kouera. When I finally reached Fatima on the telephone in Casablanca, her voice was almost hysterical. I wanted news of General Oufkir's death, but she hardly heard my question. "Oh, it's awful. This coup has brought a major tragedy to our family, Aline," she sobbed. I could hear strident voices in the background. "Our dear Ahmed was killed. He was in the King's plane."

Her news left me still more stunned. Mental images of Ahmed such a short time ago, so happy at his wedding parties, came back to me. It was hard to believe. "Oh, I'm so sorry," I said. "How is Salima?"

"You can imagine. She's completely demoralized. We're all in mourning. I'll call you when I can, but don't expect to hear from me this week."

It wasn't until Jerry arrived two days later with more American newspapers that I learned the real drama behind the taped radio messages. As soon as I heard his car on our gravel drive, I rushed out to greet him. He was already in the arched doorway of our entrance patio when I got there.

"Why, this is an Arabic palace," Jerry exclaimed, looking at the high, whitewashed walls, the white marble floor, the graceful arches and columns. For a moment he stood there, gazing through the glass walls of the house to the blue Mediterranean beyond, but impatiently I pulled him inside to a low sofa.

"Jerry," I said, "do you remember our friend Abdul, who was murdered a year ago last March? He was the first person who informed us about the possibility of a coup. Well, he's the one who designed everything in this house, inside and out—the cupolas and the minarets, even these things." I pointed to the round gilt metallic table, the rose-colored tea glasses, the silver Oriental teapot. "If you're interested in Moroccan things, I'll show you around later, but now please tell me what you know about the coup—and I hope you haven't forgotten the American newspapers. It's been impossible to get them here the last two days."

Jerry opened his briefcase. "The papers are here." He handed me a stack of clippings with long columns circled in red ink. "You have yesterday and today's papers there. A few details are different from our own version, but you knew the people. I didn't. So you can make up your own mind where the truth lies. Why don't you read them while I look around."

I took the *Times* of August 20 and started to read the headlines: MOROCCAN KING BARES AIDE'S PLOT. The story ran:

RABAT, MOROCCO, Aug. 19— King Hassan II, in a radio and television address to the Moroccan people tonight, ac- cused Gen. Mohammed Oufkir, his right-hand man, of try- ing to kill him.

I glanced up. My astonishment was such I could barely see Jerry, who was walking around the pool and gazing at the sea. Oufkir, a traitor! Oufkir, the ringleader we had been looking for! It was impossible. My heartbeat increased as I began to read again.

The General, he said, had planned to rule Morocco through Crown Prince Sidi Mohammed, who will be 9 years old Monday.

General Oufkir had masterminded a plan to shoot down the plane and make it look like an accident.

Hassan said he had personally interrogated General Kouera El-Quafi, commander of the Kenitra fighter base and one of the pilots. The King said that General Quafi, asked to name who had given him his orders, answered: "It was Oufkir, I have no reason to lie."

The plotters, it was reported, had apparently hoped that the plane would sink without a trace, and then they would announce that it had met with a serious accident. General Oufkir's reputation as a loyal soldier would have remained intact and his control of the regency would have been accepted, according to the alleged plan.

The presence of jet fighters near the Boeing, if discovered, would have been easily explained. The King customarily has an air escort when he enters and leaves Morocco by plane.

The King's brother, Prince Moulay Abdullah, would normally have headed the regency, but he was aboard the plane. He would have had to be replaced by the ruler's next-closest male relative.

Other members of the regency council would be the presiding judge of the Supreme Court, the Speaker of the National Assembly, and seven "personalities," one of whom would have been General Oufkir. He could easily have controlled the others.

Hassan said General Oufkir did not wish to establish a republic. He said no other officer of his rank had been shown to have participated in the plot because Oufkir did not wish to share power.

Of the 1,000 members of the Moroccan Air Force detained yesterday for questioning, all but 33 were reported to have been released. The 33 were said to be in shackles at a detention camp near Kenitra, 25 miles from here.

"That's today's paper," said Jerry, who had just come back in the room and was reading over my shoulder. "You didn't read yesterday's. That has a lot of juicy stuff also."

I shuffled through the stack of clippings and picked up the August 19 *New York Times* and read the outlined column on the front page: MOROCCANS SAY GENERAL, TERMED SUICIDE, LED PLOT. The report went on:

The Minister of the Interior, Dr. Mohammed Ben-Hima, said at a news conference that the General had shot himself three times early yesterday in an anteroom of the King's Summer Palace when he learned that his role in the plot had been discovered.

The charge against General Oufkir, who was quietly buried this morning in his native village high in the Atlas Mountains, came as a shock.

But as many as 1,000 men, a third of Morocco's air force and the bulk of its operational fighter wing, were being detained tonight in the inquiry now proceeding into the reasons for, and the extent of, the latest effort to kill the 43-year-old ruler.

Dr. Ben-Hima indicated that the government felt there were reasons to believe that General Oufkir was also one of the plotters who, in July of last year, launched a bloody assault on the Summer Palace at Skhirat, where the King was celebrating his 42nd birthday. Almost 100 persons died, but the King miraculously escaped.

Five of the Moroccan Army's 17 generals were killed in the fighting and four were executed. Colonels and lesser officials also lost their lives.

Dr. Ben-Hima said at his news conference that it was "painful" for him to recount the events of August 16 because General Oufkir was an old friend.

The Interior Minister said that after the attack began, he worked constantly with the General during the afternoon and evening on matters of security. During this time, he said he did not doubt General Oufkir's loyalty.

But, he went on, one of the plotters, General Kouera El-Quafi, was forced to bail out of his jet when it ran out of fuel, and was captured by the police. General Quafi, the Commander at Kenitra, 25 miles northeast of Rabat, where the fighter force of 23 F-5's is concentrated, was said to have implicated Gen. Oufkir in the plot.

There was much more in the paper. I finished reading and looked up at Jerry. "Well," I said.

He echoed, "Well."

"Now I'll show you our confidential report," Jerry said, taking some sheets of paper from his blazer pocket and waving them in front of my eyes. "But I can tell you more or less what it says."

While I poured the tea, he explained. "When the King landed, miraculously safe, at the Rabat airport of Salé, General Oufkir, who had been on a beach nearby and who had been advised of the attack, arrived at the same time. He advised the King not to go to the palace, but to hide out in the trees near the east runway, since he feared the rebel planes might try to strafe the terminal and maybe the palace too. Luckily the King followed his instructions, because a minute later the F-5's did attack both the airport and the palace. People were wounded and some were killed. But the King was safe. When no further attacks occurred, Oufkir advised the King that it would be safe to go to the palace.

"All this I read in the papers, Jerry," I complained. "Do you have more details that the paper doesn't mention?"

"Don't be impatient," Jerry said. "I'm going to tell you everything we know. Remember, we may be wrong in some things—the newspapers, too." Calmly he lit a cigarette. "The King," he began again, "was naturally furious when he landed. He demanded to know who was behind the coup and requested the names of the rebel officers at the Kenitra air base who had given the orders to shoot at his plane. By this time Oufkir had given orders for the army to surround the base. The King had requested General Kouera, who had been picked up by a government crash boat after he parachuted into the water, to be brought to him so he could interrogate him personally. As the whole murky plot began to unravel piece by piece, the King went from one shock to another." Here Jerry stopped to shake his head. "Hell," he exclaimed, "I'd hate to have been in the King's shoes when he learned who the main traitor was."

"Come on, Jerry," I prodded.

"Be calm. Let's follow the King's reasoning. By now he knew that this attempted coup and the one thirteen months before had been planned by the same person. The rebels, not having succeeded the first time, had decided to try again. The King had to find out once and for all or these coups would continue, and he realized he might not be so lucky the third time." Jerry looked at me. "So this time they had to have no doubts about who the ringleader was. In the other coup, although Medbouh was guilty, it was now obvious that he had been taking orders from someone who was still alive."

I waited impatiently for Jerry to continue.

"After receiving all the bits of intelligence, the King asked an aide to telephone General Oufkir to come to the palace. Oufkir was dining alone at home, and as soon as he received the King's request he donned his uniform and decorations, usual protocol when summoned by His Majesty, and drove to the palace."

Jerry helped himself to a cookie and poured another glass of tea. "We heard from reliable confidential sources," he went on, "that as Oufkir's car stopped inside the palace gates, and as he walked across the empty patio, a woman's voice called out. Our informer said it was easy to recognize the voice of the King's mother. It echoed loudly off the stone walls, loud enough for General Oufkir and anyone else to hear. Our informer said the tone was shrill and filled with animosity." Jerry became melodramatic as he quoted his informer.

" 'Oufkir,' the venomous voice cried out. 'We are tired of you. Tired of you and your tricks.' "

My colleague looked at me for some response. I said nothing, knowing he was arriving at the climax of his story. He, like an actor, carried on. "The General's footsteps resounded in the dark patio without faltering, not the slightest change of pace. Oufkir went up the steps and into the long hallway leading to the King's quarters, which he knew so well."

Jerry stopped for the proper dramatic pause. "And that," he said, "was the last anyone ever saw of General Oufkir alive."

"But what happened?" I asked.

Jerry looked at me and I looked at him, without saying a word. My dismay must have been obvious because he said, "It's a terrible thing, isn't it? I know you admired Oufkir, so of course it's a shock for you. But think of the King! Oufkir was the man he most trusted. To learn that he was the one who had been conspiring against him and plotting his death for several years! That's beyond comprehension."

"Does anyone know how Oufkir died?" I asked. I remembered how kind Oufkir had been when answering Carmen's and my questions about his country's history. None of the other officers had been as solicitous and helpful.

"He was shot. By whom, no one knows. Our informer tells us that when his uniform was recovered, it had three bullet holes in it. One more bullet entered the left trouser leg." Jerry paused. "The strange thing is that all the shots were in the back."

"So he must have turned around to walk away and was shot," I suggested.

"Or," said Jerry, "military personnel could have received orders to have him stand with his back toward his executioners. A deserving death for a traitor, who in no country deserves an honorable death."

"Then the report of the suicide is incorrect?"

"Who knows?" Jerry threw his hands in the air. "I'm only repeating what our informer said. Suicide or not suicide, the man is dead."

My mind jumped back to the accident in the tent, the almost fatal day of the ride along the Todra Gorges. Oufkir must have given those orders. "There are many things I understand now," I said. "For example, in the City of Roses, we were supposed to stay overnight and then were moved on after a heated argument between Oufkir and Rachid. Perhaps Rachid noticed something suspicious and reasoned that it might be dangerous to stay there. Oufkir, who had probably arranged it, wanted the group to remain. I wonder when Rachid became suspicious of Oufkir. Whenever that might have been, he needed proof or the King would never have believed him—and attempting to get that proof may have cost Rachid his life."

"Now we understand why General Oufkir dared to bring a member of the KGB illegally into Spain," Jerry went on. "Oufkir, we now know, was aligned with Libya and leftist causes. He needed favors from the Soviets, like passing on his messages to and from the Libyans to protect his identity with his own people, and had to be solicitous of them. Although I do believe that your Russian defector, Serge Lebedev, told the truth when he said that he didn't know who the leader was of the plot. In fact, I think that Oufkir did a remarkable job of keeping his identity a secret from almost everyone."

"And do you know," I said, "it's possible that no one was trying to kill me or Luis during that trip. It could have been Rachid whom Oufkir wanted to eliminate. Maybe Rachid was about to denounce him. Rachid was the one who was supposed to have sat next to me in the tent that day, not Bill Casey. And I found out days later that our car with the fixed brakes had been changed and could have been originally intended for Rachid."

"Your friend Abdul was right about the coup from the beginning. He must have known that Oufkir was the guilty one, or he probably wouldn't have been killed." Jerry stubbed out his cigarette. "Knowing too much is always dangerous in our business," he said.

Epilogue

Two weeks later Fatima telephoned, saying she would like to spend a few days in Marbella with us on her way to Paris. I was delighted. There were still many unresolved questions related to the recent coup, and probably nobody could fill me in better than Fatima. I assumed that she wanted to get away from the tragic atmosphere at home after Ahmed's death, but she mentioned that there were problems with her new boutique on the Faubourg St.-Honoré and she would have to hasten on to Paris. The Iberia plane from Casablanca to Paris stopped in Malaga, and we sent the car to meet her at the airport.

When she arrived, Luis and I were on the back patio, clipping moonflowers and banana bushes. He went to the door to greet her. "Come." He took her arm. "Let's go out on the terrace and relax while you tell us all about the recent problems in your country." They walked across the salon out to the terrace on the other side and we sat down on beach chairs next to the pool. But Fatima remained standing, looking across the sea to her country. "It looks so peaceful from here, but what horrors we've gone through!" She threw her handbag onto a table and plopped down. "You can't imagine how we're suffering because of poor Ahmed. He was so happy with Salima, and he had such a wonderful future ahead of him. The tragedy has been worse than you can possibly imagine. Ahmed fit so perfectly into our family. My father said that he was the son that he always wanted.

Though others were wounded, he was the only one killed in the King's plane—the only one! Ah, that Oufkir! Who would have believed it? All the unhappiness his ambition has brought about! The King has been magnificent. We are all so proud of his courage and strength."

"And Salima?" I asked.

"She's in despair. No one can console her. They were perfectly matched. My father is in the depths of gloom, too. It seems Salima is doomed to be unhappy." Fatima took a handkerchief from the pocket of her blue blazer and dabbed at her eyes. "We've discussed her situation at home, and even my father thinks it would now be a solution for Salima to move to Paris and take over running my shop. My father has talked to her about this and offered to provide her with a nice apartment there. She can't stay in Morocco, where everything reminds her of Ahmed. Now is when she must have something to occupy her mind. And a job is the only answer."

I asked Fatima what her reaction had been when she learned who had been responsible for the coup.

"Oufkir being the traitor was unbelievable!" she exclaimed indignantly. "A man with such an important post in the government, and so respected. I can still hardly believe it. Just think, all those men dead because of his lust for power. It makes me sick."

Fatima reached over and from her bag removed some newspaper clippings, pointing to one about Ahmed's funeral. "So soon after his wedding," she sobbed again.

The wind started to moan and bluster, echoing our gloomy thoughts. We moved into the house and stretched out Moroccan-style on carpets and banquettes in the salon. The change of scene seemed to raise Fatima's spirits.

Luis asked, "What do you think now about Rachid's accident in the souk?"

"Probably Oufkir was responsible." Fatima shrugged. "He always hated Rachid, so his death had a double advantage for him; he rid himself of a dangerous enemy and an obstacle to his plans for the coup at the same time, because we all believe that Rachid had uncovered him. That Rachid was clever. And when one remembers Oufkir's reputation for cruelty, it's easier to understand that he could have masterminded such things, don't you think?"

"I suppose so. But Oufkir must have been worried from the beginning that Rachid was going to expose him. If, as you told me, Fatima, Rachid was the head of Moroccan intelligence, he was the one person who was most apt to discover Oufkir's plot. Killing Rachid, he must have calculated, was probably the only solution."

She nodded. "And the easiest. However," she said, "Oufkir must have regretted the deaths of men like Medbouh and Ahmed, who had great respect and fondness for him. Medbouh was a traitor and Ahmed was loyal to the King, but they both died because of Oufkir. At least Ahmed died without knowing of Oufkir's treachery."

Luis looked at his watch. "Sorry, I have to go to the art exhibit of a friend at the Hotel Los Monteros. It couldn't be more inconvenient, but"—he raised his hands in the air—"the fellow's the kind of a friend who needs some help."

Fatima and I continued to chat after he left. "I think often of Omar Khalil and his little wife," I said.

"I saw Ayesha just after Omar died. She was inconsolable. Truly, I had never seen anything like it. After all her pretended indifference, she really loved him, and she told me that she had just made up her mind to settle down and to show him how much she cared, when he was killed, and it was too late. So he never knew she loved him, poor man."

"That's too bad," I said. "How did you happen to see her?"

"She was so desolate when he died that she sought me out. Me! I spoke to her on that trip only a few times, but I think she knew I was sympathetic to her, being so young and married to someone she barely knew. I had seen much more of Omar Khalil, a nice man; I liked him. So she came to see me when he died, and what she told me was very touching. She admitted that for the entire three months they were married, she ran him ragged. His other two wives were furious with her. They told him to send her back, that she was disrupting the household, and that she was too irresponsible to look after their children, that she didn't give them the respect they felt they deserved. But meanwhile,

Ayesha said, she was falling in love with Omar, but she was afraid to give him any sign of how she felt because she feared he might lose interest in her and treat her with the same indifference he treated his other wives."

"What did happen to her? And to his other wives?"

"According to our tradition daughters return to their parents if they are widowed, repudiated, or divorced. Ayesha is back with her parents now, in the City of Roses, and since Omar's other wives have children, they are being cared for by his parents. That little family has been split up with the death of its leader, like a tribe that scatters when its chief is killed. It's strange, isn't it, to think of Ayesha's life now—still a little girl and yet she's been through a marriage, and the death of her husband and widowhood, in just three months." She paused. "Anyway, these sad tales of love happen every day. You and I are lucky to be safely and happily married." There was no trace of irony in her voice. I wondered, as I always had, about her marriage to Raoul and her affair with Michel, but Fatima never hinted that such an attachment had existed. Of course I never considered mentioning what I knew.

I continued to scan the newspaper articles Fatima had handed me, and paused when I saw one with the despicable Moustapha's by-line. After all the unhappiness and the deaths of so many fine men, this amoral scum of a human being had survived. It's so unfair, I thought, but that's the way life is. As I read it, I realized that perhaps it was the clearest version yet of the coup.

"What about Moustapha Benayad?" I asked.

"As you can see, since the coup he's become pro-monarchy and writes more columns than ever—all conservative, all praising the King and his industrialization of Morocco's resources promoted by Western financing."

How ironic, I mused, as I remembered how Bill Casey and I believed Moustapha was involved in the coup. Well, I reasoned, like a jackal he had probably covered his tracks cleverly. He might not have played an important enough role to get caught, but he was still a hypocrite giving his worthless loyalty to whoever was in power.

The next day, during a walk on the beach with Fatima, I brought up Michel de Bonville's name. I wanted to know if she would confess to having seen him again, and also any information I could obtain on a KGB "illegal" agent would be of great interest to Jupiter. I tried to sound casual. "Now that poor Salima is a widow, do you think there is the possibility of Michel returning to Morocco and trying to marry her?"

Fatima turned upon me with an expression I'd never seen on her face before. Hatred and venom shot from her black, almond-shaped eyes. "To begin with," she almost snarled, "he was never in love with my sister. She was madly in love with him, but he merely used her for our family connections." For a while after that outburst she walked at my side in silence. The crunch of our bare feet on the wet sand and the low roll of waves were the only sounds. Then, with disdain, she turned to me. "The proof that he wasn't in love with Salima is that he suddenly gave up his job and went back to Paris. He left to get away from my sister."

Since I knew that was not the reason Michel had left Fatima's country, I imagined this was the explanation Michel had given her for his disappearance, which was further proof that she had seen him.

"Salima scared him off," Fatima continued. "He had been perfectly happy in Morocco until she pursued him so relentlessly."

Fatima's long, graceful fingers were nervously twisting the strap of her bathing cap. Although she tried to hide it, the mention of Michel had upset her even more than our conversation about Ahmed's death the day before. I had no doubt, as I watched Fatima twirling the bathing cap, that she was still longing for Michel. I remembered what Serge Lebedev had told me in Washington over a year ago, when he was being debriefed. "The woman Michel de Bonville enjoyed the most was Fatima," he had said. "But Salima, being more naive, was a useful ally and picked up valuable information for him." And then he had added: "But Michel is a true immoral bastard. He'll sleep with any attractive woman he can. He once told me that it was good exercise, like a two-mile jog or a long swim, but much more interesting and exciting. Salima, of course, did not understand Michel's intentions."

As I remembered Serge's words, I was reminded of Salima's frequent questions about Bill Casey.

We finished our walk on the beach with no further mention of Michel. But I noticed how anxious Fatima was to leave and get to Paris. Though not an early riser, she left on the eight o'clock plane the next morning.

I was in a quandary about my old friend. I had enjoyed our relationship much more when we were just two housewives with young children. It had been so simple. But now bits of information buzzed through my brain. Again I recalled that Salima had hinted that Fatima had been Medbouh's mistress; I had seen Michel entering Fatima's bedroom. So she had had affairs with two prominent conspirators. She had always been such a great admirer of General Oufkir. How could I be sure she had not had an affair with him, too? The thought that Fatima could have been involved in the plot struck me. I shook myself. No. That was impossible.

It must have been about six months later when I received a telephone call from Jupiter, who was in Paris. "I think you'd like to know about something that has just come to my attention," he said. "I'll be in Madrid tomorrow. Can you and Luis join me for lunch at my house around two-thirty?" Before hanging up, he added, "We'll be alone, so we can talk freely."

While we drove the fifteen minutes to Jupiter's house, set in acres of wild countryside on the outskirts of Madrid in the Moraleja, Luis and I speculated on what would be important enough to persuade Jupiter to have lunch with us alone instead of with the twenty or so guests he usually invited when he was in Madrid. The weather was lovely, the air crisp, the day sunny, one of those Madrid winter skies so blue it was almost purple. When we arrived, Jupiter was playing tennis with his professional so we had to control our impatience until we settled down to lunch. Although the wind was chilly, we were able to eat outside in a protected corner of the terrace with a view of the snow-tipped Guadarrama Mountains.

At first Jupiter postponed any serious talk. The main course was spiced marinated partridge, and then our host became a bit infuriating. He knew very well that Luis and I were dying to find out why he had asked us to this very private lunch. But he politely asked about his godson, our youngest boy, Miguel. How was he doing in school? What were his thoughts about his career? What a great tennis player! How well he played the guitar! Did he have a girlfriend? On and on, but he was inquiring about his godson, so we had to reply politely. It was not until the butler had finished serving the coffee that Jupiter finally found it comfortable to tell us the principal reason why we were there. He lit a cigar and leaned back in his chair with an amused expression on his face, looking first at Luis and then at me. "I thought," he said, "that Luis might be relieved to know, and you too, Aline"—he took another sip of his coffee, a puff on his cigar—"that you have nothing more to fear from Michel de Bonville."

Frankly I was disappointed. I was expecting something more exciting. I had not been especially worried about Michel, nor had Luis, not since we'd learned that the plotters of the Moroccan coup had been uncovered and executed. Jupiter, I knew, had received my report months ago informing him that Michel had turned up disguised as a bohemian painter in Paris under the name Michel Dupont. For me, Michel was now far enough removed from my world as not to represent any threat.

Luis did not sound concerned either when he asked, "Well, has the KGB sent him to Australia?"

"No." Another puff on his cigar.

"If you're about to tell us he's no longer in Paris, then where is he?" I asked impatiently.

Jupiter leaned forward, took another sip of coffee, replaced the cup on the saucer, looked at me, and said, "He's dead."

Jupiter's words left me speechless. Luis made no comment. We both now sensed that Jupiter's story was just beginning. He cleared his throat. "You see, Aline, I thought you might help with some suggestions about how he died."

"I don't understand," I said. "It seems to me you're the only one who could know that."

John shook his head. "I'm not able to. I don't know enough about the man's private life. And you do."

"How did he die?" Luis asked, always more practical than I.

"A heart attack," Jupiter responded. "At least that was the opinion of the doctors and that is what appeared on the coroner's report."

"Then, being a natural death, why is it so important to know about his private life?" I asked.

"Because we found out later that his death was not from natural causes." Jupiter gave me a quizzical look. "That's why I thought you might be able to help, Tiger."

Jupiter seemed to make less sense every minute. And it wasn't like him to call me by my code name either, especially in front of Luis. What had happened to my cool, controlled friend? I waited for him to continue.

"The circumstances of his death are extremely unusual," John went on.

"Do you suppose the KGB wanted to get rid of him?" I suggested. "Think about it. Michel had changed his identity and had been ordered back to the same country. The French DST is excellent—maybe they were about to uncover the fact that he was a Soviet illegal. Or maybe the KGB calculated that his cover wasn't secure, and if picked up and questioned, he might blow other agents' cover. It seems to me there are many reasons why the KGB would have wanted to kill him."

"But the KGB did not kill him," Jupiter responded.

"How do you know?"

"Because the KGB never kills that way."

Luis interrupted. "How was he killed?"

"Well, listen to the story," Jupiter went on, "and see what you think." He poured more coffee for Luis and himself and picked up his cigar again as he began to speak. "Bonville, or I should say Dupont, as he was last called, died in a *boîte* in Montmartre. It wasn't one of his usual haunts; we knew, because our men had been trailing him for weeks. He usually stayed on the Left Bank and hung out with a band of painters, drug addicts, and whores. He had little or no contact with the Residency. I suppose he was working on establishing his new identity. But the night he died, his routine changed. A well-dressed woman appeared at his apartment. They didn't come out for several hours, but when they did, they took a taxi to this small nightclub in Montmartre. We're pretty sure he'd never been there before. Maybe the

woman made the decision. Our people questioned the employ-
ees the following day and they all agreed that they'd never seen
him nor the lady before. Michel and this woman didn't ask for
anything to eat; they merely ordered two glasses of Pernod."

I was not entirely surprised to learn that John Derby knew
where Michel had spent his time. He had probably placed surveillance teams on Michel as soon as he had learned about his
presence in Paris.

John Derby continued. "According to my men, the woman
was strikingly beautiful, and very elegant, and wore large earrings with a half-moon design. She was quite tall, and slim, with
thick dark hair." My mind flashed back to the first time I had
seen Salima, standing in front of the glass display case, admiring
a pair of pendant earrings with a half-moon design. I remembered her telling me that of all the jewels her sister had in the
exhibit, these earrings were her favorites. But then I also remembered that Salima was blonde, not dark. "The couple came
in together," said Derby, "making a strange pair, the man disheveled and rough in appearance and the woman so distinguished, but they appeared to be happy and very intimate. The
woman remained for about a half hour and then left in a taxi,
alone." John Derby paused and glanced from Luis to me, realizing he had our attention. "The man complained of feeling ill
almost immediately after she left. And ten minutes later, he
slumped over on the table—dead. We obtained these details
from the waiter who served them."

"But what did he die of?" Luis asked.

Jupiter was looking at us with a wry grin. "You are aware,"
he said, "that when there is a death in a public place, an autopsy
is always done. Even when all appearances indicate it has been
a heart attack. This is normal procedure in every country. Well,
the autopsy is what makes this case so interesting, because
Michel Dupont, or Michel de Bonville, or whatever his real
name is, was poisoned. The coroner's report proved that, and
there's no doubt about it, because the French are systematic and
competent about such things."

Luis was leaning forward. "What kind of poison?"

"That's the strange part." Jupiter knocked the ash from his

cigar into a bowl at his side. The cigar had gone out, so he took time to relight it before answering." The poison was made from an innocent green flower called *gouza*. The concentrate made from the heart of the flower is a liquid, which is lethal and has fast action."

"Is that a very unusual kind of poison?" I asked.

"Not entirely," Jupiter answered. "The only thing that makes this special for us"—he gestured with the cigar—"is that this flower of death is found principally in the mountains of Morocco."

I stared at him. A million ideas crashed into each other in my brain.

Jupiter's amused voice went on. "The scientist's analysis stated that the poisonous liquid must have been administered about ten minutes before he fell dead. Probably in coffee or a strong-flavored beverage."

I felt dizzy. Luis was in a state of shock as well. In order to gain time to sort out the thoughts running through my head, I said the first words that occurred to me. "Michel was a womanizer and had affairs with many different women. . . ." I looked at Luis for help. He also had been at that luncheon in the Governor's palace. He had heard the Governor explain about the deadly plants. Both Fatima and Salima had spent much of their childhood in the mountains, and were familiar with them. Both had listened to their uncle's discussion of lethal flowers that day in Midelt. I wondered which one of us would mention it first. The idea was so terrible, so horrible. I couldn't believe what Jupiter had just told me. Michel de Bonville, alias Dupont, had been poisoned . . . by a woman. And by a poison which originated in Morocco. Serge's prediction that a woman would cause Michel's downfall was true. I looked at Jupiter. Was he pulling my leg? Had he invented the whole wild story?

"The woman?" I looked at him questioningly. "You think I might know who the woman is?"

"Well, you were in Morocco. I thought you might have some idea of where this poison had come from. You've mentioned your women friends there off and on. Think about it. A beautiful woman with lots of curly dark hair, well dressed and distinguished." He raised his eyebrows. "Of course, even if we did know, we couldn't do anything about it. Do you have any idea . . . who might be interested in killing Michel?"

Fatima, I thought immediately. How horrible. It must have been Fatima. And then I remembered that day in Marrakech. "How do I look with black hair?" Salima had laughed as she ran her hands through the fluffy black wig. From a distance no one would have been able to tell the difference.

I could tell that Luis was reading my mind. The three of us looked at each other in silence.